AQA BUSINESS STUDIES for AS
ANSWERS AND RESOURCES

AQA BUSINESS STUDIES for AS
ANSWERS AND RESOURCES

Ian Marcousé

Andrew Gillespie
Malcolm Surridge
Andrew Hammond
Naomi Birchall
Marie Brewer
Nigel Watson

HODDER
EDUCATION
PART OF HACHETTE UK

Orders: please contact Bookpoint Ltd, 130 Milton Park, Abingdon, Oxon OX14 4SB. Telephone: (44) 01235 827720. Fax: (44) 01235 400454. Lines are open from 9.00 – 5.00, Monday to Saturday, with a 24-hour message answering service. You can also order through our website www.hoddereducation.co.uk.

British Library Cataloguing in Publication Data
A catalogue record for this title is available from the British Library

ISBN: 978 0340 97574 9

First Published 2009
Impression number   10 9 8 7 6 5 4 3 2 1
Year   2014 2013 2012 2011 2010 2009 2008

Hachette UK's policy is to use papers that are natural, renewable and recyclable products and made from wood grown in sustainable forests. The logging and manufacturing processes are expected to conform to the environmental regulations of the country of origin.

Cover illustration by Oxford Designers and Illustrators.
Typeset by Servis Filmsetting Ltd, Stockport, Cheshire.
Printed in Great Britain for Hodder Education, part of Hachette UK, 338 Euston Road, London NW1 3BH by Hobbs the Printers, Totton, Hampshire.

Contents

Starting a business

Getting the start-up right

Financial planning

Finance

People in business

Operations management

Marketing and the competitive environment

Introduction to the AQA Business Studies for AS: Answers and Resources

This teacher's book is designed as an essential companion to the *AQA Business Studies for AS* textbook (ISBN 978 0 340 95864 3). The coverage of the units of the book comprises three parts:

1. It provides an introduction to each of the units in the textbook with suggestions on how you might approach teaching this area. These include ideas for visits, resources for lessons and possible teaching strategies.

2. The units contain a list of further reading and resources which will help you find additional material on each unit. These include book lists and, occasionally, website addresses. A brief account of these resources is provided, suggesting how they might be used and pointing towards the sections that are useful.

3. The bulk of the material consists of suggested answers to the questions in the textbook along with the mark schemes where appropriate. The mark schemes highlight the key skills which are assessed at AS and A level, namely

    • Knowledge and understanding

    • Application

    • Analysis

    • Evaluation

These four key skills areas are assessed separately using a levels of response marking strategy where appropriate. The allocation of marks reflects the balance towards these skill areas in AS exams.

Sample mark scheme for a 10-mark AS question

	Knowledge 2 marks	Application 2 marks	Analysis 3 marks	Evaluation 3 marks
Level 2	2 marks Good understanding of the subject content; or two answers identified.	2 marks Answer is applied effectively to the specific case.	3 marks Build-up of argument, making use of relevant business concepts.	3 marks Shows judgement in drawing conclusions from own argument.
Level 1	1 mark Some understanding of the subject content; or one answer identified.	1 mark Some relationship to the scenario (perhaps indirectly).	2-1 marks Some build-up of argument, showing grasp of cause and effect.	2-1 marks Some judgement shown in argument or weighting of language.

Within each skills category the answer must be assessed and the appropriate level of response chosen; for example, limited analysis could receive a maximum of two marks in this question. When marking students' answers it is helpful to identify each skill with the appropriate mark; for example K2, Ap1, A3, E1 is an answer which shows good knowledge and analysis, but limited application and judgement.

Introduction to the AQA Business Studies for AS: Answers and Resources

It is important to highlight the different skills through the course and for students to be clear of the differences between them. In particular analytical and evaluative skills need to be developed as these higher level skills are the most challenging and yet are crucial for the higher grades.

Students also need to recognise the demands of different types of questions (e.g. 'consider the possible factors' v 'explain the possible factors. . .') and appreciate the particular requirements of each one. It is important, therefore, that students become familiar with mark schemes such as the ones included in this book and appreciate the limitations of an approach which focuses too heavily on knowledge.

As on exam board marking schemes, possible answers are provided to each question. These are not exhaustive and students should be rewarded for any relevant point whether or not it is on the list. The ideas put forward serve purely as useful guidelines.

QWC

Quality of Written Communication in the 2008 Specification is incorporated into the general exam marking. In the case of AQA it is built into the assessment of evaluation. The decision was made to avoid following this practice within this Answer Guide as it leads to very cumbersome mark schemes. It would therefore slow down a marking process that is already a burden.

For full versions of the new mark schemes, see www.aqa.org.uk.

Updates

1. Resources

Websites are, of course, a highly moveable feast. Today's outstanding gem can lose its lustre if the owner fails to keep it up to date or decides to charge for what was once free. The authors will try to keep abreast of changes and incorporate them into reprints of this Guide. It would be hugely helpful, though, if you would share your web favourites with us and therefore a wider audience. If you have some favourite websites, please send them to Ian Marcousé, 3 Rayleigh Road, London SW19 3RE, marcouse@btopenworld.com. Careful recording of the web address is, of course, essential; it would also be great to have an indication of the unit or units each site relates to. Exactly the same principle applies to the reading lists. We will update, but would appreciate extra ideas and will incorporate them.

2. Up-to-date case studies

To keep fully up to date, nothing can beat the daily papers. For more reflective material written at the right standard, see *Business Review* magazine, Philip Allan, Market Place, Deddington, Oxford OX15 0SE. Also consider subscribing to *Topical Cases*; for details see www.a-zbusinesstraining.com.

Enterprise and Entrepreneurs

1.1 Introduction

For the opening lesson on this topic, there is no substitute for a good story. Take a really recent start-up story, for example (at the time of writing) Shaky Jakes, a hip milkshake business started by Leeds ex.Uni students in May 2008. (See www.shakyjakes.co.uk.) With a few downloaded photos from this website one can quickly pick up the business proposition (milkshakes from Ferrero Rocher to Smarties). This would be sufficient to get a good discussion going about the two young entrepreneurs' chances of success. In fact, the business introduced a loyalty card a month after opening (buy eight shakes, get one free), which suggests it took them a little while to see the importance of repeat purchase. Will our students figure out for themselves that quirky shakes may be a great novelty item, but not necessarily the basis for an ongoing business?

Even at this stage it is important to introduce the issue of risk wherever possible. You are welcome to a PowerPoint lesson focused on this issue by emailing marcouse@btopenworld.com. There is also an article on this topic in the February 2009 *Business Review* magazine.

The contents of Chapter 1 are wholly accessible to students and they could easily be set this chapter to read for homework. The Section A questions would be useful to give all the students some confidence and can be followed up by B1. Only give B2 as homework if you have already taught these students the GCSE; otherwise treat it as a potential class activity.

1.2 Further reading and resources

Title and price	Author	Publisher and ISBN	Brief account
Good Small Business Guide: How to Start and Grow Your Own Business 3rd Edition £19.99		A & C Black 2008 978 0 7136 8760 6	Terrific resource, packed with advice, comment and scepticism. Super start, with an introduction from the founder of Rachel's Organic, a section on '10 Myths about Small Businesses' followed by a 20-question self-assessment exercise. Later sections include 'Starting a Business while under 18' and 'Coping in a cash flow crisis'.
Dragons' Den: Success, from Pitch to Profit £16.99	Bannatyne, D., Meaden, D., Jones, P., Farleigh, R., Paphitis, T. and Caan, J., with Davis, E.	Collins 2008 978 0 00 726355 4	Not as good as it should be, but useful for the library. Includes: 'A lesson in franchising', 'A lesson in patents', and 'A lesson in creating a niche business'.

Anyone Can Do It: My Story £7.99	Bannatyne, D.	Orion Books 2007 978 0 7528 8189 8	Terrific book; any super-keenies could start reading it now and might devour it cover to cover. For homework, students could tackle: 'Read the ice cream start-up chapter and identify the entrepreneurial qualities shown by Bannatyne. Explain which you think was the most important; explain why'.
The Small Business Start-up Workbook £12.99	Rickman, C.	How To Books 2005 978 1 84528 038 3	Good chapters include: Chapter 3: 'Researching your market and opportunity'; Chapter 8: 'The importance of good customer service'; Chapter 9: 'How to behave – the case for ethical business'.
Against the Odds £10.99	Dyson, J.	Texere Publishing 2000 978 1587 9901 44	An ageing giant, but it's still a fantastic and very modern tale, given that all the students see the products around them. At this stage, a homework could be set on Chapter 4, the story of Dyson's development of the Ballbarrow.

1.3 Answers to workbook questions

A Revision questions
(25 marks; 25 minutes)

1. Why is 'initiative' an important quality in an entrepreneur? (**2**)

    • Entrepreneurship is about doing rather than just thinking.

    • Initiative implies doing something before others.

2. Section 1.1 lists the characteristics needed to be a successful entrepreneur. Which two from this list seem of greatest importance to:

    (**a**) a new firm facing a collapse in demand due to flooding locally (**2**)

Two from:

- determination

- passion

- the ability to cope with risk.

(**b**) a 19-year-old entrepreneur wanting to start her own airline (**2**)

Two from:

- understanding the market

- persuasive abilities

- the ability to build relationships

- the ability to cope with risk.

3. Section 1.2 mentions a restaurant that expects 60 customers per day spending £25 each, but actually gets 40 customers spending £20. Calculate the shortfall in revenue that will result from these changes. (**3**)

- Was $60 \times £25 = £1500$
  Is $40 \times £20 = £800$
  Shortfall $= £700$ a day

4. Explain two actions the government could take to encourage more people to become entrepreneurs. (**4**)

- Increase the number of grants available, perhaps especially for young entrepreneurs.

- Work to improve the quality of the advisors employed by Business Link, then advertise the availability of this support more widely.

5. Briefly explain one argument for and one against saying that entrepreneurs are born, not made. (**5**)

- *For*: some of the key entrepreneurial skills, such as determination, seem to be inbuilt, i.e. born, though some people would argue that character traits can be altered by teaching.

- *Against*: gaining an understanding of a market is clearly a skill that anyone can acquire over time.

6. Having read this chapter, explain briefly how successful or unsuccessful you think you would be as an entrepreneur. Take care to explain your reasoning. (**7**)

- A *good* answer will be a self-analysis based on comparison with the characteristics listed in 1.1.

- A *very good* answer might select just two or three of the characteristics to make the comparison.

Enterprise and Entrepreneurs

B1 Data response

(20 marks; 20 minutes)

(Refer to question on page 4 of textbook.)

1. If you were asked to advise Travis, identify four questions you would like to ask him about his business plans. **(8)**

One mark for identifying a relevant point; a further mark for development.

- What is the likely start-up cost for this business? Preferably this should take risk into account by looking at the best and worst scenario.

- How much capital do they have between them for investment? Is the whole idea a pipedream?

- How did he arrive at the Year 1 sales forecast, which appears to assume a 5% market penetration

- How did he arrive at these pricing points? Are they high or low compared with other surfboards?

2. Explain your reasoning behind one of those questions. **(3)**

Mark the answer on the basis of this marking grid:

	Knowledge 1 mark	Application 2 marks
Level 2		**2 marks** Answer is applied effectively to the specific case.
Level 1	**1 mark** Shows understanding of the subject content.	**1 mark** Some relationship to the scenario (perhaps indirectly).

Enterprise and Entrepreneurs

3. Discuss two main factors you think he should also consider before going ahead. **(9)**

	Knowledge 2 marks	Application 2 marks	Analysis 2 marks	Evaluation 3 marks
Level 2	**2 marks** Good understanding of the subject content; or two answers identified.	**2 marks** Answer is applied effectively to the specific case.	**2 marks** Build-up of argument, making use of relevant business concepts.	**3 marks** Shows judgement in drawing conclusions from own argument.
Level 1	**1 mark** Some understanding of the subject content; or one answer identified.	**1 mark** Some relationship to the scenario (perhaps indirectly).	**1 mark** Some build-up of argument, showing grasp of cause and effect.	**2-1 marks** Some judgement shown in argument or weighting of language.

Possible answers include:

- He needs to look in a mirror and ask whether he (and his father) have the qualities needed for entrepreneurial success. Where they are both lacking – perhaps in building relationships – how are they going to address the issue?

- How will they cope with the seasonality of demand (and therefore cash flow) for a product such as a surfboard (and especially a kids' board, which is very likely to be bought at the start of summer holidays).

B2 Case study

Nearly Crusshed
(30 marks; 30 minutes)

(Refer to question on page 5 of textbook.)

1. Explain what is meant by the terms:

  – cash flow **(3)**

  – business model **(3)**

Up to two marks for definition; the third mark is for some explanation.

- *Cash flow* is money in – money out, usually measured monthly; firms like to forecast it for the coming year, to identify any cash shortfalls.

Enterprise and Entrepreneurs

• *Business model* is the essence of how the business is intended to generate a profit, e.g. Manchester United charges admission, but also sells customers extra merchandise and gets still more income from selling TV rights. This is more than sufficient to cover its costs.

2. Crussh received no government support during its set-up phase. Should the government invest in the business now? Explain your answer. (6)

	Knowledge 1 mark	Application 1 mark	Analysis 2 marks	Evaluation 2 marks
Level 2			2 marks Build-up of argument, making use of relevant business concepts.	2 marks Shows judgement in drawing conclusions from own argument.
Level 1	1 mark Some understanding of the subject content; or one answer identified.	1 mark Some relationship to the scenario (perhaps indirectly).	1 mark Some build-up of argument, showing grasp of cause and effect.	1 mark Some judgement shown in argument or weighting of language.

Possible answers include:

• Why should the government invest in a successful business? Above all else, there are plenty of financiers and investors who are happy to invest in successful businesses; government only tends to be needed when finance is hard to get.

• The people who work for government are inevitably cautious about making decisions that may backfire. But businesses need quick decisions and have to take risks; government involvement might be very unhelpful.

Enterprise and Entrepreneurs

3. Discuss which of the qualities listed in Section 1.1 were important in James Learmond's case. (10)

	Knowledge 2 marks	Application 2 marks	Analysis 2 marks	Evaluation 4 marks
Level 2	2 marks Good understanding of the subject content; or two answers identified.	2 marks Answer is applied effectively to the specific case.	2 marks Build-up of argument, making use of relevant business concepts.	4-3 marks Shows judgement in drawing conclusions from own argument.
Level 1	1 mark Some understanding of the subject content; or one answer identified.	1 mark Some relationship to the scenario (perhaps indirectly).	1 mark Some build-up of argument, showing grasp of cause and effect.	2-1 marks Some judgement shown in argument or weighting of language.

Possible answers include:

• He has the ability to cope with risk, both in the initial start-up and when forced to borrow £500,000 to keep the business going in 2001; he would also have needed persuasive abilities to obtain the loan, i.e. the skill of persuasiveness and the ability to deal with risk worked together for him.

• Throughout the case there is a lot of evidence of understanding customers – what they're prepared to spend and the alternative products they look for when the British weather proves disappointing.

4a. Why did Crussh change its product range over the period 1998–2007? (4)

	Knowledge 1 mark	Application 3 marks
Level 2		3 marks Answer is applied effectively to the specific case.
Level 1	1 mark Shows understanding of the subject content.	2-1 marks Some relationship to the scenario (perhaps indirectly).

Possible answers include:

• Observing that competitors went under because they could not cope with the seasonality of the business (high sales only when the sun shines).

• There were too many financial strains caused by the impact of poor winter cash flow.

4b. How did it do so? (4)

	Knowledge 1 mark	Application 3 marks
Level 2		**3 marks** Answer is applied effectively to the specific case.
Level 1	**1 mark** Shows understanding of the subject content.	**2-1 marks** Some relationship to the scenario (perhaps indirectly).

Possible answers include:

- By developing a range of products that people buy, having been brought in by the way a fresh smoothie can 'capture the imagination' of a customer.

- By developing products for the winter market such as pea and ham soup.

Identifying Business Opportunities

2.1 Introduction

This section gives terrific scope for active learning, both in the classroom and in a foray to the local High Street. Many students may already have bright ideas of their own. The single most useful technique here is market mapping. You may have excellent opportunities locally, for example if you teach in a seaside town or in a city with a large student population. The most interesting aspect of mapping is deciding on the relevant criteria. As teachers we may be confident in suggesting that chocolate bars can be mapped on the scales: treat-everyday and older-younger. But what are the criteria for mapping the handset market or the market for social networking sites? It's a good thing for the students to see that their consumer knowledge can be of value in certain circumstances.

The other teacher-friendly topic here is franchising. The Subway website is terrific (www.subway.co.uk/business) and do remember that *Franchise World* magazine is well worth £2.75 when the topic's coming up. If you have one nearby, do try Pizza Express, whose Head Office says that all franchisees are willing to give an AM business talk to a group of students followed by the opportunity to make and cook their own pizza!

All the Workbook exercises are accessible to students. Don't underestimate the Section A questions, which are far more than simple tests of memory. Look, for example, at Question 8 (which should perhaps have been allocated more marks).

2.2 Further reading and resources

Title and price	Author	Publisher and ISBN	Brief account
Good Small Business Guide: How to Start and Grow Your Own Business 3rd Edition £19.99		A & C Black 2008 978 0 7136 8760 6	Terrific resource, packed with advice, comment and scepticism. Super start, with an introduction from the founder of Rachel's Organic, a section on '10 Myths about Small Businesses' followed by a 20-question self-assessment exercise. Later sections include 'Starting a Business while under 18' and 'Coping in a cash flow crisis'.
Developing New Business Ideas £21.99	Bragg, A. and Bragg, M.	Prentice Hall 2005 0 273 66325 9	For teachers only; has some nice diagrams, e.g. p18 'Life chance of an initial business plan'. Sections include: 'The importance of developing strong ideas' and 'The four steps in the development process'.

Identifying Business Opportunities

Unit 2

Dragons' Den: Success, from Pitch to Profit £16.99	Bannatyne, D., Meaden, D., Jones, P., Farleigh, R., Paphitis, T. and Caan, J., with Davis, E.	Collins 2008 978 0 00 726355 4	Not as good as it should be, but useful for the library. Includes: 'A lesson in franchising', 'A lesson in patents', and 'A lesson in creating a niche business'.
How They Started: How 30 Good Ideas Became Great Businesses £12.95	Lester, D.	Crimson Publishing 2007 978-1-85458-400-7	Gu chocolate puds and the Bebo network site are two super stories from the book about spotting opportunities.
The Small Business Start-up Workbook £12.99	Rickman, C.	How To Books 2005 978 1 84528 038 3	Good chapters include: Chapter 3: 'Researching your market and opportunity'; Chapter 8: 'The importance of good customer service'; Chapter 9: 'How to behave – the case for ethical business'.

2.3 Answers to workbook questions

A Revision questions

(30 marks; 30 minutes)

1. Explain how 'observation' might help a business-minded person to come up with a great new idea for starting a firm. **(3)**

   • Watching people can reveal a lot. Which shop windows do they stop and look at?

   • Seeing something that works in one place may yield an opportunity to offer the item elsewhere; in effect Innocent Drinks began because the founders had seen smoothie success in America.

2. The UK population is growing older, with a rising proportion of over-sixties. Outline two business opportunities that might arise as the population gets older. **(4)**

   • More scope for on-line shopping (with delivery) such as Tesco Direct.

   • More scope for niche opportunities in house building, or the design of products from cars to vacuum cleaners.

3. Explain in your own words the purpose of geographical mapping. **(3)**

   • To identify where your local competitors are located

   • … which might lead you to move away

- … or to move closer; it is easier to fill a restaurant in a location with many other restaurants than one where there are no others.

4. Identify three markets where age is a crucial factor in drawing up a market map. (**3**)

   - confectionery

   - magazines

   - clothes.

5. Examine two reasons why a successful, growing business might choose not to sell franchises in the business. (**6**)

   - The proprietor may be worried that franchisees may lack the necessary commitment to quality of service.

   - The proprietor might not want to have to share in the future wealth that may emerge from profitable growth.

6. Why are good franchise owners keen to inspect their franchisees regularly, even though they have no ownership stake in the franchisee businesses? (**3**)

   - To protect the image of the brand as a whole.

   - To help steer the franchisee to make the best of their business opportunity.

7. Why should a potential franchisee be very careful to research fully the background of the franchise owner? (**4**)

   - You cannot be sure that the owner's story stands up, without checking.

   - The franchise owner has a huge incentive to sell, which may conflict with your desire to buy wisely.

8. Section 2.6 talks about the importance of luck in business start-ups; outline how bad luck might damage the start of a small bakery. (**4**)

   - Rising wheat/flour prices may add to cash outflows at the most difficult part of the business start-up.

   - Another bakery may start up locally just before you do.

B1 Data response

(25 marks; 25 minutes)

(Refer to question on page 10 of textbook.)

1. Outline two pieces of small budget research Cara should carry out before taking things any further with her upmarket shoe shop in Leeds. (**6**)

Identifying Business Opportunities

	Knowledge 3 marks		Application 3 marks
Level 2	**3 marks** Good understanding of small budget research.		**3 marks** Answer is applied effectively to the specific case.
Level 1	**2-1 marks** Shows understanding of the subject content.		**2-1 marks** Some relationship to the scenario (perhaps indirectly).

Possible answers include:

- Map the market for upmarket shoe shops locally, making sure that there isn't already a shop just like the one she wants to start up.

- Check on the prices, brands, shoe sizes and other services offered by the other shoe shops locally.

2a. Outline one possible benefit to Cara of opting to become a franchisee. **(3)**

	Knowledge 1 mark		Application 2 marks
Level 2			**2 marks** Answer is applied effectively to the specific case.
Level 1	**1 mark** Shows understanding of the subject content.		**1 mark** Some relationship to the scenario (perhaps indirectly).

Possible answers include:

- There is no evidence that she has business experience, so a franchise would help her avoid some business pitfalls.

- She has relatively little capital for a retail start-up, so it will be hard for her to cope with business failure.

2b. Outline one aspect of the London shoe shop franchise that Cara should examine more carefully before signing any agreements. **(4)**

	Knowledge 1 mark		Application 3 marks
Level 2			**3 marks** Answer is applied effectively to the specific case.
Level 1	**1 mark** Shows understanding of the subject content.		**2-1 marks** Some relationship to the scenario (perhaps indirectly).

Identifying Business Opportunities

Possible answers include:

- She should look carefully at the amount of support and training they offer; would it be one-off or would the training carry on beyond the start-up phase.

- Cara will need to know exactly how the London store has built up its reputation, and the product lines they find the most successful.

3. Use the text and Figure 2.3 to discuss whether Cara is better suited to running a franchise or an independent shoe shop. **(12)**

	Knowledge 2 marks	Application 3 marks	Analysis 3 marks	Evaluation 4 marks
Level 2	**2 marks** Good understanding of the subject content; or two answers identified.	**3 marks** Answer is applied effectively to the specific case.	**3 marks** Build-up of argument, making use of relevant business concepts.	**4-3 marks** Shows judgement in drawing conclusions from own argument.
Level 1	**1 mark** Some understanding of the subject content; or one answer identified.	**2-1 marks** Some relationship to the scenario (perhaps indirectly).	**2-1 marks** Some build-up of argument, showing grasp of cause and effect.	**2-1 marks** Some judgement shown in argument or weighting of language.

Possible answers include:

- She is short of market expertise and a willingness to take tough decisions; both these shortcomings point towards franchising rather than independence.

- Yet she has a lot of creative flair and is fiercely independent – both qualities you would love to see in an independent business woman.

- Her organization makes her equipped for both types of operation, but especially the independent route.

B2 Data response

Why franchise?

(30 marks; 30 minutes)

(Refer to question on page 11 of textbook.)

1. Explain why Mal wanted to start a franchise, not an independent, business. **(4)**

Identifying Business Opportunities

	Knowledge 2 marks	Application 2 marks
Level 2	2 marks Shows clear understanding of the subject content.	2 marks Answer is applied effectively to the specific case.
Level 1	1 mark Shows some understanding of the subject content.	1 mark Some relationship to the scenario (perhaps indirectly).

Possible answers include:

- Probably 'many years as a call centre manager' made him unsure of his own expertise as a full entrepreneur (wanted freedom, but not too much).

- 'Buying into something that's already there has a clear message that risk should be lower.

2. Examine why the views of the franchisees at the exhibition may not have been typical of those of all O'Brien's franchisees. (5)

	Knowledge 1 mark	Application 2 marks	Analysis 2 marks
Level 2		2 marks Answer is applied effectively to the specific case.	2 marks Build-up of argument, making use of relevant business concepts.
Level 1	1 mark Shows some understanding of the subject content.	1 mark Some relationship to the scenario (perhaps indirectly).	1 mark Some build-up of argument, showing grasp of cause and effect.

Possible answers include:

- Would surely have been selected by O'Brien's on the basis of being happy franchisees; also, may have been well-paid for the day and keen to get more days in future; the franchisor's job is to sell franchises; that's it.

- It is generally in the interests of franchisees to make things sound good; after all, they all want customers and therefore have a vested interest in saying 'O'Brien's is great'.

3. Apart from the franchise fee, suggest three other business costs Mal would have to pay to run the sandwich shop. (3)

- One per answer – too many possibilities to list; praise students whose answers are contextualised, e.g. 'sandwich ingredients' instead of 'raw materials'.

4. Consider the list of advice given by Mark Simmonds. Discuss which aspects of this would be especially useful for Mal. (9)

	Knowledge 2 marks	Application 2 marks	Analysis 2 marks	Evaluation 3 marks
Level 2	2 marks Good understanding of the subject content; or two answers identified.	2 marks Answer is applied effectively to the specific case.	2 marks Build-up of argument, making use of relevant business concepts.	3 marks Shows judgement in drawing conclusions from own argument.
Level 1	1 mark Some understanding of the subject content; or one answer identified.	1 mark Some relationship to the scenario (perhaps indirectly).	1 mark Some build-up of argument, showing grasp of cause and effect.	2-1 marks Some judgement shown in argument or weighting of language.

Possible answers include:

- The first is the most important: don't rely on financial information given; if people are selling established franchises for figures such as £50,000, it implies that the entrepreneur probably lost money on the franchise. We haven't been told about Mal's savings, but it's reasonable to think that a call centre manager won't have a fortune to invest; he must be very careful.

- The other valuable point concerns the location; however good the franchise, a poor location can wreck the business proposition; Mal must make sure that O'Brien's wants to find him the best location in Northampton (after all, there may already be an O'Brien's in the prime spot, so they may want him out of the way).

- Both are crucial; perhaps the second is even more important than the first (as no one can predict what the actual figures will look like anyway).

5. Recommend whether or not Mal should proceed with the O'Brien's franchise. Explain your thinking. (9)

	Knowledge 2 marks	Application 2 marks	Analysis 2 marks	Evaluation 3 marks
Level 2	2 marks Good understanding of the subject content; or two answers identified.	2 marks Answer is applied effectively to the specific case.	2 marks Build-up of argument, making use of relevant business concepts.	3 marks Shows judgement in drawing conclusions from own argument.

Identifying Business Opportunities

Level 1	1 mark Some understanding of the subject content; or one answer identified.	1 mark Some relationship to the scenario (perhaps indirectly).	1 mark Some build-up of argument, showing grasp of cause and effect.	2-1 marks Some judgement shown in argument or weighting of language.

Possible answers include:

- Reasons to say yes, proceed:

  - He 'quickly decided' on franchising, so he's not ready to start a truly independent business; if it's to be a franchise, why not an O'Brien's?

  - Assuming he can afford an investment of £40,000+, he can feel comfortable that he's not loading himself up with bank debt; compared with the costs of, say, a McDonald's franchise, this is not too pricey.

- Reasons to say no:

  - He seems to be nowhere close to making a final decision; one trip to a franchise exhibition is hardly research; he should go and visit a few actual franchisees at their franchise outlet, to get a broader understanding about how successful the franchises are.

  - Paying out 9% of turnover is a huge price to pay, especially when it comes on top of many other start-up costs; he should not agree to buy the franchise without getting on the street and asking passers-by how much they would pay for an O'Brien's chicken salad sandwich compared with a Subway one and compared with one made by Hampton Farm (a made-up name to see if 'O'Brien's' adds any value).

For full marks students must make a justified decision (I'd say no, if that was all the information available).

Protecting Business Ideas

3.1 Introduction

The best way to prepare for this section of the course is to read *Against The Odds* by James Dyson. It shows just how tough the business world can be, and illustrates the need to be able to afford to protect a patent. In the 15 years Dyson spent developing his floor-cleaner, he spent £1.5 million taking out (and fighting to enforce) patents. This was almost as big a sum as the £2 million on the development itself.

Teaching this topic has been made much easier by *Dragons' Den*. The 'Dragons' regularly ask about how an idea will be protected and they show a lot of understanding of patent and trademark rules. There have been many instances of this, but it's hard to beat the calamitous James Seddon performance with the egg cooker. There's some very good stuff about patents as James explains his patent to James Farleigh. Go to www.eggxactly.com and you can get the 14-minute complete clip from the programme.

Within the Workbook, the Section A questions are valuable, especially 3, 4 and 5. Section A plus B1 would make a good homework.

3.2 Further reading and resources

Title and price	Author	Publisher and ISBN	Brief account
Good Small Business Guide: How to Start and Grow Your Own Business 3rd Edition £19.99		A & C Black 2008 978 0 7136 8760 6	Nice and brief on patents, copyright and trademarks, pages 27-39.
Against the Odds £10.99	Dyson, J.	Texere Publishing 2000 978 1587 9901 44	An ageing giant, but it's still a fantastic and very modern tale, given that all the students see the products around them. At this stage, a homework could be set on Chapter 15, especially the section headed: New Technology.
How They Started: How 30 Good Ideas Became Great Businesses £12.95	Lester, D.	Crimson Publishing 2007 978-1-85458-400-7	The case on Vitabiotics is a good story, and has some excellent material on patents.
FT Guide to Business Start Up 2008 £19.99	Williams, S.	Prentice Hall 2007 978 0273 14873	Chapter 11 'Beating the Pirates' is thorough without being too daunting. Especially useful on trademarks.

'Patents'	Coates, G.	Business Review, 9 (4), April 2003	Sounds old, but it's a good article and the material doesn't really date.

3.3 Answers to workbook questions

A Revision questions

(20 marks; 20 minutes)

1. Briefly explain why Michael Reeves should be able to build a very successful business based on the patent explained in Section 3.2. **(4)**

    • If his competitors can find no way round the patent, Reeves will have a huge competitive advantage; he can charge a price premium over competitors yet still enjoy high sales.

    • As golfers tend to be quite wealthy, they will be able to afford to pay higher prices to guarantee their personal safety.

2. Explain why an entrepreneur may struggle if the success of a new business relies on a patented invention. **(4)**

    • Patents are expensive to obtain and to protect.

    • Breaking a patent isn't a criminal offence, so you have to be willing to take offenders to court yourself.

3. Look at Figure 3.1 and identify:

    (a) two countries where the number of patents rose in 2005 **(1)**

       • China and South Korea

    (b) two countries where the number of patent applications fell in 2005 **(1)**

       • UK and India

4. Briefly explain why it might disappoint the British government to see that the number of patent applications in Britain has been falling. **(3)**

    • It implies that British firms are becoming less innovative and may point to slower economic growth in future.

5. For each of the following, identify whether the IP issue relates to patent, copyright or trademark:

    (a) Galaxy has designed a new pack for its Celebrations brand. **(1)**

       • Trademark

(b) Burberry has come up with a new way to get solar power from a tartan cap, sufficient to keep an iPod powered all day long. (**1**)

  • Patent

(c) Lacoste has developed a new, completely distinctive scent for men. (**1**)

  • Trademark

(d) You have just copied a tennis game from your friend's Wii console. (**1**)

  • Copyright

6. Why may intellectual property be more important today than 50 years ago? Briefly explain your answer. (**3**)

  • As brands and differentiation are much more important today, so is IP, especially trademarks. Although copyright is no different for authors today than 50 years ago, computer software and digital music make copyright a bigger issue.

B1 Data response

(20 marks; 20 minutes)

(Refer to question on page 14 of textbook.)

1. Explain in your own words the meaning of the word patent. (**3**)

  • Protection for an inventor, discouraging others from copying the invention; it is granted by government, usually for a period of 20 years; it helps encourage inventors to invent.

2. Examine the likely reasons why James Seddon applied for a patent on the technical innovations within the Eggxactly product. (**7**)

	Knowledge 2 marks	Application 2 marks	Analysis 3 marks
Level 2	**2 marks** Good understanding of the subject content; or two answers identified.	**2 marks** Answer is applied effectively to the specific case.	**3 marks** Build-up of argument, making use of relevant business concepts.
Level 1	**1 mark** Some understanding of the subject content; or one answer identified.	**1 mark** Some relationship to the scenario (perhaps indirectly).	**2-1 marks** Some build-up of argument, showing grasp of cause and effect.

Protecting Business Ideas

Possible answers include:

- The way the egg is cooked involves a series of technical innovations by James, so he had the opportunity to take out patents.

- As the owner of a small business, James thought he needed as much protection as possible to avoid copycat products by industry giants such as Russell Hobbs.

- He had invested more than two years of time (unpaid) into the business and therefore thought he and his family deserved the full rewards from his invention.

3. Discuss whether James is likely to lose out as a result of waiting over a year before applying for patents in the rest of the world. **(10)**

	Knowledge 2 marks	Application 2 marks	Analysis 3 marks	Evaluation 3 marks
Level 2	**2 marks** Good understanding of the subject content; or two answers identified.	**2 marks** Answer is applied effectively to the specific case.	**3 marks** Build-up of argument, making use of relevant business concepts.	**3 marks** Shows judgement in drawing conclusions from own argument.
Level 1	**1 mark** Some understanding of the subject content; or one answer identified.	**1 mark** Some relationship to the scenario (perhaps indirectly).	**2-1 marks** Some build-up of argument, showing grasp of cause and effect.	**2-1 marks** Some judgement shown in argument or weighting of language.

Possible answers include:

- There is a serious possibility that some other business may beat him to the US or Japanese market with a copy of his own product; if this happens he will be unable to do anything about it (but they won't then be able to sell their products in the UK).

- Fortunately, until the product hits the UK market, no one may take the Eggxactly idea seriously enough to be bothered to complete the technical work on the product; and, after all, James has a huge head start as he really understands the technology.

- Is he *likely* to lose out? Quite possibly, but perhaps not probably; and, after all, if he was too short of cash to complete the patent applications, he must have needed that cash to make a success of the product itself.

Protecting Business Ideas

B2 Data response

(25 marks; 25 minutes)

(Refer to question on page 15 of textbook.)

1. Explain whether the above issue is about breaking copyright or trademark law. (**4**)

   • Trademark is about logos and other 'badges of origin'. Copyright isn't about the badge, it's about the substance, the content, e.g. of the writing within a book, or the lyrics or music within a song. This case is about copyright.

2. Outline two possible reasons why 18-24 year olds may be the 'worst culprits'. (**4**)

   • They may simply be heavier users of the music and therefore more likely to buy but also more likely to illegally download.

   • Younger adults have grown up with digital music and may therefore be more expert at downloading it illegally.

3. Discuss whether John Enser is right to urge the music industry to cut its prices for officially downloaded music. (**8**)

	Knowledge 1 mark	Application 2 marks	Analysis 2 marks	Evaluation 3 marks
Level 2		**2 marks** Answer is applied effectively to the specific case.	**2 marks** Build-up of argument, making use of relevant business concepts.	**3 marks** Shows judgement in drawing conclusions from own argument.
Level 1	**1 mark** Some understanding of the subject content; or one answer identified.	**1 mark** Some relationship to the scenario (perhaps indirectly).	**1 mark** Some build-up of argument, showing grasp of cause and effect.	**2-1 marks** Some judgement shown in argument or weighting of language.

Possible answers include:

   • Yes, because the industry is unwise to put itself in a position of threatening its customers with legal action; far better to make the music cheap enough to be affordable – especially, perhaps, older tracks. Business success comes from repeat purchase and customer loyalty; high prices and threats are hardly the way to achieve this.

   • It is understandable, though, that the industry feels that people have no legal or moral right to 'steal' the IP of creative musicians; a professional writer might only have a handful of big hits in his/her career; pretty harsh to have the royalties 'stolen'.

4. Evaluate whether young people are likely to listen to the appeal by the BPI spokesman against 'downloading songs free'. **(9)**

	Knowledge 2 marks	Application 2 marks	Analysis 2 marks	Evaluation 3 marks
Level 2	**2 marks** Good understanding of the subject content; or two answers identified.	**2 marks** Answer is applied effectively to the specific case.	**2 marks** Build-up of argument, making use of relevant business concepts.	**3 marks** Shows judgement in drawing conclusions from own argument.
Level 1	**1 mark** Some understanding of the subject content; or one answer identified.	**1 mark** Some relationship to the scenario (perhaps indirectly).	**1 mark** Some build-up of argument, showing grasp of cause and effect.	**2-1 marks** Some judgement shown in argument or weighting of language.

Possible answers include:

- It is not possible to hold back a tide, so perhaps the BPI should accept that many people (not just the young) feel that they have a right to everything free that is on the Internet; just as no one would think about copyright issues when watching a YouTube clip, so no one worries about downloads of songs; accordingly, young people are very unlikely to listen to an 'appeal'.

- The only thing that might change behaviour is a series of well-publicised arrests and trials of ordinary people downloading music; but that carries its own risks for the music industry.

Developing Business Plans

4.1 Introduction

The topic of business plans needs to be dealt with not only as part of the specification, but also as a key integrating theme. It will provide the heart of the Unit 1 exam, providing scope to test students' ability to examine and critique material and to evaluate the chances of business success.

Although there is no requirement that students should 'do' a business plan, there is a great deal of scope for using a cut-down version of a business plan to engage student interest. This could start off with little more than getting them doing two-slide (max) presentations to include:

- their new business idea, its niche, its customers and its competition
- an outline plan for making the idea happen: location, staffing, finding and keeping customers.

Needless to say, all the high street banks publish material containing checklists and questionnaires covering the same kind of material as presented in this unit. Later in the term, you might organise your class into small teams and encourage them to develop a product or service idea, research the potential market, consider the skills they have to offer, identify operating resources required, and prepare a finance proposal. Presentations to the rest of the group, to the Head Teacher, to a friendly bank manager or to an outside business contact can all provide a fitting climax to this study task.

4.2 Further reading and resources

Title and price	Author	Publisher and ISBN	Brief account
Tips and Traps for Writing a Business Plan £10.99 (bargain!)	Balanko-Dickson, G.	McGraw Hill 2007 978 0 07 146751 3	Lots of super snippets and lists that will help in lessons, e.g. Seven Stages in Deciding Prices. Good sections include: 'Common Mistakes in Writing a Business Plan' and 'Working with Professional Advisors'. Useful tips such as 'Avoid breakevenitis'.
FT Guide to Business Start Up 2008 £19.99	Williams, S.	Prentice Hall 2007 978 0273 14873	Chapter 6 is a succinct, six-page introduction to business plans – ideal for the early stages of the course.
How to Fund Your Business: The Essential Guide to Raising Finance to Start and Grow Your Business £14.99	Parks, S.	Prentice Hall 2006 978 0273 70624 3	This is a much better book than you'd expect; oddly it's especially good on business plans (and weaker at raising finance). Chapter 2 is terrific: 'What Do Funders Want?'; also Chapter 4 'Preparing Your Plan'.

How to Prepare a Business Plan, 5e £12.99	Blackwell,. E.	Kogan Page 2008 978 0 7494 4981 0	Key features: 'Is a cash flow forecast of any real use'?; 'How not to write a business plan'. Useful comparisons between opening service and manufacturing businesses (helpful for Application).
Entrepreneurship and Small Business £34.99(!)	Burns, P.	Palgrave 2007 978 140 394 7338	Look beyond the price and get one for the staff room; it's terrific. Here, the gem is p380 'The Banker's View' and p381 'The Investor's View'.
The Small Business Start-up Workbook £12.99	Rickman, C.	How To Books 2005 978 1 84528 038 3	Good chapters include: Chapter 3 'Researching Your Market and Opportunity'; Chapter 8 'The Importance of Good Customer Service'; Chapter 9 'How to Behave – the Case for Ethical Business'.
A-Z AS Business Studies Worksheets – photocopiable pack plus VLE £95.00	Marcouse, I.	A-Z Business Training Ltd* 2008	AQA Worksheets 9 (Business Plan) and 30 (Evaluating a Business Plan) will be useful. They provide a variety of suitable AS questions and answers. *To order, go to www.a-zbusinesstraining.com

4.3 Answers to workbook questions

A Revision questions

(30 marks; 30 minutes)

1. Explain in your own words the meaning of the term 'business plan'. (3)

   • A plan setting out how to turn a business idea into a successful start-up.

   • This should provide full details of the business proposition, its distinctive characteristics, the resources needed for success and how and when they are to be used.

2. Why may young entrepreneurs need a business plan more than middle-aged ones? Briefly explain your answer. (3)

   • The less the level of experience, the more the entrepreneurs will need to prove that they have thought through the whole process from start to (successful) finish.

Developing Business Plans

- For example, it's far more important for a first-time boss to write out a plan for hiring staff than for someone with years of personnel experience.

3. Some people think that a business plan aimed at 'dragon' investors should be different from one aimed at bankers. Outline two ways in which a plan aimed at investors might be different from one aimed at a banker. **(4)**

   - One aimed at investors would emphasise the upside potential rather than the downside risk, e.g. the scope for building a global business or the opportunities for a series of additional products.

   - Investors would be interested in exit routes, i.e. how and when to expect to make their profit, e.g. 'I plan to float the business on the stock market within three years'.

4. Why might an entrepreneur find it easier to write a business plan for a second business start-up than for his/her first? **(4)**

   - There are so many mistakes to be made; many will be made second time as well, but others can be learnt from, e.g. being too optimistic about sales.

   - In the first plan, a lot will be speculation, e.g. about how much lighting costs in a shop; second time around there will be real knowledge.

5. Re-read the table of benefits and problems in Table 4.1 and decide whether the following entrepreneurs should take time to write out a full business plan. Explain your reasons.

   (a) A 30 year old, previously a teacher, who needs to borrow a small sum to help finance the launch of a night club. **(3)**

      - Yes, should have a full plan, because although the sum to be borrowed is small, the investment is likely to be considerable, and the risks (nightclub) are massive; the 30 year old risks losing his/her life savings; in addition, any bank is going to insist on seeing a business plan before lending a penny towards a night club launch.

   (b) A 50 year old, previously an accountant, who can personally finance the start-up of a business producing digital radios. **(3)**

      - No need, as there's no external capital, and the accountant will presumably have a clear idea about the cash flows involved; nevertheless, the accountant would probably benefit from setting out a clear plan for positioning, marketing and personnel.

6. How might Business Link help someone draw up a good business plan? **(3)**

   - Provide an experienced head and a second look at the data.

   - The advisor should know what bank managers are looking for.

7. If you were to open your own business after completing your A Levels, do you think you would complete a business plan? Explain your answer with reference to your own strengths and weaknesses. **(7)**

Developing Business Plans

• Suggested marking process:

Up to 3 marks for the self-analysis.

Up to 3 marks for relating features of a business plan to own strengths/weaknesses.

Up to 3 marks for the concluding argument.

BUT TO A MAXIMUM OF 7 MARKS, i.e. allow students different ways to achieve the maximum mark.

B1 Data response

(20 marks; 20 minutes)

(Refer to question on pages 19–20 of textbook.)

1. Look carefully at the graph for the first four months of the life of the business. Are the directors borrowing the right sum of money? Explain your answer. (**4**)

    • No, because the £80,000 covers the three months before opening, but will not cover the £10,000 of negative cash flow in the first operational month (month 4). The business needs to borrow a sum closer to £60,000, allowing a £10,000 contingency fund.

2. If the cash flow forecast proves correct, are the directors right to say that the £40,000 can be repaid by the end of the first year? Explain your answer. (**4**)

    • Yes, because they have forecast total cash inflows of £470,000 and total cash outflows of £465,000. Assuming that the directors' £40,000 will still be in the business at the end, there should be no difficulty in repaying the bank.

3. Discuss why a banker might be concerned to read, 'As shown in the cash flow table, we will be able to repay the sum in full…'? (**7**)

	Knowledge 1 mark	Application 2 marks	Analysis 2 marks	Evaluation 2 marks
Level 2		2 marks Answer is applied effectively to the specific case.	2 marks Build-up of argument, making use of relevant business concepts.	2 marks Shows judgement in drawing conclusions from own argument.
Level 1	1 mark Some understanding of the subject content; or one answer identified.	1 mark Some relationship to the scenario (perhaps indirectly).	1 mark Some build-up of argument, showing grasp of cause and effect.	1 mark Some judgement shown in argument or weighting of language.

Possible answers include:

- The quote shows certainty ('will be able to repay'), but a cash flow forecast is no more than a guess that looks into the future; the wording makes it look as if the directors believe that their guesstimates are facts.

- The situation is especially uncertain as the business idea is a new restaurant; all new business start-ups are insecure, but none are as insecure as a new restaurant.

4. Explain why the directors might be wise to borrow rather more capital than they believe they will need to finance the first year of the business. (5)

	Knowledge 1 mark	Application 2 marks	Analysis 2 marks
Level 2		**2 marks** Answer is applied effectively to the specific case.	**2 marks** Build-up of argument, making use of relevant business concepts.
Level 1	**1 mark** Shows some understanding of the subject content; or one answer identified.	**1 mark** Some relationship to the scenario (perhaps indirectly).	**1 mark** Some build-up of argument, showing grasp of cause and effect.

Possible answers include:

- So many things can go wrong, e.g. delayed opening; staffing problems; tough competition locally; therefore it's hugely helpful to have a contingency fund.

- Banks are not kind to firms that come back quickly, asking for more cash, i.e. if the directors ask for an overdraft in month 3, the bank is very unlikely to provide it.

B2 Data response

(20 marks; 20 minutes)

(Refer to question on page 20 of textbook.)

1. Explain how Judith's start-up might have been helped by the business plan. **(5)**

	Knowledge — 2 marks		Application 3 marks
Level 2	**2 marks** Good understanding of the subject content		**3 marks** Answer is applied effectively to the specific case.
Level 1	**1 mark** Shows understanding of the subject content.		**2-1 marks** Some relationship to the scenario (perhaps indirectly).

Possible answers include:

- She lacks experience, having spent 25 years in catering.

- It would have been a valuable part of a process that started with 18 months' planning.

2. Outline one feature of the start-up that raises questions about the effectiveness of this business plan. **(3)**

- 'Hitch in supplies' suggests that either they had done too little research into suppliers, or perhaps that they struck it lucky in that they were given a second chance that allowed them to start manufacturing.

3. Examine two features of the start-up that might have been less effective without the help of Business Link West Midlands. **(6)**

	Knowledge 3 marks		Application 3 marks
Level 2	**3 marks** Good understanding of the subject content; or two answers identified, showing understanding.		**3 marks** Answer is applied effectively to the specific case.
Level 1	**2-1 marks** Shows understanding of the subject content.		**2-1 marks** Some relationship to the scenario (perhaps indirectly).

Possible answers include:

- The direct help given with the business plan would have been useful, and may have given the bank manager confidence in the data; without the help things would have been tougher.

- Impartial advice is vital; the most important person at start-up is the entrepreneur; Judith has to be prevented from kidding herself about how easy it will all be.

4. From the evidence available, how likely is it that Judith's business will succeed? **(6)**

   - It sounds well-planned, and with an original product.

   - Judith sounds sensible, willing to learn and to take advice.

   - Both her husband and her Business Link advisor seem helpful.

   - So the evidence points to a high chance of success, but there are no certainties with business start-up.

Key Concepts in Business Start-Up

Unit 5

5.1 Introduction

This chapter covers three concepts:

1   opportunity cost, which is the cost of missing out on the next best alternative

2   transforming inputs into outputs, i.e. the process of turning resources into finished products

3   risk: the chance of a misfortune occurring.

All three are important and all are concepts that are widely applicable throughout the subject.

1. Opportunity cost should be introduced in relation to business start-up. The issue is: what is the entrepreneur missing out on as a result of the decision to start a business. Clearly there are financial and also work/life balance issues to consider. Many entrepreneurs kid themselves that they are adopting a more laid-back lifestyle than the '9-5 rat race' – and find themselves instead on a treadmill. The founder of 'The Fabulous Bakin Boys' gives a good account of hard work in the feature in *How They Started* (see below). The start-up of One Water (*Business Review*, September 2006) shows the trade-offs of security and income when starting an enterprise.

2. What the AQA Spec calls, clumsily, 'Transforming inputs into outputs' is really the value chain. So be alert to articles about the costs of production, especially in developing countries. For example, the BBC series *Blood, Sweat and T-shirts* revealed that the labour cost in a shirt made in India might be as low as 12p. If you can take students through the full trail from harvested cotton through to the £50 Paul Smith T-shirt, all well and good.

3. Risk is at the heart of Unit 1. Students need to learn to treat it objectively, weighing it up rather than shying away from it. It should be possible to create classroom situations where students are stating whether they would, or would not, invest in a new business idea. It is no problem if a student is risk-averse as long as s/he recognises it. The problem in an exam is when a student shies away from recommending a course of action when there is 'a chance of failure'.

The Section A exercises provide worthwhile coverage of the text. In addition the B2 exercise is worth tackling as it covers all three concepts within the same (real) context.

5.2 Further reading and resources:

Title and price	Author	Publisher and ISBN	Brief account
From Acorns: How to Build a Brilliant Business 2nd Edition £9.99	Woods, C.	Prentice Hall 2007 978 0 273 71252 7	The book starts with The Entrepreneur's Ten Commandments, one of which is: 'Cost your own time properly.

Key Concepts in Business Start-Up

			Your business's scarcest resource? Your time. Only spend it on the areas where you add the most value. Cost your own time properly – you might be willing to work for 50p an hour, but you won't find anyone else who will'. It's good on opportunity cost and risk.
Entrepreneurship and Small Business £34.99	Burns, P.	Palgrave 2007 978 140 394 7338	The section on risk (p304) emphasises the value of Ansoff's matrix, e.g. as a way to analyse the risks of start-up (how much experience has the proprietor in that particular market, and with those products?).
Against the Odds £10.99	Dyson, J.	Texere Publishing 2000 978 1587 9901 44	There's a super section in the chapter called 'We ruv G-Force'. Dyson put his first dual cyclone cleaner on the market in Japan at £1200 retail (25 years ago!), but because of huge distribution mark-ups, he received just £20 per machine (10 per cent of the ex-factory price).
How They Started: How 30 Good Ideas Became Great Businesses £12.95	Lester, D.	Crimson Publishing 2007 978-1-85458-400-7	Inputs into outputs: Glasses Direct – James Murray-Wells realised at Uni that the output price of High Street specs was absurd 'for some glass and wire'. He found a manufacturer who could supply subscription specs for £6 – and set up his hugely successful website.

Key Concepts in Business Start-Up

5.3 Answers to workbook questions

A Revision questions

(25 marks; 25 minutes)

1. Explain in your own words why time is an important aspect of opportunity cost. **(3)**

    • Time can only be used once, so the more time spent in the office, the less the time spent with the family. A choice is needed between different uses of the scarce resource – time.

2. Give two ways of measuring the opportunity cost to you of doing this homework. **(2)**

    • Typical answers – 'enjoying myself' (fair point); watching TV; carrying on inane conversations on Facebook; doing other homework; helping around the house (perhaps pass that one on to parents ASAP).

3. Outline one opportunity cost to a restaurant chef/owner of opening a second restaurant. **(3)**

    • Less (or no) time to make sure the first restaurant is running smoothly.

    • Less cash to invest in the first restaurant (is it starting to look a little shabby?).

4. State whether the following are P(rimary), S(econdary) or T(ertiary):

    a) Cadbury's chocolate (S)

    b) Sainsbury's (T)

    c) A pick-your-own-strawberries business (P with shades of T)

    d) Ryanair (T) **(4)**

5. If an exam question is about the location of a business, why is it important to know if the business is in the primary, secondary or tertiary sector? **(3)**

    • Primary businesses have to be located where the resources are.

    • Secondary can be located near resources or near the market, depending on cost implications.

    • Tertiary: many need to be close to the customer/market, e.g. retailing, cleaning, building repair, car repairs; but internet-based ones can be anywhere.

6. Why may a successful entrepreneur be good at 'moderate risk taking' rather than 'high risk taking'? **(3)**

    • Although a 'Dragon' investor can split his/her capital across many high-risk ventures, hoping that one or two hit the jackpot, the individual entrepreneur may have only one shot at success/failure. Therefore s/he needs the risks to be moderate, so that the chances of success are relatively high.

7. Identify one risk from each of the following business decisions. Briefly explain what you think the risk is:

a) doubling the advertising budget when a firm's sales haven't increased compared with last year (**2**)

- The risk is of loss-making, as happened to Land of Leather in early 2008; a huge advertising campaign yielded little response from consumers, leaving the business in a serious loss-making position.

b) a bakery switching to a new supplier of flour (**2**)

- The risk is of disruption, e.g. late deliveries, or deliveries of the wrong types of flour or deliveries of sub-standard flour.

c) an entrepreneur borrowing £80,000 secured against his house, when interest rates are nice and low at 3.25% (**3**)

- Interest rates can go up as well as down! The risk is that rising interest rates may make the fixed costs of the business too high – and then risk the entrepreneur losing the house because of the difficulty of making the interest payments.

B1 Data response

(10 marks; 15 minutes)

(Refer to question on page 24 of textbook.)

1. Outline three opportunity cost issues within this short passage. (**6**)

- The opportunity cost of starting the business was losing £55,000 a year of stable salary.

- To this is added the potential earnings (and status) that would come from promotion, given his 'very good' career prospects.

- Opportunity cost of time was accepting an extra 5 hours per working day (losing out, therefore on family and social time).

2. Outline the possible impact on James of the increase in the workload. (**4**)

- Might cause problems at home, especially if he has a young family.

- Might cause burnout, especially if work pressures stop him sleeping.

- But he may love the excitement and the pressure – which is easy to enjoy if the business is going well.

B2 Data response

(20 marks; 25 minutes)

(Refer to question on page 25 of textbook.)

1. Is the work of the Ugandan villagers in the primary, secondary or tertiary sector? (**1**)

- Primary

2. What would be the opportunity cost of the farmers who put 'countless hours of work into forming a new cooperative'? (**3**)

   • Those involved directly in the talks would have struggled to farm their own land as effectively as those who ignored the talks; this may have affected short-term earnings.

3. Outline one risk for the farmers and one risk for the Fairtrade organisation in forming a new cooperative with high guaranteed prices for the coffee beans. (**6**)

   • Risk for farmers is that the agreed price premium might not pay them for the extra costs/crop losses that might result from going organic, e.g. pest damage.

   • Risk for Fairtrade is that if the world price of coffee was to slump, the price agreed with the farmers may prove too high for western retail buyers.

4a Into which of the three sectors will the Gumutindo cooperative move if it starts its own production plant? (**1**)

   • Secondary

4b Discuss whether producing coffee ready for sale would definitely increase the income levels of the 3000 members of the cooperative. (**9**)

	Knowledge 2 marks	Application 2 marks	Analysis 2 marks	Evaluation 3 marks
Level 2	**2 marks** Good understanding of the subject content; or two answers identified	**2 marks** Answer is applied effectively to the specific case.	**2 marks** Build-up of argument, making use of relevant business concepts.	**3 marks** Shows judgement in drawing conclusions from own argument.
Level 1	**1 mark** Some understanding of the subject content; or one answer identified.	**1 mark** Some relationship to the scenario (perhaps indirectly).	**1 mark** Some build-up of argument, showing grasp of cause and effect.	**2-1 marks** Some judgement shown in argument or weighting of language.

Possible answers include:

   • There is a real possibility that it would increase incomes, though only if effective branding can be produced to make sure that value is added by moving from coffee beans to a packet of coffee.

   • There is also a possibility that coffee farmers will prove far less efficient at roasting, grinding and packing coffee than full-time manufacturers; in this case, any extra revenue generated will be swallowed up by extra costs, leaving no one any better off.

   • It is not possible to be sure what will happen, but it will probably not be of benefit unless the Fairtrade organisation invests in some strong branding and pack designs for Gumutindo coffee.

Choosing the Right Legal Structure

6.1 Introduction

The format of the Unit 1 exam makes it likely that this will be quite a live topic for short answer questions. When appraising a business plan it will also be necessary to grasp the implication of starting a business as a partnership as compared with a limited company. So although this is an unexciting topic, the chapter is especially worth reading (especially the Evaluation).

The Workbook section A question 4 gives a good model for what should probably be quite a detailed class activity. Students should have plenty of opportunities to think about what the right structure is for a new business. In particular it would be good if students had an answer to the B1, 1b question: 'Why are there so many more sole traders than limited companies?' It is a good pointer to the fact that most people starting their own business aspire more to self-employment than to empire-building.

The most important concept within this section of the specification is limited versus unlimited liability. Examiners are regularly shocked to see how poorly this is understood at A Level. It is a topic that should form an important part of Unit 1 revision.

6.2 Further reading and resources

Title and price	Author	Publisher and ISBN	Brief account
From Acorns: How to Build a Brilliant Business 2nd Edition	Woods, C.	Prentice Hall 2007 978 0 273 71252 7	Super section on pages 78 and 79 which tackles the question: Why would anyone in their right mind *not* want to limit their liability?
Starting Your Own Business: The Good, the Bad and the Unexpected £12.99	Lester, D.	Crimson Publishing 2008 978 1 85458 401 4	Chapter 11 contains a terrific introduction to business organisations. Only pity is that the chapter includes Limited Liability Partnerships, which will muddy the student waters.
FT Guide to Business Start Up 2008 £19.99	Williams, S.	Prentice Hall 2007 978 0273 14873	Clear and authoritative on legal structure, with a particularly clear account of sole traders and private limited companies.

Choosing the Right Legal Structure

6.3 Answers to workbook questions

A Revision questions

(25 marks; 25 minutes)

1. Explain two differences between a sole trader and a partnership. **(4)**

    • Sole trader is entirely owned by one person; partnership by 2 or more.

    • Therefore risks, responsibilities and workload are shared.

2. In your own words, try to explain the importance of establishing a separate legal entity to separate the business from the individual owner. **(4)**

    • The value is that potential liabilities rest with the company (the separate legal entity) and cannot be passed on to the owners (the shareholders); consequently the owners enjoy limited liability.

3. You can start a business today. All you have to do is tell the Inland Revenue (the taxman). Outline two risks of starting in this way. **(4)**

    • You will have unlimited liability because you are technically operating as a sole trader.

    • It sounds too impulsive; business start-up is risky, so it should have some careful preparation/ research before rushing in.

4. Briefly discuss whether each of the following businesses should start as a sole trader, a partnership or a private limited company.

    a) a clothes shop started by Claire Wells with £40,000 of her own money plus £10,000 from the bank; it is located close to her home in Wrexham **(3)**

    • This could be started as a private limited company to create a full guarantee of no personal losses beyond Claire's £40,000; but many people would start this as a sole trader, because the risks of default are very low and everything seems to be within Claire's control.

    b) a builders started by Jim Barton and Lee Clark, who plan to become the number one for loft extensions in Sheffield; they've each invested £15,000 and are borrowing £30,000 from the bank. **(3)**

    • It could be a partnership, but the risk-profile is so high that it would be foolish not to make this a limited company; 67% of the capital is borrowed (compared with 20% for Claire Wells) and the big ambitions (number one in Sheffield) imply the need for extra inputs of capital in future.

5. Explain the possible risks to a growing business of making the jump from a private limited company to 'going public', then floating its shares on the stock market. **(5)**

    • The sudden influx of cash from the float coincides with a sudden increase in external scrutiny and pressure; with the media and City analysts sniffing around, the pressure is on to invest this cash quickly (many of the building societies that 'floated' in the 1980s and 1990s made staggering mistakes with their early investments – the cash was burning a hole in their pockets).

- Rapid growth is always risky; with a sudden injection of a lot of cash, businesses often attempt a great leap forward, perhaps by making their first takeover bid for another company; as most takeovers fail, this is certainly risky.

6. In what way may the type of business organisation affect the image of the business. (2)

- It sounds more established/formal to have Ltd after your name than nothing; and makes the business seem much bigger if it is TIB plc than TIB Ltd.

B1 Data response

(20 marks; 20 minutes)

(Refer to question on page 31 of textbook.)

1 (a) Calculate the number of sole traders in the UK; then calculate the number of limited companies. (3)

- 66% of 3,600,000 = 2,376,000
  24% of 3,600,000 = 865,000

(b) Explain two possible reasons why there are so many more sole traders than companies. (6)

	Knowledge 2 marks	Application 2 marks	Analysis 2 marks
Level 2	**2 marks** Shows clear understanding of the subject content, or two reasons identified.	**2 marks** Answer is applied effectively to the specific case.	**2 marks** Build-up of argument, making use of relevant business concepts.
Level 1	**1 mark** Shows some understanding of the subject content; or one answer identified.	**1 mark** Some relationship to the scenario (perhaps indirectly).	**1 mark** Some build-up of argument, showing grasp of cause and effect.

Possible answers include:

- Starting up as a sole trader is cheap and easy, and requires no expert work by an accountant – all that will be needed is a properly completed income tax return for the individual; these figures are about all businesses; in fact many *should* form a limited company, but at this early stage the entrepreneur has not thought hard enough about the risks involved.

- If a person starts a small shop with no intention of building it into a chain of stores, a sole trader organisation makes good sense.

2. What proportion of British businesses operate with unlimited liability? **(1)**

• 76%

3. Dr Fraser's research also shows that one in five businesses is principally owned by a woman and 93% are owned by white, 7% by non-white ethnicity.

(a) Examine two possible reasons why women are so much less likely to own a business than men. **(6)**

	Knowledge 2 marks	Application 2 marks	Analysis 2 marks
Level 2	**2 marks** Shows clear understanding of the subject content, or two reasons identified.	**2 marks** Answer is applied effectively to the specific case.	**2 marks** Build-up of argument, making use of relevant business concepts.
Level 1	**1 mark** Shows some understanding of the subject content; or one answer identified.	**1 mark** Some relationship to the scenario (perhaps indirectly).	**1 mark** Some build-up of argument, showing grasp of cause and effect.

Possible answers include:

• It may be lack of opportunity; there is some evidence that banks have traditionally been biased against women entrepreneurs; it may also be that venture capital providers feel more comfortable with male businesspeople; a further possibility is that the famously long hours involved in starting a business are more off-putting to women than to men.

• It may be lack of desire; women may have less interest in business start-up, perhaps because society's attitudes to 'thrusting/dynamic' women is equivocal; women may have less of a drive to 'prove themselves' – often the motive for male entrepreneurs.

b) The % figures for non-white business ownership are slightly below the number of non-whites in the population (between 8 and 9%). Outline two reasons that might explain this. **(4)**

• It may be due to lower wealth levels, making it harder to start a business.

• It may be due to discrimination among bankers/investors.

Choosing the Right Legal Structure

B2 Data response

(20 marks; 25 minutes)

(Refer to question on page 32 of textbook.)

1a The name of the business is Devoted 2 Vintage. Does that suggest it's a sole trader or a private limited company? **(1)**

- A sole trader (no Ltd after name)

1b Bearing in mind your answer to 1a, outline two factors Bernice should remember about the legal structure of the business she is running. **(6)**

	Knowledge 3 marks	Application 3 marks
Level 2	**3 marks** Shows clear understanding of the subject content, and identifies two factors.	**3 marks** Answer is applied effectively to the specific case.
Level 1	**2-1 marks** Shows understanding of the subject content.	**2-1 marks** Some relationship to the scenario (perhaps indirectly).

Possible answers include:

- It gives her no personal protection from creditors if the business fails, i.e. she has unlimited liability; because her business is fashion-orientated, it is relatively high risk, so she is taking quite a chance.

- She is also vulnerable if she takes a holiday and leaves someone else in charge; if that person makes disastrous mistakes in Bernice's name (buying a ghastly line of clothes), the liability effectively rests with Bernice.

2. As Bernice expands the business to develop online, should she consider changing the legal structure of the business? If so, why and how? **(6)**

	Knowledge 3 marks	Application 3 marks
Level 2	**3 marks** Shows clear understanding of the subject content.	**3 marks** Answer is applied effectively to the specific case.
Level 1	**2-1 marks** Shows understanding of the subject content.	**2-1 marks** Some relationship to the scenario (perhaps indirectly).

Choosing the Right Legal Structure

Possible answers include:

- Yes, because online represents expansion, and the more stretched she is, the greater the chance of a bad mistake being made.

- She should change to a private limited company; it's not that expensive and it will help her sleep at night.

3. Discuss how well Bernice has done so far in setting up her first business. (7)

	Knowledge 1 mark	Application 2 marks	Analysis 2 marks	Evaluation 2 marks
Level 2		2 marks Answer is applied effectively to the specific case.	2 marks Build-up of argument, making use of relevant business concepts.	2 marks Shows judgement in drawing conclusions from own argument.
Level 1	1 mark Some understanding of the subject content; or one answer identified.	1 mark Some relationship to the scenario (perhaps indirectly).	1 mark Some build-up of argument, showing grasp of cause and effect.	1 mark Some judgement shown in argument or weighting of language.

Possible answers include:

- Strengths include: spotting a gap; understanding the market; showing initiative; responding to market trends.

- Weaknesses include starting as an unlimited liability business and – perhaps – rushing to start a business based on her own passion without stopping to check that customers locally were as keen.

Market Research

7.1 Introduction

Market research presents the teacher with a microcosm of the challenges and difficulties of this AS Level. Many students come with a comfortable, common-sense understanding. They 'know it' already. What they know is likely to be a squidgy mixture of street interviewers, product demonstrators and a Pepsi Challenge-style mixture of the two. Market research findings will be subject to scepticism on the grounds that 'people are in a hurry' and 'everyone lies'.

It is not easy to move towards an understanding of the logic, precision and mathematics of sampling, questionnaire design and the analysis and interpretation of survey findings. Yet success in this task can represent a major step forward for a student. No essay reader could fail to be impressed by the ability to analyse a marketing problem using an academic approach to market research. Partly for that reason, there is a strong case for teaching research towards the beginning of the marketing syllabus. Without it, there are few marketing case studies that can be tackled impressively.

7.2 Further reading and resources

Title and price	Author	Publisher and ISBN	Brief account
Essentials of Marketing £32.99	Blythe, J.	Prentice Hall 2005 978 027 369 3581	The chapter on market research is practical and accessible. It doesn't explain different sampling methods, but apart from this is a very good match for the Spec.
Good Small Business Guide: How to Start and Grow Your Own Business 3rd edition £19.99		A & C Black 2008 978 0 7136 8760 6	Useful four-page section on market research; worth copying for all. Starts on p228.
Entrepreneurship and Small Business £34.99	Burns, P.	Palgrave 2007 978 140 394 7338	Pages 146-150 give a super introduction to research. It's strong on purposes and light on methods; and is very focused on the small business sector.
FT Guide to Business Start-Up 2008 £19.99	Williams, S.	Prentice Hall 2007 978 0273 14873	Chapter 2 'Who Will Buy?' is useful, covering market size and share as well as a broad overview of market research. Especially good for secondary research.

7.3 Answers to workbook questions

A Revision questions

(35 marks; 35 minutes)

1. State three ways in which a cosmetics firm could use market research. **(3)**

    • To identify the main target market.

    • To identify the image of each of the main brands.

    • To find out how brand loyal the users are.

2. Outline three reasons why market research information may prove inaccurate. **(6)**

    • The sample may be too small for statistical validity.

    • The interviewers may be unconsciously biased.

    • Respondents may say what they believe the interviewer wants to hear.

3. Distinguish between primary and secondary research. **(3)**

    • Primary is first hand research gathered directly from your target audience, e.g. by an interview. Secondary is second-hand, such as from a book or a government report.

4. What advantages are there in using secondary research rather than primary? **(3)**

    • Cheaper to gather.

    • May be on a much larger (perhaps national rather than local) scale.

    • Less likely to be biased towards your point of view.

5. Which is the most commonly used sampling method? Why may it be the most commonly used? **(4)**

    • Quota sample is the most commonly used because it is the cheapest (and fastest) way of achieving a representative sample.

6. State three key factors to take into account when writing a questionnaire. **(3)**

    • Ensure that the questions meet all your research objectives.

    • Avoid writing questions which lead the respondent towards a particular answer.

    • Ensure that each question is clear and precise.

7. Explain two aspects of marketing in which consumer psychology is important. **(4)**

    • When conducting market research it is important to understand consumer psychology.;

- When conducting interviews it is important that psychologists do not sway the consumer.

8. Outline the pros and cons of using a large sample size. (**4**)

- Pros: increases the reliability of the findings, i.e. gives a higher confidence level.

- Cons: more expensive and takes longer, meaning less of the research budget is left for other surveys.

9. Identify three possible sources of bias in primary market research. (**3**)

- The interviewer probing for the answers he/she wants.

- Questionnaires that lead consumers to certain answers.

- Low response rates.

- Small sample size.

10. Why may street interviewing become less common in the future? (**3**)

- The increased sampling from databases (such as from the Tesco Clubcard) means there is less need for street interviewing.

B1 Market research assignment

(30 marks; 30 minutes)

(Refer to question on page 39 of textbook.)

1 Write a questionnaire based upon the above details, bearing in mind the advice given in Section 7.5. (**12**)

	Knowledge 4 marks	Application 4 marks	Analysis 4 marks
Level 2	**4-3 marks** Good understanding of the subject content; or accurate questions asked.	**4-3 marks** Answer is applied effectively to the specific case.	**4-3 marks** Build-up of argument, making use of relevant business concepts.
Level 1	**2-1 marks** Shows some understanding of the subject content.	**2-1 marks** Some relationship to the scenario (perhaps indirectly).	**2-1 marks** Some build-up of argument, showing grasp of cause and effect.

As an example of a (very good) questionnaire:

Questionnaire on Hampton Health Foods

Good morning, I wonder if you could spare a few moments to answer a few questions?

1. How often do you eat breakfast cereal nowadays?

   Once a month (or less)   _____

   Two or three times a month   _____

   One or two times a week   _____

   Three to six times a week   _____

   Once or more a day   _____

2. Which of the following brands have you eaten in the past month?

   Jordan's Original Crunchy   _____

   Kelloggs Bran Flakes   _____

   Kellogs Fruit N Fibre   _____

   Shredded Wheat   _____

   Any other cereal   _____ (please specify the brand)

3. Hampton Health Foods is considering introducing a new breakfast cereal. The company is looking at three possibilities. For each in turn, will you tell me whether the product sounds absolutely right for you, quite right for you, not quite right, or absolutely wrong:

	Absolutely right	Quite right	Not quite right	Absolutely wrong
Cracker: an extra-crunchy mix of oats and almonds	_____	_____	_____	_____
Fizzz: crunchy oats which fizz in milk	_____	_____	_____	_____
St James: a luxury mix of oats, cashews and pecan nuts	_____	_____	_____	_____

4. How often do you think you might buy each of the three products:

	Once a week	2 or 3 times a month	About once a month	Less often
Cracker: an extra-crunchy mix of oats and almonds	_____	_____	_____	_____
Fizzz: crunchy oats which fizz in milk	_____	_____	_____	_____
St James: a luxury mix of oats, cashews and pecan nuts	_____	_____	_____	_____

5. Approximately what price would you expect each one of the three would be for a large pack?

	Over £2	£1.76–2.00	£1.50–1.75	Under £1.50
Cracker: an extra-crunchy mix of oats and almonds	_____	_____	_____	_____
Fizzz: crunchy oats which fizz in milk	_____	_____	_____	_____
St James: a luxury mix of oats, cashews and pecan nuts	_____	_____	_____	_____

6. Are there any things you <u>dislike</u> about each product and brand name?

Cracker: an extra-crunchy
mix of oats and almonds

_____

Fizzz: crunchy oats which
fizz in milk

_____

St James: a luxury mix of oats,
cashews and pecan nuts

_____

7. Are there any things you <u>like</u> about each product and brand name?

Cracker: an extra-crunchy
mix of oats and almonds

_____

Fizzz: crunchy oats which
fizz in milk

_____

St James: a luxury mix of oats,
cashews and pecan nuts

_____

8. Would you please tell me which of the following age categories you fit into?

15–24 _____   25–34 _____   35–44 _____

45–54 _____   55–64 _____   65+ _____

9. Could you please tell me the occupation of the head of household?

_____

10. Record here whether male _____ or female _____

2. Explain which sampling method you would use and why. (6)

	Knowledge 2 marks	Application 2 marks	Analysis 2 marks
Level 2	**2 marks** Good understanding of the subject content.	**2 marks** Answer is applied effectively to the specific case.	**2 marks** Build-up of argument, making use of relevant business concepts.
Level 1	**1 mark** Shows some understanding of the subject content.	**1 mark** Some relationship to the scenario (perhaps indirectly).	**1 mark** Some build-up of argument, showing grasp of cause and effect.

Possible answers include:

• Quota sample based upon secondary information on the profile of the target market.

• Stratified sample based purely on people who eat (or buy?) breakfast cereals; this is probably the most cost-effective as it focuses on real cereal eaters.

• Random sample conducted by visiting homes chosen from the electoral register, e.g. every twentieth name – ensures all types of customer, including those who are not currently eating cereals.

3. Interview six to eight people using your questionnaire, then write a 200-word commentary on its strengths and weaknesses. (12)

	Knowledge 3 marks	Application 3 marks	Analysis 3 marks	Evaluation 3 marks
Level 2	**3 marks** Good understanding of the subject content.	**3 marks** Answer is applied effectively to the specific case.	**3 marks** Build-up of argument, making use of relevant business concepts.	**3 marks** Shows judgement in drawing conclusions from own argument.
Level 1	**2-1 marks** Some understanding of the subject content.	**2-1 marks** Some relationship to the scenario (perhaps indirectly).	**2-1 marks** Some build-up of argument, showing grasp of cause and effect.	**2-1 marks** Some judgement shown in argument or weighting of language.

Possible answers include:

- whether research objectives have been met

- clarity of the questions

- the use of open and closed questions

- bias.

B2 Data response

(20 marks; 30 minutes)

(Refer to question on pages 39–40 of textbook.)

1. Outline whether the sample size of 150 was appropriate in this case. (**4**)

   - Possibly yes, to keep the costs down, though 150 may be a little bit small a sample size given the unclear findings of question 2.

   - It was appropriate to have a small-ish sample in case the findings were clear-cut. As they aren't, another, bigger sample may be needed.

2. Examine the marketing director's conclusion that 'none of the new product ideas has done brilliantly, but happy that there's one clear winner'. (**7**)

	Knowledge 2 marks	Application 2 marks	Analysis 3 marks
Level 2	**2 marks** Good understanding of the subject content.	**2 marks** Answer is applied effectively to the specific case.	**3 marks** Build-up of argument, making use of relevant business concepts.
Level 1	**1 mark** Shows some understanding of the subject content.	**1 mark** Some relationship to the scenario (perhaps indirectly).	**2-1 marks** Some build-up of argument, showing grasp of cause and effect.

Possible answers include:

- Actually, they have *all* done really badly; the only interesting answer is 'might buy once a week', and no more than 5% have chosen any one of the three flavours; surely the Marketing Director should be questioning the whole strategy.

- It isn't clear which idea is 'the clear winner' chosen by the Marketing Director. It should be 'Muesli yoghurt', because that has more than double the result achieved by the other flavours for 'once a week'; people saying something as vague as 'might try' is as valueless as 'never'.

Market Research

3a Explain one method of qualitative research that could be used in this case. **(3)**

- In-depth, one-to-one interviews with those saying 'buy once a week'; this would help reveal exactly what they want from the brand, to help assess its potential.

3b Analyse two ways in which qualitative research might help the marketing director. **(6)**

	Knowledge 2 marks	Application 2 marks	Analysis 2 marks
Level 2	**2 marks** Good understanding of the subject content.	**2 marks** Answer is applied effectively to the specific case.	**2 marks** Build-up of argument, making use of relevant business concepts.
Level 1	**1 mark** Shows some understanding of the subject content.	**1 mark** Some relationship to the scenario (perhaps indirectly).	**1 mark** Some build-up of argument, showing grasp of cause and effect.

Possible answers include:

- Give psychological insights into why dog owners buy what they buy; for instance, it may be that they like to pretend that they don't give their pets treats (risk of making them fat/unhealthy), whereas they do.

- The quantitative research is not convincing; more information is needed before making a decision.

Understanding Markets

8.1 Introduction

In many ways students struggle most with things that are obvious. 'Understanding markets' sounds too straightforward to be worth learning. Yet there are several concepts here that are of great value to students: market segmentation, market growth and share and the different types of market. The key is cases rather than theory, i.e. finding ways to apply the material effectively.

The Workbook Section A questions are especially helpful as homework. B2 is also worthwhile, but it would be best to use it for a classroom exercise, especially if your students are numerically challenged.

8.2 Further reading and resources

Title and price	Author	Publisher and ISBN	Brief account
Start Your Business Week by Week £14.99	Parkes, S	Prentice Hall 2005 0 273 69447 2	Chapter 7 is a useful introduction to understanding markets. It's unsophisticated, but that's quite helpful.
Essentials of Marketing £32.99	Blythe, J.	Prentice Hall 2005 978 027 369 3581	Although the book's best bit is the extended Boston Matrix on p135 (including a dodo!), chapter 4 on segmentation, targeting and positioning is useful in understanding markets.
Good Small Business Guide: How to Start and Grow Your Own Business 3rd edition £19.99		A & C Black 2008 978 0 7136 8760 6	Useful four-page section called 'Profiling Your Competitors' and a further three-page section on 'Feedback from Customers'.
Starting Your Own Business: The Good, the Bad and the Unexpected £12.99	Lester, D.	Crimson Publishing 2008 978 185 458 401 4	Pages 38-45 are good on understanding your market, and start to look at the difficulty of predicting the size of the business opportunity.

8.3 Answers to workbook questions

A Revision questions

(35 marks; 30 minutes)

1. Outline three features of the market for fast food near to where you live. (**6**)

One mark per relevant point + 1 for development; example answer:

- Affected by local art college, so it's geared to small independents, not the mass market.

- Busy town centre, so there's a huge range of fast food catering for every niche.

- At the local primary school, an ice cream van arrives for the end of every day.

2. Section 8.2 lists five factors determining the demand for a product: price, incomes, actions of competitors, marketing activities and seasonality. Identify which two of these would most heavily affect sales of:

   a) strawberries

   - Seasonality; price (incomes is also OK)

   b) easy Jet tickets to Barcelona

   - Price, actions of competitors

   c) tickets to see Newcastle United

   - Seasonality, income

   d) DFS furniture

   - Marketing activities; seasonality (**8**)

3. Explain in your own words the difference between market size by volume and market size by value. (**2**)

   - By volume is the number of units sold; by value is the total spending on all the units sold.

4a Toyota's share of the UK car market is about 6%. If it continues with that share, how many UK car sales would that amount to in 2020; and how many would there be in China in 2020, assuming the same market share? (**4**)

   - 6% of the UK market will be 156,000 cars in 2020

   - 6% of the Chinese market will be 1,200,000 in 2020

4b Outline two ways Toyota might respond to that sales difference. **(4)**

  • They will spend far more on marketing activities in China than Britain.

  • They may switch production for Toyota, Derby to Toyota, Shanghai.

5. Why might a shoe shop focusing on 'Little Feat' be able to charge higher prices per pair than a general shoe shop? **(2)**

  • Any specialism, with depth and breadth of stock to go with it, enables a retail business to charge more, i.e. it adds value for the customer (masses of stock for small feet).

6. Explain in your own words how the market for shoes could be segmented. **(3)**

  • Could be by age, by social class, by income, by height (shorter people want higher heels) or by fashion.

7. Look at Table 8.3. Discuss which business should be happier with its market position: Walkers or Pampers. **(6)**

  • Pampers should be very happy, as its 61% of the disposable nappy market gives it a very safe position compared with Walkers.

  • But the much greater market size gives Walkers a higher sales value than Pampers; the acid test would be – which is the more profitable?

B1 Data response

(15 marks; 15 minutes)

(Refer to question on page 45 of textbook.)

1. Outline two reasons why a whole market may shrink in size, as happened to CD sales in the first half of 2007. **(4)**

	Knowledge 2 marks	Application 2 marks
Level 2	2 marks Shows clear understanding of the subject content.	2 marks Answer is applied effectively to the specific case.
Level 1	1 mark Shows some understanding of the subject content.	1 mark Some relationship to the scenario (perhaps indirectly).

Possible answers include:

  • Customers may stop buying because there is a superior technology available elsewhere, e.g. iPod downloads.

  • Lower consumer incomes could lead to a reduction in demand throughout a market.

2. ChoicesUK collapsed as the market declined. Explain two ways in which it might have set about boosting its market share (to combat the decline in the market as a whole). **(6)**

Knowledge 3 marks		Application 3 marks
Level 2	**3 marks** Shows clear understanding of the subject content.	**3 marks** Answer is applied effectively to the specific case.
Level 1	**2-1 marks** Shows some understanding of the subject content.	**2-1 marks** Some relationship to the scenario (perhaps indirectly).

Possible answers include:

- Price cutting, though this would have been very dangerous in a market dominated by HMV.

- It might have tried to move into a niche where sales were declining rather more slowly, e.g. country music; the problem was that the pace of change was so rapid (10% sales fall in six months) that ChoicesUK probably wasn't able to move quickly enough.

3. In the past, more than half the annual sales of ChoicesUK have taken place in the three months before Christmas. Should the Directors have kept the business going a few months more? **(5)**

Knowledge 2 marks		Application 3 marks
Level 2	**2 marks** Shows clear understanding of the subject content.	**3 marks** Answer is applied effectively to the specific case.
Level 1	**1 mark** Shows some understanding of the subject content.	**2-1 marks** Some relationship to the scenario (perhaps indirectly).

Possible answers include:

- No doubt they would have loved to do so; presumably they were forced to cease trading because they ran out of money.

- If they were running out of money it was the directors' duty to shut the business down asap.

B2 Data response

(30 marks; 35 minutes)

(Refer to question on pages 45–6 of textbook.)

1a What was the grocery market size and market growth in 2007? **(2)**

- Market size: £128.2 billion

- Market growth: 4%

1b Identify three possible reasons why sales at Somerfield fell in 2007. **(3)**

- Prices too high; service too poor; product range too narrow.

2a Show the workings to calculate that a 0.2% share of the UK grocery market equals £256.4 million. **(3)**

- £128.2bn × 0.2/100 = £256.4 million

2b Use the figures and the bar chart to work out the value of the UK 2007 sales of Lidl. **(2)**

- £128.2 billion × 2.2 = £282.04bn / 100 = £2.82bn

2c Examine two *possible* reasons why Lidl enjoyed the biggest sales growth within the grocery market in 2007. **(6)**

	Knowledge 1 mark	Application 2 marks	Analysis 3 marks
Level 2		2 marks Answer is applied effectively to the specific case.	3 marks Build-up of argument, making use of relevant business concepts.
Level 1	1 mark Shows some understanding of the subject content.	1 mark Some relationship to the scenario (perhaps indirectly).	2-1 marks Some build-up of argument, showing grasp of cause and effect.

Possible answers include:

- Consumers may have been looking to trade down, given tougher economic times; this gains some confirmation from the strong performance from Aldi, another discount retailer.

- There may also have been a change to Lidl's sales strategy, e.g. offering a wider range of goods at discount prices, or offering better-known brands at a discount.

3a Outline two ways in which Tesco may benefit from being the grocery market leader. **(4)**

- Bigger discounts from suppliers due to buying in greater bulk (therefore lower costs per unit).

• Developers of property centres will be especially keen to welcome Tesco as a tenant, so Tesco may get special deals.

3b Ten years ago, Sainsbury's was the UK grocery market leader. Discuss whether it could return to that position within the next ten years. **(10)**

	Knowledge 2 marks	Application 2 marks	Analysis 3 marks	Evaluation 3 marks
Level 2	2 marks Good understanding of the subject content; or two answers identified.	2 marks Answer is applied effectively to the specific case.	3 marks Build-up of argument, making use of relevant business concepts.	3 marks Shows judgement in drawing conclusions from own argument.
Level 1	1 mark Some understanding of the subject content; or one answer identified.	1 mark Some relationship to the scenario (perhaps indirectly).	2-1 marks Some build-up of argument, showing grasp of cause and effect.	2-1 marks Some judgement shown in argument or weighting of language.

Possible answers include:

• Very hard to imagine; Sainsbury's seems too stuck in a middle-class niche; it would require a complete change of strategy, yet does it have the staff who could make a switch to being a mass-market retailer?

• Also hard to imagine because it would require Tesco to make a series of dreadful errors, such as allowing senior management to focus too much on overseas (especially the U.S.).

• More positively, if Sainsbury's came out with a new type of store, focused more on younger people and families, with a greater emphasis on making life easier rather than more complicated (Jamie Oliver recipes), there may be scope for significant market share gains.

• A betting person would probably put their money on Tesco rather than Sainsbury's for the next ten years, though.

Sources of Finance

9.1 Introduction

In effect this topic breaks down into three parts:

- Obtaining finance for start-up

- Finance for running or building a small business

- Finance for larger businesses (and the finance expansion)

The focus must be on finance for small firms, but the information here will have to serve students for the full two years. Therefore plcs and company flotation need to be dealt with.

Although *Dragons' Den* can provide some hugely useful clips for the classroom, there is a risk overall that students will imagine that the business world works in this way. Examiners would inevitably be impressed by students who realise that venture capital is an unlikely option for a new small firm. The heart of the matter is that most start-ups are financed primarily by the entrepreneur (or the extended family). In these days of web start-ups, the initial investment is as much time as money. For instance, although Glasses Direct eventually needed a lot of finance, James Murray-Wells did all the development and testing from his bedroom, by developing an e-commerce website for his low-price specs.

In teaching, it is always worth bearing in mind the three key ways to analyse a question about sources of finance:

1. The split between internal and external sources.

2. The split between loan capital and share capital.

3. The (less clear-cut) difference between short and long-term sources of capital.

Students who are able to break down the options in that way will be in a strong position in the exams

9.2 Further reading and resources

Title and price	Author	Publisher and ISBN	Brief account
From Acorns: How to Build a Brilliant Business 2nd Edition £9.99	Woods, C.	Prentice Hall 2007 978 0 273 71252 7	The blessedly short chapter on 'Raising Finance' is by far the best as an introduction to students – it's accurate and wise, but without technical detail or obscure sources.
FT Guide to Business Start Up 2008 £19.99	Williams, S.	Prentice Hall 2007 978 0273 14873	Chapter 24 is quite friendly on the subject of 'raising the money', but it's frustrating to see a book present CDFIs

			(Community Development Finance Initiatives) as if they're as common as bank loans. Covers the Loan Guarantee Scheme well.
How to Fund Your Business: The Essential Guide to Raising Finance to Start and Grow Your Business £14.99	Parks, S.	Prentice Hall 2006 978 0273 70624 3	Chapter 1 'An Overview' is helpful – worth getting students to read. Later on, the book has too much detail – often on arcane financing options.
Starting Your Own Business: The Good, the Bad and the Unexpected £12.99	Lester, D	Crimson Publishing 2008 978 185 458 401 4	Chapter 12 is great for a teacher but – like most of the books listed here – there are too many obscure sources of finance to give the chapter to students.
Entrepreneur-ship and Small Business £34.99 (!)	Burns, P.	Palgrave 2007 978 140 394 7338	Chapter 15 is worth reading. It includes some gems such as a favoured bankers' acronym for judging the worth of loan applicants: CAMPARI – Character, Ability, Management, Purpose (of loan), Amount, Repayment, Insurance.

9.3 Answers to workbook questions

A Revision questions

(30 marks; 30 minutes)

1. Describe the problem caused to a company if a major customer refuses to pay a big bill. **(3)**

    • It will affect cash flow and could make the company unable to pay its own bills.

2. Why do banks demand collateral before they agree to provide a loan? **(2)**

    • If the business is unable to pay back the loan they will have something to sell to recoup the money lent.

3. Outline two ways in which businesses can raise money from internal sources. **(4)**

    Up to two marks for each suggestion:

- Improving cash flow by paying creditors later or getting debtors to pay sooner.

- Retaining profit.

- Selling assets.

4. What information might a bank manager want when considering a loan to a business? **(4)**

- A business plan outlining the past performance of the business and its future expectations. This will include a past and forecast profit and loss account, balance sheet and cash flow forecast.

5. Read the 'Application' report on Northern Rock. Explain the two mistakes made by the bank. **(4)**

Two marks for each mistake identified.

- The bank had expanded rapidly.

- The bank financed long-term projects with short-term finance.

- The finance was not adequate or appropriate. The bank was not prepared for the lack of availability of short-term loans in the commercial market.

6. Outline two sources of finance that can be used for long-term business development. **(4)**

Up to two marks for each suggestion:

- long-term loan

- selling shares

- retained profit

7. Explain why a new business might find it difficult to get external funding for its development. **(5)**

One mark per reason. Up to four marks for explanation:

- May have no collateral.

- No track record.

- New businesses are risky so investors are cautious.

- Takes time to build up profitability so investors may have to wait for a return.

8. Outline one advantage and one disadvantage of using an overdraft. **(4)**

Up to two marks for an advantage; two marks for a disadvantage.

- Advantages include: easy to arrange; business only uses the lending that it needs at any one time; flexible form of borrowing; immediately available once organised.

- Disadvantages include: very expensive; can be withdrawn by the bank at any time; may encourage the business to be careless about cash flow.

Sources of Finance

B1 Activity

(25 marks; 30 minutes)

(Refer to question on page 51 of textbook.)

1. If your £75,000 was at stake, what research would you carry out before investing in James Seddon's 'Eggxactly'. Explain your reasoning. **(8)**

	Knowledge 2 marks	Application 3 marks	Analysis 3 marks
Level 2	**2 marks** Shows clear understanding of the subject content.	**3 marks** Answer is applied effectively to the specific case.	**3 marks** Build-up of argument, making use of relevant business concepts.
Level 1	**1 mark** Shows some understanding of the subject content.	**2-1 marks** Some relationship to the scenario (perhaps indirectly).	**2-1 marks** Some build-up of argument, showing grasp of cause and effect.

Possible answers include:

- Secondary research into trends in the way eggs are eaten, and in the overall consumption of eggs at home; is this a growing or declining market? Then try to find comparable figures for big markets overseas such as America (as sales of 'zillions' could only come from a worldwide market).

- Research into the sales of gadgets such as sandwich toasters; how many have been sold? What were the Year 1 sales? And what is the level of sales today?

- Research into the prices of comparable kitchen gadgets; what price could households be expected to pay?

2. Outline the risks being taken on by the investors of £75,000. Are they wise? **(6)**

	Knowledge 1 mark	Application 2 marks	Analysis 1 mark	Evaluation 2 marks
Level 2		**2 marks** Answer is applied effectively to the specific case.		**2 marks** Shows judgement in drawing conclusions from own argument.

Sources of Finance

Level 1	1 mark Some understanding of the subject content; or one answer identified.	1 mark Some relationship to the scenario (perhaps indirectly).	1 mark Some build-up of argument, showing grasp of cause and effect.	1 mark Some judgement shown in argument or weighting of language.

- Clearly it's a very risky investment, because they don't really know whether the Eggxactly works!

- But for £75,000 they are getting a 40% stake in a business that might prove hugely successful; this is a highly innovative product backed by a patent that could give high profits for 20 years before the patent runs out.

- Are they wise to offer their money? Yes, given that they can afford to lose £37,500 each if it fails, while giving themselves the chance of making millions if it succeeds.

3. The £75,000 investment was share capital in exchange for 40% of James Seddon's business. Discuss whether James Seddon should accept the offer or turn it down. (11)

	Knowledge 2 marks	Application 2 marks	Analysis 3 marks	Evaluation 4 marks
Level 2	2 marks Good understanding of the subject content; or two answers identified.	2 marks Answer is applied effectively to the specific case.	3 marks Build-up of argument, making use of relevant business concepts.	4-3 marks Shows judgement in drawing conclusions from own argument.
Level 1	1 mark Some understanding of the subject content; or one answer identified.	1 mark Some relationship to the scenario (perhaps indirectly).	2-1 marks Some build-up of argument, showing grasp of cause and effect.	2-1 marks Some judgement shown in argument or weighting of language.

Yes he should because:

- Getting a technically innovative product to the market is inevitably expensive, so he will need that £75,000; also, the text says the patent is 'pending', so more money may need to be spent firming it up.

- James Seddon is a 'computer software expert', so he lacks experience in a sector such as consumer/retail sales; the expertise of the Dragons could be very helpful.

But he should be cautious because:

- For £75,000 he is being expected to give away 40% of a business that might generate sales of 'zillions'; this is a huge price to pay.

Judgement marks should come from the logic of the student's own argument, but in fact James Seddon eventually turned the Dragons down.

B2 Data response

Mayday Printers

(20 marks; 30 minutes)

(Refer to question on page 52 of textbook.)

1   Prepare a report for the board, outlining the advantages and disadvantages of each proposal. End your report with a clear recommendation. (**20**)

Report format: (2)

	Content 4 marks	Application 4 marks	Analysis 4 marks	Evaluation 6 marks
Level 2	**4-3 marks** Candidate offers two or more advantages and 2 or more disadvantages.	**4-3 marks** Candidate uses the context thoughtfully.	**4-3 marks** At least one effective argument constructed.	**6-4 marks** Well-supported conclusions that stem from the student's arguments.
	2 marks Candidate offers two advantages or disadvantages.	**2 marks** Candidate applies knowledge effectively to the circumstances.	**2 marks** Some analysis of argument.	**3-2 marks** Sound judgement shown in answers and conclusions.
Level 1	**1 mark** Candidate offers a single relevant argument or shows limited knowledge.	**1 mark** Candidate attempts to apply knowledge to the circumstances.	**1 mark** Limited development of argument.	**1 mark** Some judgement shown in response.

Relevant answers might include the following:

- Credit should be given in Analysis for the use of the figures. Annual cost of loan will be £12,000. Annual cost of leasing will be £18,000. Revenue £20,000. Does this leave enough for other costs? So will the project be profitable?

- Buying the machine is cheaper, less strain on the cash flow. But the loan must be repaid. Also the business must maintain the machine. This is an extra cost. If the machine breaks down the leasing company will replace/repair it. If buying the machine they will have a fixed asset but need to allow for depreciation.

• Will the business grow in future years?

• Is there any other way? Perhaps a smaller machine initially. Easier if leasing.

• As revenue is unlikely to be evenly spread will cash flow be a problem? Already tight occasionally.

• Can they get staff? They are already paying a premium price for overtime.

Location Factors for a Business Start Up   Unit 10

10.1 Introduction

The central theme for teaching should be the need for location decisions to be made following analysis of quantitative and qualitative factors. Students who have just studied break-even have the perfect tool in their hands: comparing location A versus B on the grounds of their fixed costs, variable costs, selling price and then potential demand.

Of course, that would not be the place to start. Use the short but sweet section in the book *From Acorns* to help students focus on how a decision might be made. Then provide some case material for students to have to make and justify a location choice. The September 2008 *Business Review* has a short article called 'An Ice Dream' which is backed (in the *Teachers' Notes*) by a location simulation.

From that intuitive basis for decision making, move on to rehearse break-even with your students by providing some data on two different locations, perhaps for a coffee or sandwich bar. The books listed below will be helpful.

In the Workbook, the questions in Section A plus case B1 will be the most valuable at this stage.

10.2 Further reading and resources

Title and price	Author	Publisher and ISBN	Brief account
From Acorns: How to Build a Brilliant Business 2nd Edition £9.99	Woods, C.	Prentice Hall 2007 978 0 273 71252 7	Just four pages on location, but terrific stuff. The entire focus is on service businesses: online or retail. Page 94: 'Your Place or Mine?'.
FT Guide to Business Start Up £19.99	Williams, S.	Prentice Hall 2007 978 0273 14873	Chapter 17 is a sensible look at 'Choosing your workplace'. OK for students to read, though it's not one of the book's better chapters.
Starting and Running a Sandwich-Coffee Bar: An Insider Guide £12.99	Miller, S.	How To Books Ltd 2002 978 185703 805 7	Pages 52-68 take a serious look at the key issues about a retail start-up. Tackles head-on the most important strategic point: look for a virgin site or cluster where competition already exists?

| *Starting Your Own Business: The Good, the Bad and the Unexpected* £12.99 | Lester, D. | Crimson Publishing 2008 978 185 458 401 4 | Chapter 13 ('Where to start your business') is full of good advice; strong on government support, but remains rooted in real practice. A super complement to a text-book treatment of the subject. Very focused on the tertiary sector. |

10.3 Answers to workbook questions

A Revision questions

(30 marks; 30 minutes)

1. Explain what is meant by the 'quantitative' factors that may influence a firm's choice of location. **(3)**

    • Factors to which a money sum can be attached, e.g. rent or the cost of wages locally.

2. Describe one factor that would be important to a manufacturing firm but not a retail firm when choosing a location. **(2)**

    • Whether the business process was bulk-increasing or bulk-reducing.

3. Explain why a firm relying on mail order may not locate in a high rent area. **(2)**

    • A mail order business does not need to be physically close to its customers, so it would choose a location with low costs (but high accessibility, e.g. for delivery drivers).

4. How might the use of just-in-time production influence the location of a business? **(3)**

    • Need to be close to suppliers

    • Need to have reliable road links, e.g. not dependent on the M25 (or the M62)

5. State two factors that would influence the location of a firm that employs a labour-intensive process. **(2)**

    • Need to be in an area where wage-rates are low

    • Need to be located close to an area with a high population density

6. How may selecting the least-cost location improve a firm's competitive ability? **(4)**

    • It will help the business keep costs low enough to be able to charge relatively low prices to customers.

7. Explain two reasons why a firm may decide to choose a location near to its supplier. **(4)**

    • To keep delivery costs down – especially important if the process is bulk-reducing.

    • To help make a JIT system work effectively.

8. Identify two qualitative factors that may influence a firm's choice of location. **(2)**

    • Location may be near to the owner's own home.

    • The location may be in a cluster of comparable businesses, because clients expect a merchant bank to be in the City of London, or Leeds, or Edinburgh.

9. Explain how a cheap location for a new service industry may represent a 'false economy'. **(4)**

    • Many services need a location that is super-convenient to customers, e.g. a hotel by the station or a pizza place where office workers can easily get to. Good locations are expensive, but might be great value for money if they are in the right place for gaining high sales.

10. What is meant by the term footloose? Identify two factors that may prevent a business from being footloose **(4)**

    • Footloose is the willingness of a business to change location, i.e. has few or no ties to the local area.

    • A firm is prevented from being footloose if it has:

    – a real commitment to the local community

    – a real need for the specialist labour that lives close to the business, e.g. film people living near to Soho, London – the centre of the media industries.

B1 Activity

(Refer to question on page 57 of textbook.)

There are no marks allocated to this activity and therefore no mark scheme.

B2 Data response question

(20 marks; 20 minutes)

(Refer to question on page 58 of textbook.)

1. What factors should John take into account before moving his production into the industrial unit? **(6)**

	Knowledge 3 marks	Application 3 marks
Level 2	**3 marks** Good understanding of the subject content; or two answers identified.	**3 marks** Answer is applied effectively to the specific case.
Level 1	**2-1 marks** Shows understanding of the subject content.	**2-1 marks** Some relationship to the scenario (perhaps indirectly).

Possible answers include:

- The effect on profit, due to the extra fixed costs.

- The effect on him of the extra travelling time to/from work (offset against the benefit of no longer having work intertwined with home life).

- Will there be extra space that will enable him to produce more efficiently?

2. Explain how John's profits could be affected by his decision to move to the industrial unit. **(4)**

	Knowledge 1 mark	Application 3 marks
Level 2		**3 marks** Answer is applied effectively to the specific case.
Level 1	**1 mark** Shows understanding of the subject content.	**2-1 marks** Some relationship to the scenario (perhaps indirectly).

Possible answers include:

- The extra fixed costs will lower the profit, unless production levels can be increased.

- Higher production levels will provide an opportunity to bulk-buy, which will lower variable costs per unit and therefore should boost profit.

3. What are the benefits of selling the radios via a mail-order company? **(5)**

- No fixed costs from hiring a sales force (plus managers); distribution is only a variable cost.

• Mail order enables you to find out a lot of detail about the gender, age and region orders are coming from; that should help with further product development.

4. What qualitative factors may be behind John's decision to relocate production from the garage to the industrial unit? **(4)**

• Quality of life at home may be improved, e.g. more space for any kids.

• He may feel that a business address sounds more professional than '16 Lavender Gardens'.

Employing People

11.1. Introduction

In the past, chapters on employing people have tended to focus on the process of recruitment and selection, ignoring the decision of whether or not to employ in the first place. Students need to appreciate that deciding if and when to take on new workers is a delicate balancing act, especially for new businesses. Extra staff may allow owners to devote more time to core activities, driving the business forward and generating profit. However, it may not be possible to generate the sales needed to cover additional costs straightaway, meaning that some way of bridging the gap temporarily will need to be found.

Once the decision to employ new staff has been taken, the key words to consider are adequate and appropriate. Traditionally, the majority of employees have been full-time and permanent. However, such arrangements may not suit the needs of every business, especially those that are either small or newly established. Students need to be able to consider the circumstances and individual needs of different business, and recommend employment solutions that match them.

For homework, the most engaging Workbook student activity is B1 'The Gourmet Chocolate Pizza Company'.

11.2. Further reading and resources

Title and price	Author	Publisher and ISBN	Brief account
From Acorns: How to Build a Brilliant Business 2nd Edition £9.99	Woods, C.	Prentice Hall 2007 978 0 273 71252 7	Chapter 22 on 'Taking on staff' is terrific. It starts with: Can you afford not to employ someone? using opportunity cost within the argument. Brill.
Starting Your Own Business: The Good, the Bad and the Unexpected £12.99	Lester, D.	Crimson Publishing 2008 978 185 458 401 4	Chapter 15 is terrific on 'Taking on staff'- well worth copying or using as a homework supplement to Unit 11 of Business Studies.
Start and Run Your Own Business: The Complete Guide to Setting Up and Managing a Small Business £12.99	Le Marinel, A.	How to Books Ltd 2004 1 85703 988 2	Chapter 9 contains clear and practical advice on how businesses should go about employing new staff. NB This book is not as good as the others on this list.

Employing People

Unit 11

Start Your Business Week by Week £14.99	Parks, S.	Prentice Hall 2005 0 273 69447 2	The Week 8 – Management chapter gives a concise overview of the main points to consider when establishing an initial management team within a small firm.

In addition, the following web site addresses may be helpful:

Site	Web address	Brief account
smallbusiness.co.uk	www.smallbusiness.co.uk	Free registration gains access to a number of guides and case studies containing advice on employment issues for small businesses.
Business Link	www.businesslink.gov.uk	Contains lots of free guides on employment, including 'recruitment' and 'employing different types of worker'.
ACAS	www.acas.org.uk	Lots of useful free resources, including downloadable advisory booklets on a number of HR issues, including employment rights.
Business Start-ups	www.startups.co.uk	The 'Taking on Staff' section of this website has a number of useful case studies and video clips.

11.3 Answers to workbook questions

A Revision questions

(40 marks; 40 minutes)

1. Outline three reasons why a small business may need to take on additional staff. (6)

    • To respond to increased workload due to increased demand.

    • To gain access to skills that the business lacks currently and which are required in order to perform more effectively.

    • To concentrate on completing the day-to-day activities involved in running the business, so that owners have more time for planning and marketing the business.

© Hodder Education 2008

2. Suggest two reasons why the owner of a small business might be reluctant to employ more staff. (2)

   • The cost

   • The risk of appointing someone who is unsuitable

3. Explain why a business should consider any plans to expand the workforce in relation to its wider objectives. (4)

   • It may be some time before the cost of an increased workforce results in any significant increase in revenue, leading to a short-term reduction in profits.

   • New staff will almost certainly be needed to handle increased workload if the objective is growth.

4. Examine two advantages of employing part-time staff to a small, expanding business. (6)

   • It helps to keep costs down when there is no need for full-time cover.

   • It increases a firm's flexibility to cater for predicted fluctuations in demand.

   • It may attract a wider pool of job applicants – some workers with the necessary skills may not be interested in working full-time (e.g. those with dependants or who are already claiming pensions).

   • The opportunity to work part-time may increase staff motivation and reduce absenteeism and labour turnover.

5. Suggest two reasons why an over-reliance on part-time staff could, in fact, increase the costs of a business. (4)

   • It is likely to mean increased training and administration costs.

   • It may also create communication and coordination problems if part-time staff do not work together.

6. Briefly explain what is meant by a fixed-term contract. (2)

   • A fixed-term contract is one where workers are employed for a pre-determined time or until a specific task or set of tasks has been completed.

7. Analyse the main advantages and disadvantages of using temporary workers for a domestic cleaning business. (6)

   • Advantages: Probably cheap to hire, as the staff won't be looking for a living, permanent wage; easy to move them on if they are underperforming.

   • Disadvantages: May lack commitment, encouraging, for example, opportunistic pilfering; may require an expensive management layer of supervisors.

8. Suggest one suitable method of dealing with the following staff shortages:

   a) providing cover for a receptionist on two weeks' holiday **(1)**

   - (temporary) agency staff, to avoid the need for adding staff to a payroll for such a short time

   b) providing extra sales assistance at a delicatessen on Saturdays **(1)**

   - part-time permanent, assuming increased sales were not likely to be short-term

   c) providing additional waiters and kitchen staff at a restaurant over the busy Christmas period **(1)**

   - staff on temporary contracts as demand is likely to fall once the festivities have finished

9. Suggest one benefit and one drawback to a small business from using consultants to provide specialist skills. **(4)**

   - Benefit: they provide an opportunity to obtain specialised skills temporarily.

   - Disadvantage: frequent or lengthy use of consultants may be more expensive and less effective than consulting permanent employees.

10. Briefly explain the main risks for a small business from failing to adhere to legislation regarding the employment of workers. **(3)**

    - The cost of fines imposed if income tax is not collected.

    - The cost and possible compensation resulting from being taken to an employment tribunal, e.g., if part-time staff are treated differently to those on permanent contracts.

    - The bad publicity that may be generated as a result, having a negative impact on the business's ability to recruit in future.

Employing People

B1 Activity

(20 marks; 25 minutes)

(Refer to question on pages 63–4 of textbook.)

1. Outline three qualities possessed by Helen Ellis that helped her establish her business. **(6)**

	Knowledge 3 marks	Application 3 marks
Level 2	**3 marks** 3 qualities explained briefly but accurately	**3 marks** Relevant points applied in detail to the case.
Level 1	**2-1 marks** Only one quality explained or qualities identified but not explained, showing limited understanding.	**2-1 marks** Limited attempt to apply points to the case.

Relevant answers might include:

- Dedication – Helen would have had to carry on working in the evenings and at weekends in order to get the business established.

- Organisation skills – Helen had experience of working from home, which requires a great deal of self-discipline and ability to establish a routine.

- Ability to spot opportunities and develop ideas – Helen took an existing product from the USA and modified it to match UK consumer tastes more closely.

- Ability to handle customers, suppliers and employees – all of these groups need to be managed effectively if Helen's business is to succeed.

2. Describe one advantage and one disadvantage to Helen's business from employing new staff. **(6)**

	Knowledge 3 marks	Application 3 marks
Level 2	**3 marks** Three qualities explained briefly but accurately.	**3 marks** Relevant points applied in detail to the case.
Level 1	**2-1 marks** Only one quality explained or qualities identified but not explained, showing limited understanding.	**2-1 marks** Limited attempt to apply points to the case.

- Advantages:

  - Someone to share the workload – this may give Helen more time to develop ideas for moving the business forward.

  - Access to new skills, experience etc – this may allow the business to function more efficiently.

Employing People

• Disadvantages:

- Cost of paying wages to additional members of staff – may reduce profits if additional revenue generated is insufficient to cover these additional costs.

- More of Helen's time will need to be devoted to meeting legal obligations as an employer – leaving less time to develop the business.

3. Examine the benefits of appointing a new member of staff on a temporary contract initially. **(8)**

	Knowledge 2 marks	Application 2 marks	Analysis 4 marks
Level 2	**2 marks** One or more benefit explained, showing good understanding.	**2 marks** Relevant points consistently applied to the case.	**4-3 marks** Good analysis of identified advantage and disadvantage.
Level 1	**1 mark** One or more benefit identified, but not explained, showing limited understanding.	**1 mark** Some attempt to apply point(s) to the case.	**2-1 marks** Limited analysis of identified advantage and/ or disadvantage.

Temporary contract – where workers are employed for a pre-determined time or until a specific task or set of tasks is completed.

Relevant answers might include:

• A temporary contract would have allowed Helen the opportunity to gain access to extra help to deal with the business's increasing workload, as demand for chocolate pizzas increased. However, there may have been some uncertainty as to whether sales would have continued to grow in the long-term, so a temporary contract will avoid the costs of having to make workers redundant.

• Issuing temporary contracts initially would have given Helen the chance to assess how suitable the new recruit was to the business, for example, did she have a good work ethic and agree with Helen's vision for the business? As the new worker proved to be suitable, she was offered a permanent contract.

Employing People

B2 Activity

(25 marks; 30 minutes)

(Refer to question on page 64 of textbook.)

1. Briefly explain how contracted workers differ from employees. **(6)**

	Knowledge 3 marks	Application 3 marks
Level 2	**3 marks** Clear explanation of both terms showing good understanding.	**3 marks** Relevant points applied in detail to the case.
Level 1	**2-1 marks** Some explanation of both terms, or clear explanation of one term, showing some understanding.	**2-1 marks** Limited attempt to apply points to the case.

- A contracted worker is an individual (or firm) who provides agreed services to a business, such as accountancy, human resources or IT, for a set fee over a period of time. An employee, on the other hand, works for an organisation under a contract of employment in return for a salary or wage. A firm has a number of legal responsibilities for its employees, which do not apply to contracted workers, for example, National Insurance contributions, holiday and sickness payments. In the case of System Associates, a team of contractors acted as content editors. This allowed the company to successfully complete a project for London Connects, despite its permanent staff already operating at full capacity.

2. Analyse two benefits to a small company like Systems Associates of using contractors. **(7)**

	Knowledge 2 marks	Application 2 marks	Analysis 3 marks
Level 2	**2 marks** One or more relevant benefit(s) explained.	**2 marks** Relevant points consistently applied to the case.	**3 marks** Good analysis of identified benefit(s).
Level 1	**1 mark** One or more relevant benefit(s) identified.	**1 mark** Some attempt to apply point(s) to the case.	**2-1 marks** Limited analysis of identified benefit(s).

Relevant benefits might include:

- Employing temporary workers allowed System Associates to secure the London Connect contract, despite its existing workforce being at full capacity. Any delay may have resulted in the contract being awarded to a rival firm, resulting in a missed opportunity to generate sales and profits.

- Employing the contractors on a temporary basis means that the company could assess the skills and attitude of each of the workers, allowing them to choose the two most suitable for employing on a permanent basis.

3. Assess the impact of continuing to increase the size of the workforce on the long-term success of Systems Associates. (12)

	Knowledge 3 marks	Application 3 marks	Analysis 3 marks	Evaluation 3 marks
Level 2	**3 marks** Relevant issue(s) explained, showing good understanding.	**3 marks** Arguments are consistently applied to the case material.	**3 marks** Good analysis of question, arguments are fully developed.	**3 marks** Judgement offered with limited justification; some structure evident; some use of technical terms.
Level 1	**2-1 marks** Relevant issue(s) identified but not explained, showing limited understanding.	**2-1 marks** Limited attempt to apply arguments to the case material.	**2-1 marks** Limited analysis of question.	**2-1 marks** Some judgement offered but unjustified; ideas communicated in a simplistic way; limited use of technical terms.

- Positive impact:

  - Increasing the number of permanent employees (whether part-time) or full time is likely to be more cost effective than having to frequently recruit and select temporary or contract staff.

  - Increasing the number of permanent employees may also help to maintain the company's current culture, as well as a team of loyal and motivated staff.

  - It may not always be possible to attract the correct number of contractors with the necessary skills. This may mean that the business fails to meet deadlines or the quality of work provided suffers.

- Negative impact:

  - Increasing the number of permanent staff will significantly increase the company's overall costs – these overheads may not be sustainable if demand for the company's services began to fluctuate or fall.

  - An expanding workforce may lead to communication and coordination problems – this is even more likely if the majority of workers are part-time or temporary.

Calculating Revenue, Costs and Profit Unit 12

12.1 Introduction

It is sensible to start with revenue rather than costs, as the calculations are more intuitive. At all stages, bear in mind the student tendency to confuse 'price' and 'cost'. Make it clear that although lots of shoppers say, 'It costs £10', we have to say, 'Its price is £10'.

Understanding the categories of costs provides essential underpinning knowledge for later topics such as break-even analysis and contribution. Students' problems with fixed and variable costs should never be underestimated. In the accompanying Workbook, the acid test is question 5 in section B1. If students can get that right, then they really understand the difference between fixed and variable costs. *(Ed: I would not expect any more than 1 in 10 students to get this right, unaided.)*

Ultimately the successful student will be the one who cannot only complete the calculations but can also use profit intelligently in written analysis. To achieve this these topics invite a practical approach. Students can become familiar with the concepts, necessary calculations and graphs by carrying out a variety of practical tasks as an integral part of the learning process.

The Workbook has a good range of activities. A meaty homework would be Section A plus B1. If you want a written approach, B3 is the one to go with.

12.2 Further reading and resources

Note that this is a barren area for wider reading. Most books about small firms refer to direct costs and overheads, or want to go into too much detail about all the different costs. Best to stick to A Level text books and *Business Review*, though do note *Starting Your Own Business*, below.

Title and price	Author	Publisher and ISBN	Brief account
FT Guide to Business Start-Up £19.99	Williams, S.	Prentice Hall 2007 978 0273 14873	Excellent on 'How to Increase Profits' (Unit 2), but overly complex approach in the book for Unit 1.
Starting Your Own Business: The Good, the Bad and the Unexpected £12.99	Lester, D.	Crimson Publishing 2008 978 185 458 401 4	Chapter 6 is good on the subject of revenue and profit. Worth getting better students to read it, though probably after you've covered revenue, costs and break-even. Many small business books refer to direct costs and overheads, whereas this one uses our terminology: fixed and variable costs.
Entrepreneurship and Small Business £34.99	Burns, P.	Palgrave 2007 978 140 394 7338	Interesting material in here for teachers, but its treatment of the material is a long way away from an AS classroom.

12.3 Answers to workbook questions

A Revision questions
(30 marks; 30 minutes)

1. Why might business initially receive relatively low revenues from a product newly introduced to the market? **(3)**

    • low sales as product unfamiliar to consumers

    • penetration price to allow product to gain market share

    • low output

2. State two circumstances in which a company may be able to charge high prices for a new product? **(2)**

    • If the product is advanced and is unlikely to face competition in the short-term.

    • If consumers place a high value on the product.

3. For what reasons might a firm seek to maximise its sales revenue? **(4)**

    • If costs are not sensitive to the level of sales, then maximising revenues will increase profits.

    • Maximising sales revenue (through low prices) may help a product to establish itself.

4. If a business sells 4000 units of Brand X at £4 each and 2000 units of Brand Y at £3 each, what's its total revenue? **(4)**

    • $(£4 \times 4000)$
    $+ (£3 \times 2000)$
    $= £22,000$

5. State two reasons why firms have to know the costs they incur in production. **(2)**

    • to help set prices

    • to help plan cash outflows when a big order is being completed

6. Distinguish, with the aid of examples, between fixed and variable costs. **(4)**

    • Fixed costs do not vary directly with the level of output and examples include rent and rates. Variable costs <u>do</u> vary directly with output – when a business's output rises, costs associated with fuel and raw materials are likely to rise as well.

7. Explain why fixed costs can only alter in the long term. **(3)**

    • Because the costs are not related to output, they are a function of time, for example, hiring a member of staff whose salary is a permanent fixture.

8. Give two reasons why profits are important to businesses. (2)

   • they act as a measure of a business's success

   • profits attract further investment by shareholders

9. Outline one advantage and one disadvantage that may result from a business deciding to lower the proportion of profits it distributes to its owners. (4)

   • Advantage: more funds retained for reinvestment within the organisation.

   • Disadvantage: investors may be less willing to buy the company's shares if the returns are lower.

10. State two purposes for which a business's profits might be used. (2)

    • retained within the company for future investment

    • paid to shareholders in the form of dividends

B1 Calculation practice questions

(30 marks; 25 minutes)

(Refer to question on page 71 of textbook.)

1. During the summer weeks Devon Ice Cream has average sales of 4000 units a week. Each ice cream sells for £1 and has variable costs of 25p. Fixed costs are £800.

   a) Calculate the total costs for the business in the summer weeks. (3)

   $$
   \begin{aligned}
   \bullet \text{ Total costs} &= \text{fixed costs} + (\text{variable costs per unit} \times \text{quantity}) \\
   &= £800 \quad + (25p \times 4000) \\
   &= £1800
   \end{aligned}
   $$

   b) Calculate Devon Ice Cream's weekly profit in the summer. (3)

   $$
   \begin{aligned}
   \text{Profit} &= \text{revenue} - (\text{fixed costs} + \text{variable costs}) \\
   &= (£1 \times 4000) - £1800 \\
   &= £2200
   \end{aligned}
   $$

2a If a firm sells 200 widgets at £3.20 and 40 squidgets at £4, what is its total revenue? (3)

   • Total revenue $= (£3.20 \times 200) + (£4 \times 40) = £800$

2b Each widget costs £1.20 to make, while each squidget costs £1.50. What are the total variable costs? (3)

   • Total variable costs $= (£1.20 \times 200) + (£1.50 \times 40) = £300$

2c If fixed costs are £300, what profit is the business making? (3)

   • The business makes a profit of $£800 - £600 = £200$

3. 'Last week our sales revenue was £12,000 which was great. Our price is £2 a unit, which I think is a bit too cheap.'

 a) How many unit sales were made last week? (**2**)

   • £12,000/£2 = 6,000 units

 b) If a price rise to £2.25 cuts sales to 5600 units, calculate the change in the firm's revenue. (**4**)

   • New revenue = 5600 × £2.25 = £12,600
   Answer = +£600

4. BYQ Co has sales of 4000 units a month, a price of £4, fixed costs of £9000 and variable costs of £1. Calculate its profit. (**4**)

 • Revenue = £16,000
  Total costs = £9000 + £4000
  Profit = £3000

5. At full capacity output of 24,000 units, a firm's costs are as follows:

   managers' salaries £48,000
   materials   £12,000
   rent & rates   £24,000
   piece-rate labour   £36,000

 a) What are the firm's total costs at 20,000 units? (**4**)

   • Fixed costs are £72,000 (salaries + rent)
    At 24,000, variable costs are £48,000 (materials and piece-rate labour)
    So v.c.p.u. = £2 per unit
    Therefore, at 20,000 units, total costs are (£2 × 20,000) + £72,000 = £112,000

 b) What profit will be made at 20,000 units if the selling price is £6? (**1**)

   • Profit = £8000

B2 Case study

Cleaning up
(25 marks; 30 minutes)

(Refer to question on pages 71–2 of textbook.)

1. Which of Mary's two prices would provide her with the higher monthly revenue? (**3**)

 • At £5: 100 × £5 = £500
  At £4: 125 × £4 = £500
  Neither. They're both the same.

Calculating Revenue, Costs and Profit Unit **12**

2. Calculate Mary's monthly profits (or losses) in each case. (**6**)

- At £5: $100 \times £5 - (\{£0.5 \times 100\} + £350) = £100$
  At £4: $125 \times £4 - (\{£0.5 \times 125\} = £350) = £87.50$

3. Analyse two possible reasons why Mary's financial forecasts might not prove to be accurate. (**7**)

	Knowledge 2 marks	Application 2 marks	Analysis 3 marks
Level 2	2 marks Shows clear understanding of the subject content.	2 marks Answer is applied effectively to the specific case.	3 marks Build-up of argument, making use of relevant business concepts.
Level 1	1 mark Shows some understanding of the subject content.	1 mark Some relationship to the scenario (perhaps indirectly).	2-1 marks Some build-up of argument, showing grasp of cause and effect.

Possible answers include:

- She had no experience as an entrepreneur or as a window-cleaner, so she could easily be wrong on both the revenues and the costs, e.g. underestimating how long it takes to get the job done, and to get from one house to the next.

- Circumstances can change, e.g. if consumer spending starts to fall, people may cut back on luxuries such as window cleaning.

4. Analyse the case for and against Mary charging £5 per household for her window cleaning service. (**9**)

	Knowledge 2 marks	Application 3 marks	Analysis 4 marks
Level 2	2 marks Shows clear understanding of the subject content.	3 marks Answer is applied effectively to the specific case.	4-3 marks Build-up of argument, making use of relevant business concepts.
Level 1	1 mark Shows some understanding of the subject content.	2-1 marks Some relationship to the scenario (perhaps indirectly).	2-1 marks Some build-up of argument, showing grasp of cause and effect.

Possible answers include:

- Charging £5 yields more profit, and because both prices yield a dreadful profit per month, no one else should be drawn into this market – in which case she should opt for the more profitable price.

- Better by far, though, would be to forget the idea completely unless there is a realistic chance of getting householders to use the service more often than once a month.

B3 Case study

Chalfont Computer Services Ltd
(25 marks; 30 minutes)

(Refer to question on page 72 of textbook.)

1. What is meant by the term 'variable costs'? **(2)**

    • costs that vary as output varies **(2)**

    • costs that can go up and down **(0)**

2. Calculate Robert's forecast profits for his first three months' trading. **(5)**

	Revenue	–	Total costs	=	Profit	**(1)**
Jan:	$40 \times £40$	–	$([40 \times £15] + £1000)$	=	£0	**(1)**
Feb:	$50 \times £40$	–	$([50 \times £15] + £1000)$	=	£250	**(1)**
Mar:	$60 \times £40$	–	$([60 \times £15] + £1000)$	=	£500	**(1)**
			Total profit for the 3 months	=	£750	**(1)**

3. Robert estimates that if he cut his prices by 10% he would have 20% more customers each month. Calculate the outcome of these changes and whether this would benefit Robert. **(8)**

	Revenue	–	Total costs	=	Profit	
Jan:	$48 \times £36$	–	$([48 \times £15] + £1000)$	=	£8	**(2)**
Feb:	$60 \times £36$	–	$([60 \times £15] + £1000)$	=	£260	**(2)**
Mar:	$72 \times £40$	–	$([72 \times £15] + £1000)$	=	£512	**(2)**
			Total profit for the 3 months	=	£780	**(1)**
			Extra profit from price cut	=	+£30	**(1)**

4. Examine the case for and against a bank lending Robert £10,000 on the basis of his forecast profits. **(10)**

	Knowledge 2 marks	Application 4 marks	Analysis 4 marks
Level 2	**2 marks** Shows clear understanding of the subject content.	**4-3 marks** Answer is applied effectively to the specific case.	**4-3 marks** Build-up of argument, making use of relevant business concepts.
Level 1	**1 mark** Shows some understanding of the subject content.	**2-1 marks** Some relationship to the scenario (perhaps indirectly).	**2-1 marks** Some build-up of argument, showing grasp of cause and effect.

Possible answers include:

- The big question is whether the sales increase is seasonal (and therefore temporary) or incremental, as repeat custom build from the January start. If £250 a month is all that can be expected, it will take 40 months to repay the loan. But if the sales can be expected to stay at or around 82 (the April figure), the monthly profit of $(82 \times £25) - £1000 = £1050$ would mean the loan can be repaid in less than 10 months.

In fact, though, no bank would lend to Robert purely on forecast profits, no matter how glittering, because he has not started up a business before and his entire research appears to be based on people he spoke to in his local pub!

Break-even Analysis

13.1 Introduction

This is an important topic within the finance and accounts section of the syllabus and one requiring a good understanding of concepts such as fixed and variable costs. It is important that students should already be confident with revenues, costs and profit (see Chapter 12). No modern A Level syllabus would require students to draw a break-even chart in an exam, but exam questions will probe understanding of the chart and the ability to show the impact of changing variables such as price or fixed costs. It is often helpful to introduce the notion of contribution as part of the process of teaching this topic.

Teaching this topic can be helped by adopting a practical approach and giving students regular activities to complete. Students need to be able to give some assessment of the value of the technique of break-even in a variety of circumstances. It is advisable that this is covered once the concept has been mastered. This will assist them when they are called upon to write analytically or evaluatively with respect to break-even analysis.

For homework, the best combination of questions from the Workbook is Section A plus B2.

13.2 Further reading and resources

Title and price	Author	Publisher and ISBN	Brief account
Good Small Business Guide: How to Start and Grow Your Own Business 3rd Edition £19.99		A & C Black 2008 978 0 7136 8760 66	Curiously, the four pages called 'Understanding the role of price' (p155) are the best on break-even. It also specifically covers the difference between price and cost.
Starting Your Own Business: : The Good, the Bad and the Unexpected £12.99	Lester, D.	Crimson Publishing 2008 978 185 458 401 4	Chapter 6 is good on the subject of revenue, profit and break-even. Worth getting better students to read it, though probably after you've covered revenue, costs and break-even. Many small business books refer to direct costs and overheads, whereas this one uses our terminology: fixed and variable costs.

Entrepreneurship and Small Business £34.99	Burns, P.	Palgrave 2007 978 140 394 7338	Pages 131-5 contain some interesting material on break-even and pricing. Not for your students, but potentially useful for you – especially with a view to stretching the most able.
A-Z AS Business Studies Worksheets – photocopiable pack plus VLE £95.00	Marcouse. I.	A-Z Business Training Ltd* 2008	AQA Worksheets 5, 6, 11, 23 and 70 will be useful for this section of the course. They'll provide a wide variety of suitable AS questions (and answers) *To order, go to www.a-zbusinesstraining.com
Business Case Studies 3rd Edition £17.99	Marcouse, I. and Lines, D.	Longman 2002 0 582 40636-6	Case Study 16 'A Small Business Start-Up' requires the drawing of a simple break-even chart within an accessible start-up context.

13.3 Answers to workbook questions

A Revision questions

(25 marks; 25 minutes)

1. What is meant by the term 'break-even point'? (**2**)

    • The level of output at which total revenue equals total costs. Hence the business makes neither a profit nor a loss.

2. State three reasons why a business might conduct a break-even analysis. (**3**)

    • To estimate the future level of output they need to produce.

    • To assess the impact of changes in costs on profits and/or the volume required to break-even.

    • To support an application for finance from a bank or other financial institution.

3. List the information necessary to construct a break-even chart. **(4)**

    - selling price

    - fixed costs

    - variable costs per unit

    - maximum capacity of the business

4. How would you calculate the contribution made by each unit of production that is sold? **(2)**

    - Subtract the variable cost of producing a single unit from its selling price.

5. A business sells its products for £10 each and the variable cost of producing a single unit is £6. If its monthly fixed costs are £18,000 how many units must it sell to break even each month? **(3)**

    - Break-even output = Fixed costs/contribution per unit **(1)**
      Contribution per unit = £4

    - Break-even = £18,000/£4 **(1)** = 4,500 units **(1)**

6. Explain why the variable cost and total revenue lines commence at the origin of a break-even chart. **(3)**

    - If a firm does not produce any output it will not incur any variable costs (fuel, materials, etc.), nor will it earn any revenue since it does not have any products to sell. For these reasons variable costs and total revenue lines on a break-even chart commence at the origin.

7. What point on a break-even chart actually illustrates break-even output? **(2)**

    - Break-even point on the chart occurs at that level of output where the total revenue line crosses (and equals) the total costs line.

8. Explain how, using a break-even chart, you would illustrate the amount of profit or loss made at any given level of output. **(2)**

    - Profits are shown on the break-even graph at outputs in excess of break-even output. They are shown by the vertical distance between the total revenue line and the total cost line. Losses occur below break-even output and are shown by the vertical distance between the total cost line and the total revenue line.

9. Why might a business wish to calculate its margin of safety? **(2)**

    - The margin of safety is a useful guide to a business because it illustrates the amount by which output and sales can fall from their current level before the business reaches break-even output. A firm with a low safety margin should consider strategies for enabling prices to be increased or costs to be cut.

10. A business is currently producing 200,000 units of output annually, and its break-even output is 120,000 units. What is its margin of safety? **(2)**

    - The margin of safety equals current output less break-even output. Thus in this case it is 80,000 units.

B1 Data response

(45 marks; 60 minutes)

(Refer to question on page 80 of textbook.)

1a Construct the break-even chart for Paul's planned business. **(9)**

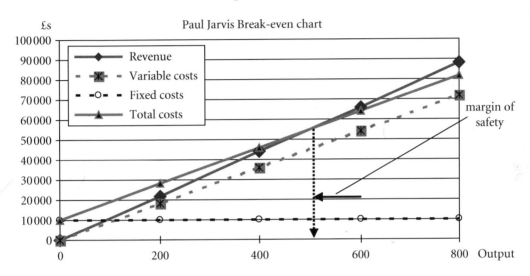

Paul Jarvis Break-even chart

1b State, and show on the graph, the profit or loss made at a monthly sales level of 600 customers. **(4)**

- Profit at 600 customers is £2000; the scale of this graph cannot show that, but it should be the vertical difference between revenue and total costs at 600 units.

1c State, and show on the graph, the margin of safety at that level of output. **(4)**

- The margin of safety is demand minus break-even. If demand is 600 units and break-even is 500 units, the safety margin = 100 units.

2. Paul's market research shows that, in his first month of trading, he can expect 450 customers at his hotel.

(a) If Paul's research is correct, calculate the level of profit or loss he will make. **(5)**

- He will make a loss of $(£110 \times 450) - ([£90 \times 450] + £10,000) = £1000$

(b) Illustrate this level of output on your graph and show the profit or loss. **(3)**

- Again, no can do – it's the vertical distance between the revenue and total costs at 450 units.

3. Paul has decided to increase his prices to give an average revenue per customer of £120.

(a) Draw the new total revenue line on your break-even chart to show the effect of this change. **(3)**

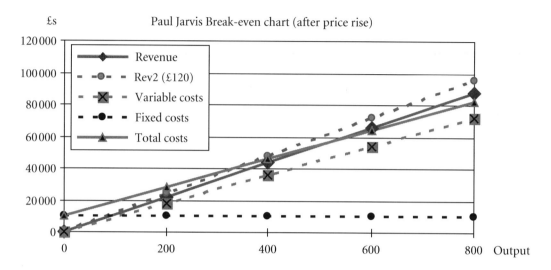

£s Paul Jarvis Break-even chart (after price rise)

Legend:
- Revenue
- Rev2 (£120)
- Variable costs
- Fixed costs
- Total costs

Output

(b) Mark on your diagram the new break-even point. **(1)**

- The new break-even is 333 units, which can be indicated by a downward vertical line to cut the horizontal axis.

(c) Calculate Paul's new break-even number of customers to confirm the result shown on your chart. **(6)**

- Fixed costs £10,000; Contribution per unit = £120 − £90 = £30;
  New break-even = £10,000/£30 = 333 units

4. Paul is worried that his break-even chart may be 'misleading'. Do you agree with him? Justify your view. **(10)**

	Knowledge 2 marks	Application 2 marks	Analysis 3 marks	Evaluation 3 marks
Level 2	2 marks Good understanding of the subject content.	2 marks Answer is applied effectively to the specific case.	3 marks Build-up of argument, making use of relevant business concepts.	3 marks Shows judgement in drawing conclusions from own argument.
Level 1	1 mark Some understanding of the subject content.	1 mark Some relationship to the scenario (perhaps indirectly).	2-1 marks Some build-up of argument, showing grasp of cause and effect.	2-1 marks Some judgement shown in argument or weighting of language.

- Yes because:

  - He is new to the industry and therefore cannot be sure about the variable costs per customer, nor even about the effective average price achieved.

  £110 for every room; some days he'll fill half the rooms at £110, and then accept bulk bookings for the rest of the rooms at perhaps only £60 per room; if this happened regularly, he should have a revenue line that shows two different degrees of steepness.

- No because:

  - A break-even chart is never any more than a broad indication of the factors that lead to profit or loss; it isn't specific enough to 'mislead'.

  - As long as he has given as much thought as he can to providing accurate data, it should be of help.

B2 Data response

(30 marks; 40 minutes)

(Refer to question on page 81 of textbook.)

1. What is a break-even chart? (**4**)

Possible answers:

  - A graph setting out the forecast costs and revenues associated with a given product.

  - It allows profits or losses to be read off at each level of output.

  - It illustrates the level of output necessary to cover costs (i.e. to break-even).

2. Calculate the following:

   (**a**) the variable cost of producing 1000 T-shirts (**2**)

   (**b**) the contribution earned through the sale of one T-shirt (**4**)

     - The variable cost of producing 1000 T-shirts is £20,000.

     - The contribution from the sale of a single T-shirt is £15 (£35 – £20).

3. Shelley has decided to manufacture the shirts in Poland. As a result the variable cost per T-shirt (including commission and distribution costs) will fall to £15 per T-shirt. However, fixed costs will rise to £12,000.

   (**a**) Calculate the new level of break-even for Shelley's T-shirts.

     - Break-even = Fixed costs/contribution per unit (**1**)
       Contribution per unit is now £35 – £15 (**1**) = £20 (**1**)

       New break-even is £12,000/£20 (**1**) = 600 (**1**) units (**1**)

(b) Calculate the margin of safety if sales are 1000 T-shirts per month.

> • Safety margin = sales – break-even point (1)
>
> Sales (1000) – break-even (600) (1) = 400 (1) units (1)

Give six marks for correct answer to (a) and four marks for correct answer to (b).

4. Should Shelley rely on break-even analysis when taking business decisions? Justify your view. (10)

	Knowledge 2 marks	Application 2 marks	Analysis 3 marks	Evaluation 3 marks
Level 2	**2 marks** Good understanding of the subject content; or two answers identified.	**2 marks** Answer is applied effectively to the specific case.	**3 marks** Build-up of argument, making use of relevant business concepts.	**3 marks** Shows judgement in drawing conclusions from own argument.
Level 1	**1 mark** Some understanding of the subject content; or one answer identified.	**1 mark** Some relationship to the scenario (perhaps indirectly).	**2-1 marks** Some build-up of argument, showing grasp of cause and effect.	**2-1 marks** Some judgement shown in argument or weighting of language.

• Yes because:

– Break-even analysis is a simple, easily communicated technique, i.e. easily explained to people like her sales staff.

– It is helpful to know the minimum 'target', i.e. the figure you really don't want to fall below.

– In this case, her UK break-even point is £11,250/£15 = 750 units, so it is helpful to know that the move to Poland cuts the break-even point by 150 units.

• Perhaps not, because:

– Break-even measures profit, but Shelley must also think about her cash flow; it might be great to be in Poland (cost-wise), but the cash-flow implications of the move might be dangerous.

– Shelley should also remember to consider qualitative factors, e.g. how will her staff (and, potentially, customers) feel about the move to Poland?

Cashflow Management and Forecasting Unit 14

14.1 Introduction

Most students are happy preparing cash flow forecasts and the majority understand the care that is needed with regard to the timing of cash in and out flows. The problems that students have difficulty with in exams are:

- preparing the cash flow if the figures given are not in a form they are used to

- interpreting the cash flow data

The style of modern exams makes it unlikely that any student would have to prepare a cash flow forecast from scratch. Examiners prefer to give a cash flow forecast with gaps that have to be filled in; this sounds easy but does not prove so. Students' main problems are with:

- confusion between entries and totals (or sub-totals)

- confusion between monthly cash flow and cumulative (or 'Year-to-date') figures

As the new Unit 1 exam is to be rooted in Business Plans, cash flow forecasts are to become more important than ever. Students need to be able to manipulate the numbers but also write intelligently about the difference between forecast and fact, and the reason why cash flow is such an important consideration at the birth of a business.

In the Workbook, exercise B1 would be good to use in the classroom, then the A questions plus B3 would make a good homework task (plenty for students to think about without creating too onerous a marking load).

14.2 Further reading and resources

As with other finance topics, cash flow is hard to get students to read up in wider literature. There is too much variety in the use of terms and too much detail in the spreadsheets used. In the books mentioned below, only one is really approachable for wider student reading at this stage and that is the one by Steve Parks.

Title and price	Author	Publisher and ISBN	Brief account
Good Small Business Guide: How to Start and Grow Your Own Business 3rd Edition £19.99		A & C Black 2008 978 0 7136 8760 6	Good sections on 'Addressing cash flow problems' (p146) and 'Coping in a cash flow crisis' (p149) – but both are more appropriate for Unit 2's look at cash flow.
Starting Your Own Business: The Good,	Lester, D.	Crimson Publishing 2008 978 185 458 401 4	High time students read Chapter 6 of this book, called 'How

Cashflow Management and Forecasting Unit 14

the Bad and the Unexpected £12.99			much money will you need?'. It contains some terrific wisdom on cash flow, though also goes into profit and break-even.
Start Your Business Week by Week £14.99	Parks, S.	Prentice Hall 2005 0 273 69447 2	Pages 140–144 are unusually good. It's all kept simple and approachable. These pages would work well as a class presentation exercise, i.e. get a couple of students to read the pages, discuss them with you, then do a class presentation.
Entrepreneurship and Small Business £34.99	Burns, P.	Palgrave 2007 978 140 394 7338	Pages 167–8 'Cash Flow and Death Valley' is a nicely evocative way of pointing out the cash flow difficulties inherent in business start-up.

14.3 Answers to workbook questions

A Revision questions

(30 marks; 30 minutes)

1. What is meant by 'cash flow'? (**2**)

    • Cash flow is the flow of money into and out of the business in a given time period.

2. Why is it important to manage cash flow? (**4**)

    • Businesses need to ensure they have sufficient money coming into the business to pay for any debts as they become due.

    • Cash flow problems can result in suppliers stopping supplies.

    • Creditors may also take a business to court to claim unpaid money.

    • More positively, it is also important to know when surplus cash is to be generated by the business, enabling expansion to take place.

3. What is a cash flow forecast? (**3**)

    • A cash flow forecast shows the expected future flow of money into and out of the business. The flows are normally shown on a monthly basis.

4. Explain two limitations of cash flow forecasts. (4)

  • They rely on estimates and are only as good as the figures they are based on. Estimates of sales or costs may be wrong. Timing of cash receipts or expenditure may be wrong.

5. Give two reasons why a bank manager might want to see a cash flow forecast before giving a loan to a new business. (2)

  • To ensure that the business has sufficient cash to pay interest on the loan and repay the capital.

  • To be reassured that the business is aware of the need for cash flow management.

6. How might a firm benefit from delaying its cash outflows? (3)

  • The firm receives the money earlier so may not need to borrow.

  • Reduced exposure to bad debts.

  • It avoids the costs of pursuing debtors.

7. What problems might a firm face if its cash flow forecast proved unreliable? (3)

  • A risk it might run over its overdraft limit (which could threaten the survival of the business).

  • Might not be able to pay its suppliers (or staff) when necessary – threatening a refusal to supply.

8. How might a firm benefit from constructing its cash flow forecasts on a computer spreadsheet? (4)

  • Once the system has been set up it is easier and quicker to prepare forecasts:

    – Easier to do variance analysis.

    – Easier to prepare several scenarios so can be more aware of alternative outcomes.

    – Can send electronically to colleagues in an instant.

9. Identify two actions a firm could take to improve its cash flow position. (2)

  • Run a sale, offering stock at a discount, for cash.

  • Delay spending money, e.g. on new office carpets.

10. Why is it especially hard for a first-time entrepreneur to produce an accurate cash flow forecast? (3)

  • Lack of experience in knowing how long customers take to pay.

  • Can't be sure which suppliers will (eventually) provide some credit.

  • Can't know the actual level of sales, nor the seasonal timings.

Cashflow Management and Forecasting

B1 Cash flow

(20 marks; 20 minutes)

(Refer to question on page 88 of textbook.)

Complete the cash flow table below to find out:

1 the company's forecast cash position at the end of June (**18**)

2 the maximum level of overdraft the owners will need to negotiate with the bank before starting up. (**2**)

Cash flow table (all figures in £000s)

	Jan	Feb	Mar	Apr	May	June
Cash at start	40,000					
Cash in		12,000	16,000	20,000	25,000	24,000
Cash out	45,000*	16,000	18,000	20,000	22,500	22,000
Net cash flow	(5000)	(4000)	(2000)	0	2500	2000
Opening balance	0	(5000)	(9000)	(11,000)	(11,000)	(8500)
Closing balance	(5000)	(9000)	(11,000)	(11,000)	(8500)	(6500)

Cash position at end of June is minus £6500.

They need to arrange an overdraft of at least £11,000.

* students may assume that the £10,000 overheads will be paid in January. This should be taken as correct. In which case the June answer will be minus £16,500 and the overdraft requirement £21,000.

Cashflow Management and Forecasting Unit 14

B2 Data response

Merlin Construction

(30 marks; 30 minutes)

(Refer to question on page 89 of textbook.)

1. Construct a cash flow forecast for the business for the January to September. **(10)**

Month £s	Jan	Feb	March	April	May	June	July	August	Sept
Inflow									
Loan	130,000								
Sales					120,000				120,000
Total inflow	130,000				120,000				120,000
Outflow									
Building	100,000								
Materials		10,000	10,000	10,000	10,000	10,000	10,000	10,000	10,000
Loan Interest	1,000	1,000	1,000	1,000	1,000	1,000	1,000	1,000	1,000
Wages	4,000	4,000	4,000	4,000	4,000	4,000	4,000	4,000	4,000
Other expenses	1,000	1,000	1,000	1,000	1,000	1,000	1,000	1,000	1,000
Total outflow	106,000	16,000	16,000	16,000	16,000	16,000	16,000	16,000	16,000
Monthly balance	24,000	(16,000)	(16,000)	(16,000)	104,000	(16,000)	(16,000)	(16,000)	104,000
Opening balance	0	24,000	8,000	(8,000)	(24,000)	80,000	64,000	48,000	32,000
Closing balance	24,000	8,000	(8,000)	(24,000)	80,000	64,000	48,000	32,000	136,000

- 1 mark for loan (OK if included in opening balance)

  2 marks for sales

  1 mark for each expenditure line (5 marks)

  2 marks for correct closing balance.

  (1 mark for correct technique but incorrect calculation.)

2. Outline two significant features of this cash flow forecast. **(6)**

- Three marks for each feature identified. Possible answers:

  – Cash flow problems in March and April. Overall the business is profitable and the cash flow situation is healthy.

- Based on estimates so could be wrong. Cash flow is very dependent on sales: if they are not made then there will be problems.

3. Discuss two possible courses of action. (8)

  • One mark for each suggestion plus up to three marks for discussion.

  - Use an overdraft for the period of the cash shortfall. Provides additional cash. Flexible but expensive.

  - Negotiates larger initial loan. Makes additional cash available. Additional interest costs but provides a safety net.

  - Sells the flats earlier. Brings in revenue earlier. May not be possible, depends on market.

  - Obtain longer credit for the materials. This will delay some expenditure. Depends on supplier and credit rating of firm.

4. Examine two ways in which the cash flow forecast might be unreliable. (6)

	Knowledge 2 marks	Application 2 marks	Analysis 2 marks
Level 2	**2 marks** Good understanding of the subject content.	**2 marks** Answer is applied effectively to the specific case.	**2 marks** Build-up of argument, making use of relevant business concepts.
Level 1	**1 mark** Shows some understanding of the subject content.	**1 mark** Some relationship to the scenario (perhaps indirectly).	**1 mark** Some build-up of argument, showing grasp of cause and effect.

Possible answers include:

  • Sales might not be made or they could be later than expected.

  • Unexpected problems might delay the project.

  • Costs might change, e.g. interest rates may increase or more labour may be needed than expected.

B3 Data response

D&S Jewellers

(25 marks; 25 minutes)

(Refer to question on page 89 of textbook.)

Cash flow forecast for D&S Jewellers

Month (£s)	September	October	November	December	January	February
Cash inflow						
From cash sales	12000	16000	20000	80000	6000	5000
From credit sales	5000	6000	10000	14000	50000	2000
Total cash in	17000	22000	30000 a	94000 b	56000 c	7000 d
Cash outflow						
Security costs	3000	3000	3000	4000	3000	3000
Buying jewellery stocks	10000	25000	55000	5000	0	2000
Rent	9000	0	0	9000	0	0
Wages	8000	8000	8000	8000	8000	8000
Other expenses	1000	1000	1000	1000	1000	1000
Total outflow	31000	37000	67000	27000	12000	14000
Monthly balance	(14000)	(15000)e	(37000)f	67000g	44000h	(7000)i
Opening balance	8000	(6000)j	(21000)k	(58000)l	9000m	53000n
Closing balance	(6000)o	(21000)p	(58000)q	9000r	53000s	46000t

1. Explain two problems Sujugan may have had in drawing up this cash flow forecast for D&S Jewellers. **(6)**

   – Three marks for each problem identified. Problems might include:

   – lack of experience

   – incorrect figures

   – sales are estimates

   – they may not have the same experience as other jewellery shops

2. Complete the job for Sujugan by working out the missing figures a–t. (10)

- a = £30,000   b = £94,000   c = £56,000   d = £7000   e = (£15,000)

  f = (£37,000)   g = £67,000   h = £44,000   i = (£7000)   j = (£6000)

  k = (£21,000)   l = (£58,000)   m = £9000   n = £53,000   o = (£6000)

  p = (£21,000)   q = (£58,000)   r = £9000   s = £53,000   t = £46,000

3. What would you recommend that Danielle and Sujugan do about this forecast? Explain the reasons behind your answer. (9)

	Knowledge 2 marks	Application 3 marks	Analysis 4 marks
Level 2	2 marks Good understanding of the subject content; or two answers identified.	3 marks Answer is applied effectively to the specific case.	4-3 marks Build-up of argument, making use of relevant business concepts.
Level 1	1 mark Shows some understanding of the subject content.	2-1 marks Some relationship to the scenario (perhaps indirectly).	2-1 marks Some build-up of argument, showing grasp of cause and effect.

Possible answers include:

- The business has a cash flow problem in September, October and November. Suggestions could be a loan or an overdraft. Overdraft is shorter term but expensive. Loan is longer term, which they may not need. It would give them longer-term cover but would need to be paid back and interest payments factored into costs.

- Overdraft facility should be longer than for the three months in case the figures are wrong. Do they have any flexibility on when goods have to be paid for? As sales are retail they are unlikely to be able to bring forward payment for the goods sold.

- Overall, though, their position looks great, as long as they can get through the next few months (building stocks for the Christmas rush).

Setting Budgets

15.1 Introduction

As with all financial concepts, keep the numbers easy – don't make the maths a stumbling block to understanding. Indeed, this unit is largely non-numerate – the key thrust being what is a budget, and why firms should budget for the future. Unit 17, Using Budgets, is more likely to bring examination questions that require numerate answers. I would try to teach at least one lesson on the topic of budgets without showing any numbers.

Beware lines of logic that say budgets motivate – there is a catch. Budgets are only likely to motivate if the budget holder has had some input in the process of setting the budget – and if they see the targets as realistic. Awareness of this problem should help your students overcome the common weakness of overly generic lines of argument failing to score more than only low level analysis marks.

For AQA, remember that this content will be examined in a small business context. It is therefore worth stressing the following points from the unit:

a) New businesses are likely to be short of cash, so budgeting may enable more effective control of cash outflows.

b) For one-person start-ups, time spent on budgeting may be poorly used; the sole trader should know his/her costs well enough to keep on top of them; getting on the phone to drum up business may be a far better use of time. When there are staff involved, though, for example, for a new restaurant, budget-setting may be critical in controlling costs and in incentivising sales staff.

15.2 Further reading and resources

Title and price	Author	Publisher and ISBN	Brief account
Running Your Own Business 6th Edition £14.99	Leach, R. and Dore, J.	Management Books 2000 Ltd 2008 978 18525 26023	Short but sweet on budgeting. Pages 82 and 83 would form the basis of a good lesson. (NB this reference is to the 5th edition, available at time of writing, but a 6th is published in August 2008; look up budgeting in the index.)
A-Z AS Business Studies Worksheets – photocopiable pack plus VLE £95.00	Marcouse. I.	A-Z Business Training Ltd* 2008	AQA Worksheets 7 (Budgets) and 8 (Budgets and Variances) provide coverage in this area. They provide suitable AS questions and answers. *To order, go to www.a-zbusinesstraining.com

Setting Budgets

15.3 Answers to workbook questions

A Revision questions

(30 marks; 30 minutes)

1. Explain the meaning of the term budgeting. **(2)**

   • A process of setting targets for costs and revenues for a future time period.

2. List three advantages that a budgeting system brings to a company. **(3)**

   • helps prevent overspending

   • provides a yardstick against which performance can be measured

   • allows spending power to be delegated

3. Why is it valuable to have a yardstick against which performance can be measured? **(3)**

   • Exceeding targets can bring motivation through a sense of achievement, whilst failure to meet targets allows corrective measures to be taken in the future.

4. What are the advantages of a zero-based budgeting system? **(3)**

   • It forces managers to be more efficient about the allocation of resources because they have to justify every pound they ask for.

   • It prevents the common phenomenon of annual budget increases.

5. Briefly explain how most companies actually set next year's budgets. **(3)**

   • Take last year's budget and adjust it slightly, perhaps adding a little to allow for inflation.

6. Why should budget holders have a say in the setting of their budgets? **(4)**

   • People will be more committed to reaching a target they believe can be met.

   • Budget holders are on the spot and may have particular knowledge of their area that is not available at Head Office level.

7. Complete the budget statement by filling in the gaps: **(8)**

	January	February	March	April
Income	4200	4500	4000	**4000**
Variable costs	1800	**2000**	2000	1800
Fixed costs	1200	1600	**2100**	1600
Total costs	3000	3600	4100	**3400**
Profit	**1200**	900	**(100)**	600

   • Answers in bold (one mark per correct answer)

8. Amend the budget statement completed in question 7 to show the income levels needed to generate a profit of £1000 per month, assuming there is no change in costs. (**4**)

	January	February	March	April
Income	**4000**	**4600**	**5100**	**4400**
Variable costs	1800	2000	2000	1800
Fixed costs	1200	1600	2100	1600
Total costs	3000	3600	4100	3400
Profit	1200	900	(100)	600

- Answers in bold (one mark per correct answer)

B1 Data response

(30 marks; 30 minutes)

(Refer to question on pages 94–5 of textbook.)

1. Complete the budget statement by filling in the gaps: (**4**)

	Jan–Mar	Apr–Jun	Jul–Sep	Oct–Dec
Shop sales	200	3000	5000	2000
Lake fees received	0	22000	25000	2800
Stock	2500	1000	2500	1000
Wages	1000	5000	5000	1000
Overheads	1000	4000	6000	4000
Profit	**(4300)**	**15000**	**16500**	**(1200)**

- Answers in bold (**4**)

2. Adjust the budget to show the effect of a 50% increase in shop sales in the third quarter and a 25% increase in wages in quarter 4. (**4**)

	Jan–Mar	Apr–Jun	Jul–Sep	Oct–Dec
Shop sales	200	3000	**7500**	2000
Lake fees received	0	22000	25000	2800
Stock	2500	1000	2500	1000
Wages	1000	5000	5000	**1250**
Overheads	1000	4000	6000	4000
Profit	(4300)	15000	**19000**	**(1450)**

- Answers in bold (**4**)

Setting Budgets

3. Explain why a budgeting system helps KB Wetsports to:

   (a) control expenses (6)

   (b) motivate staff (6)

	Knowledge 3 marks	Application 3 marks
Level 3	3 marks Candidate shows good understanding of budgeting **and** identifies one relevant point **or** identifies two points and shows limited understanding of budgeting.	
Level 2	2 marks Candidate shows good understanding of budgeting **or** identifies two relevant points.	3 marks Candidate applies knowledge effectively to *KB Wetsports'* circumstances.
Level 1	1 mark Candidate shows some understanding of budgeting **or** identifies one relevant point.	2-1 marks Candidate attempts to apply knowledge to *KB Wetsports'* circumstances.

(a) Budgeting will help to keep a close eye on the wages budget when sorting out staffing rotas and avoid overstaffing.

Setting targets for shop sales should help to avoid overstocking the shop, thus tying up more working capital than is necessary.

(b) Shop staff may be motivated to try to hit their sales targets

All staff may be committed to keeping overheads low and may therefore see the need to keep wastage to a minimum.

4. To what extent is budget-setting a crucial element of a successful small business start-up such as KB Wetsports? (**10**)

	Knowledge 2 marks	Application 2 marks	Analysis 3 marks	Evaluation 3 marks
Level 3			**3 marks** Good quality analysis of role played by budget setting in start-ups.	**3 marks** Candidate offers judgement plus full justification.
Level 2	**2 marks** Candidate shows good understanding of budgeting **or** identifies two relevant points.	**2 marks** Candidate applies knowledge effectively to *KB Wetsports'* circumstances.	**2 marks** Sound analysis of role played by budget setting in start-ups.	**2 marks** Candidate offers judgement plus limited justification.
Level 1	**1 mark** Candidate shows some understanding of budgeting **or** identifies one relevant point.	**1 mark** Candidate attempts to apply knowledge to *KB Wetsports'* circumstances.	**1 mark** Limited analysis of role played by budgeting in start-ups.	**1 mark** Candidate offers undeveloped judgement based on evidence.

• Yes because:

- Start-ups always seem short of cash, and budgeting may help monitor and control cash flows more carefully.

- The entrepreneurs will find it hard to decide whether they are performing successfully without any targets against which success can be measured. As Kurt and Brian may lack experience of running their own business, this could be very helpful.

• No because:

- For a start-up, estimates may be so far off as to be useless. There is no mention that Kurt and Brian have relevant business experience that would help them to set realistic budgets.

- Setting budgets could take Kurt and Brian away from more important tasks such as customer service and brand building.

• Overall:

In this case a simple budgeting system, which should avoid taking up too much management time, would bring benefits. However, Kurt and Brian may need to adjust the budgets regularly in the early stages of the business as they develop a feeling for exactly where their targets should be set.

Setting Budgets

B2 Data response

(20 marks; 25 minutes)

(Refer to question on page 95 of textbook.)

1. Identify and explain three pieces of evidence from the text that demonstrate the problems for firms that operate without a budget. (**9**)

   • Up to three marks per point

   – Over 40% feel they can spend what they want. The lack of a budget does nothing to breed a culture of cost control – this hits the bottom line.

   – 88% aren't influenced by cost. It is therefore obvious that they will be influenced by other factors, such as luxury, that drive up overheads.

   – £1.3bn that doesn't need to be spent is £1.3bn of lost profit that firms could use more productively and profitably.

2. Explain how a small business might benefit from setting expenditure budgets for its business travel. (**5**)

	Knowledge 3 marks	Application 2 marks
Level 3	**3 marks** Candidate shows good understanding of budgeting **and** identifies one relevant point **or** identifies two points and shows limited understanding of budgeting.	
Level 2	**2 marks** Candidate shows good understanding of budgeting **or** identifies two relevant points	**2 marks** Candidate applies knowledge effectively to *small businesses'* circumstances.
Level 1	**1 mark** Candidate shows some understanding of budgeting **or** identifies one relevant point	**1 mark** Candidate attempts to apply knowledge to small businesses' circumstances.

   • No unexpected surprises when expense claims are handed in makes financial control easier.

   • Can still empower staff to choose own arrangements, just offer an upper limit. This may minimise the annoyance for staff used to 'making their own arrangements'.

   • Money tends to be tighter in smaller firms.

Setting Budgets

3. Outline two problems a business might have in setting a travel budget (6)

	Knowledge 3 marks	Application 3 marks
Level 2	**3 marks** Candidate shows good understanding of budgeting **or** identifies two relevant points.	**3 marks** Candidate applies knowledge effectively to travel budgets.
Level 1	**2-1 marks** Candidate shows some understanding of budgeting **or** identifies one relevant point	**2-1 marks** Candidate attempts to apply knowledge to travel budgets.

- Unpredictability of the need for many trips. Much business travel may be made in order to grab an opportunity while you can – frequently an unexpected opportunity.

- Changes in costs charged by airlines, hotels and rail companies may be dramatic and unpredictable.

Assessing Business Start-Ups

16.1 Introduction

This is perhaps the most important chapter of the book so far. It is the one that integrates the issues within Unit 1 and focuses on how to evaluate a business plan. The issue of risk in business start-up is compared with the ups and downs of Cadbury's track record at launching new products. This seems a helpful way to ensure that students appreciate just how difficult it is to succeed in bringing something new to the market. Sections 16.5 and 16.6 of the chapter are especially useful.

The most frequent line of questioning, though, will focus on assessing the strengths and weaknesses of a business plan. Section 16.4 does this quite concisely and suggests including in the teaching programme a term that is not in the Spec: the 'business model'. This enables a student to distinguish between the heart of the business plan (the model) and the rights and wrongs of how the plan sets out the mechanics of turning the idea into an actual business.

Given the importance of this chapter, it is recommended that students do the Section A questions plus exercises B1 and B2. Also, please note that Unit 48 is a mock exam paper for Unit 1, which also has a student answer and an examiner's commentary on the student's performance.

16.2 Further reading and resources

Title and price	Author	Publisher and ISBN	Brief account
Good Finance Guide for Small Businesses £14.99		A & C Black 2007 978 0 7136 8209 0	Pages 7-9 have a super section on 'Approaching Business Angels' which gives a good idea of how investors appraise business plans.
From Acorns: How to Build a Brilliant Business 2nd Edition £9.99	Woods, C.	Prentice Hall 2007 978 0 273 71252 7	Pages 46-52 are useful to give an idea of how to appraise a business plan.
Good Small Business Guide: How to Start and Grow Your Own Business 3rd Edition £19.99		A & C Black 2008 978 0 7136 8760 6	Pages 318-320 look at 'Analysing Your Business's Strengths, Weaknesses, Opportunities and Threats'; a very useful way of appraising a new business idea.

Starting Your Own Business: The Good, the Bad and the Unexpected £12.99	Lester, D.	Crimson Publishing 2008 978 185 458 401 4	Chapters 7 and 8 give a genuine insight into what to look for when appraising a business idea and/or plan.
Business Case Studies 3rd Edition £17.99	Marcouse, I. and Lines, D.	Longman 2002 0 582 40636-6	Case Study 78 'The 3-in-1 Washing Machine' remains a nice, light, integrated case on start-up. Should generate plenty of discussion.

16.3 Answers to workbook questions

A Revision questions

(25 marks; 25 minutes)

1. Outline two entrepreneurial qualities shown by Duncan Goose. **(2)**

   • initiative

   • passion

   • ability to build relationships

   • ability to cope with risk

2. Explain in your own words why it is wise to have doubts about some of the businesses that call themselves 'social enterprises'. **(4)**

   • They may be using 'social' or 'environmental' clothing to hide a business that is really just finding a clever way to differentiate the business or brand, i.e. to help boost profits.

   • A free market is one in which entrepreneurs seek out ways to make a profit; if that is through green imagery, so be it; the socially concerned consumer should read the small print of the social claim made by any company (or charity).

3. Outline two ways to assess whether a business start-up has been a success. **(4)**

   • Whether it has met its own objectives, e.g. building one water pump per day.

   • Whether it provides enough profit to provide the income the entrepreneur needs, plus sufficient to reinvest in business improvements, i.e. to make its success sustainable.

4. Explain why potential investors would want to hear about the business model before reading a business plan. **(4)**

   • A business model shows how the business idea translates meeting a customer need into generating profitable revenue.

   • If the concept is not credible, the details of execution are irrelevant.

5. Outline two possible reasons why an established firm such as Cadbury can achieve no better than a one in seven success rate when launching new products. **(4)**

   • In a stable, long-established market such as chocolate, the market is saturated and almost every niche has been filled (or there is a long trail of dead brands that have tried to fill it).

   • Customers in a market such as this love to try new brands (and may buy them enthusiastically for weeks) but still revert back to traditional brand loyalties over time; so the producer believes they have a hit (e.g. Wispa, Fuse and KitKat Chunky) but sales slide away.

6. Look again at Figure 16.1. If the entrepreneur had thought hard about the risks of starting a new restaurant, how might s/he have done things differently? Outline two points. **(5)**

   • Arranged at the outset for a bigger overdraft – the planned £20,000 contingency was not enough.

   • The entrepreneur should have made much more cautious forecasts of demand in year 1; it can take a long time to build up demand with a new business such as a restaurant (word of mouth has to spread).

B1 Data response

(20 marks; 25 minutes)

(Refer to question on page 101 of textbook.)

1. Assess whether the dinner ladies showed poor market analysis, good analysis but poor execution, or bad luck. Explain your answer. **(6)**

	Knowledge 2 marks	Application 4 marks
Level 2	**2 marks** Shows clear understanding of the subject content.	**4-3 marks** Answer is applied effectively to the specific case.
Level 1	**1 mark** Shows some understanding of the subject content.	**2-1 marks** Some relationship to the scenario (perhaps indirectly).

Possible answers include:

   • Their market analysis seems to have been sound.

- Their mistake was to be aware of the importance of the summer weather (in keeping them going through the winter) but to have failed to prepare themselves financially, e.g. to have found enough start-up capital to see them through whatever the weather.

- Nevertheless it was horribly bad luck to face 'the wettest summer on record' in their opening year; no one would have been prepared for that; overall, then, their difficulties can be put down to bad luck.

2a If the cash position for the winter looks worrying, examine two forms of finance that would be appropriate in this case, and could be arranged before the winter starts. **(8)**

	Knowledge 3 marks	Application 3 marks	Analysis 2 marks
Level 2	**3 marks** Shows clear understanding of the subject content.	**3 marks** Answer is applied effectively to the specific case.	**2 marks** Build-up of argument, making use of relevant business concepts.
Level 1	**2-1 marks** Shows some understanding of the subject content.	**2-1 marks** Some relationship to the scenario (perhaps indirectly).	**1 mark** Some build-up of argument, showing grasp of cause and effect.

Possible answers include:

- An overdraft only requires you to pay interest when you actually need to use the facility; whereas a loan might require paying interest for three years, even though the finance was needed only for the first winter; the flexibility of overdrafts usually makes them ideal for small firms.

- The friend who put in £8000 may have more capital. This would be a better source than an outsider – who may exploit their weak position in the way that the 'Dragons' demand 50% of a business in return for relatively small investments. Perhaps they will have to sell another 20%, leaving themselves with 60% and therefore still in control.

2b Explain which form of finance would be more suitable, and why. **(6)**

	Knowledge 2 marks	Application 4 marks
Level 2	**2 marks** Shows clear understanding of the subject content.	**4-3 marks** Answer is applied effectively to the specific case.
Level 1	**1 mark** Shows some understanding of the subject content.	**2-1 marks** Some relationship to the scenario (perhaps indirectly).

Possible answers include:

- The ideal would be the overdraft because it is flexible; but in the circumstances of a new business at a difficult time it may be impossible to persuade any bank to provide an overdraft. However, they must try this route – hopefully they could arrange an overdraft before winter starts.

- If the overdraft option fails (and assuming that they themselves have no other source of capital) they should return to the friend and ask for more capital in exchange for a higher share stake.

B2 Data response

(25 marks; 30 minutes)

(Refer to question on pages 101–2 of textbook.)

1a Identify the business objective at Glasses Direct. **(1)**

- 'Get very big very fast'

1b Explain why this objective may have helped encourage staff to provide 'great customer service'. **(5)**

	Knowledge 2 marks	Application 3 marks
Level 2	**2 marks** Shows clear understanding of the subject content.	**3 marks** Answer is applied effectively to the specific case.
Level 1	**1 mark** Shows some understanding of the subject content.	**2-1 marks** Some relationship to the scenario (perhaps indirectly).

Possible answers include:

- The realisation that growth required a high level of repeat business and would be helped by good word of mouth (free) publicity.

- If the objective had been 'Get rich quick', staff may have been less concerned about customer service, and more interested in, for example, selling add-ons such as sunglasses or fancy frames.

2. Look at the six personal objectives in Section 16.2. Outline which one of them you believe was most important for Jamie when starting Glasses Direct. (5)

	Knowledge 2 marks		Application 3 marks
Level 2	**2 marks** Shows clear understanding of the subject content.		**3 marks** Answer is applied effectively to the specific case.
Level 1	**1 mark** Shows some understanding of the subject content.		**2-1 marks** Some relationship to the scenario (perhaps indirectly).

Possible answers include:

- The three most plausible of the six are 'own boss', 'build something' and 'show what I can do'.

- Based on the stated objective of 'very big very fast' it is possible to drop 'own boss' from the list.

- As 'build something' successfully would automatically achieve 'show what I can do', it seems the best explanation for Jamie's motives.

3. Glasses Direct seems to have enjoyed a relatively untroubled start-up. Outline two risks that the company faced, even though things turned out well. (6)

	Knowledge 3 marks		Application 3 marks
Level 2	**3 marks** Shows clear understanding of the subject content.		**3 marks** Answer is applied effectively to the specific case.
Level 1	**2-1 marks** Shows some understanding of the subject content.		**2-1 marks** Some relationship to the scenario (perhaps indirectly).

Possible answers include:

- It might have faced fierce competition if a business such as Boots had started up its own Boots Direct rival; in the early stages, with relatively weak finances, Jamie would not have been able to withstand such a blow; fortunately big firms such as Boots often think and act slowly.

- Given that he was fresh from University, Jamie couldn't really know at the outset whether he would have the skills required to manage and motivate staff effectively; fortunately he seems not to have suffered from what is often a difficult problem for entrepreneurs.

4. As Glasses Direct was growing satisfactorily, discuss whether Jamie was right to sell around 50% of the shares in exchange for the £2.9 million of fresh capital. (8)

Assessing Business Start-Ups

	Knowledge 1 mark	Application 2 marks	Analysis 2 marks	Evaluation 3 marks
Level 2		**2 marks** Answer is applied effectively to the specific case.	**2 marks** Build-up of argument, making use of relevant business concepts.	**3 marks** Shows judgement in drawing conclusions from own argument.
Level 1	**1 mark** Some understanding of the subject content; or one answer identified.	**1 mark** Some relationship to the scenario (perhaps indirectly).	**1 mark** Some build-up of argument, showing grasp of cause and effect.	**2-1 marks** Some judgement shown in argument or weighting of language.

Possible answers include:

- This is hard to answer without knowing what all the financing alternatives were, but he presumably had to choose whether to grow slowly from internal sources plus family, or grow faster at the expense of half the shares.

- If his decision was that half of a lot is more than all of a little, that may well have been right.

- The reason one can say that he was right to sell, though, was that it was a way to achieve his objective of 'Get very big very fast' (which is a way to ensure that even Boots will not be able to push Glasses Direct out of this market in future).

Using Budgets

17.1 Introduction

As a twin to Unit 15 (setting budgets), the content of this unit should flow naturally from Unit 15. With students understanding why budgets are set, they can now explore how budgets are used. Numbers will start to appear, but it still makes sense to stick to nice rounded numbers on any worked examples or other exercises you give to students. This should maintain the confidence of students with weaker numeracy skills.

It can be surprisingly hard for some students to grasp the need for budgets as a means of delegating spending power – surely the boss controls the purse strings? Indeed in small firms, especially those with an autocratic leader this may well be the case. However, simple use of a workforce statistic, such as RBS has over 100,000 employees worldwide and annual costs to budget each year of around £14 billion, can offer the insight required to crack this nut. This example can be extended to show how variance analysis, linked with management by exception, means that budgets do provide the only realistic way of monitoring/overseeing finances in such large organisations.

It may help to initially encourage students to label variances as good or bad, then attach the terms favourable and adverse (the terms preferred for AQA exams). This can help to overcome a vocabulary hurdle while trying to explain the basic principle behind variance identification.

A key question remains: should this part of the course be taught in Unit 2 or in Unit 1? Most staff will probably decide to teach budgeting as a whole, including variance analysis. After all, what is the purpose of budgeting without a comparison with actual data? As Unit 1 is relatively uncrowded, there is nothing to lose by teaching this material earlier in the year; but much to gain in terms of student understanding.

When using the Workbook materials, it is sensible to bear in mind that students will need practice in class and for homework. In effect there are three activities here: Section A, B1 and B2. You may wish to keep Section A for the revision period.

17.2 Further reading and resources

Title and price	Author	Publisher and ISBN	Brief account
Running Your Own Business 6th Edition £14.99	Leach, R. and Dore, J.	Management Books 2000 Ltd 2008 978 18525 26023	Short but sweet on budgeting. Pages 82 and 83 would form the basis of a good lesson. (NB this reference is to the 5th edition, available at time of writing, but a 6th is published in August 2008; look up budgeting in the index.)
Business Review, November 2004	Wolinski, J.	Philip Allan	Good article on budgeting; covering the rationale and the analysis through variances.

Using Budgets

A-Z AS Business Studies Worksheets – photocopiable pack plus VLE £95.00	Marcouse, I.	A-Z Business Training Ltd* 2008	AQA Worksheets 7 (Budgets) and 8 (Budgets and Variances) provide coverage in this area. They provide suitable AS questions and answers *To order, go to www.a-zbusinesstraining.com
Business Case Studies 3rd Edition £17.99	Marcouse. I. and Lines, D.	Longman 2002 0 582 40636-6	Case Study 22 'Budgeting in Harrogate' is a very accessible case on budgeting and simple variance.

17.3 Answers to workbook questions

A Revision questions

(40 marks; 40 minutes)

1. Explain the meaning of the term budgeting. (**3**)

   • A process of setting targets for costs and revenues for a future time period.

2. What are the two main advantages that using a budgeting system brings to a company? (**2**)

   • allows the delegation of spending power

   • can be used to monitor performance

3. Why is it valuable to have a yardstick against which performance can be measured? (**3**)

   • Exceeding targets can bring motivation through a sense of achievement, whilst failure to meet targets allows corrective measures to be taken in the future.

4. How might a firm respond to an increasingly adverse variance in labour costs? (**4**)

   • Find ways to reduce the variance. This could involve imposing greater controls on labour costs, reducing staffing levels or overtime rates.

   • They may also wish to check the viability of the budgeted figure.

5. Explain what is meant by 'a favourable cost variance'. (**2**)

   • The actual costs for a time period are lower than the budgeted costs for that period.

6. Why is management by exception a useful time-saving measure for management? (**4**)

   • It allows busy managers to focus their time only on problem areas and really successful areas, looking for causes of variances. This can allow them to learn lessons that can be spread throughout the organisation. It negates the need to look carefully at every budget.

7. Explain two drawbacks of budgeting. **(4)**

   • Setting and monitoring budgets takes up management time that carries an opportunity cost.

   • Targets can be unrealistic and therefore demotivate budget holders.

   • Budgeting may encourage short-term decisions, taken solely to hit targets, that may actually be harmful in the long term.

8. Briefly explain why a shop with a favourable income variance might expect some cost variances to be adverse. **(4)**

   • Selling more is likely to push up costs, such as stock and staffing levels if the shop is busier than expected.

9. Look at the following table, then answer the questions that follow it:

   (a) May – Budgeted profit = £1300
   May – Actual profit = £1100
   June – Budgeted profit = £1500
   June – Actual profit = £1600 **(4)**

   (b) i)   June
   ii)   Isn't one
   iii)   June
   iv)   June
   v)   June
   vi)   May
   vii)   May
   viii) June
   ix)   May
   x)   June **(10)**

B1 Data analysis

(20 marks; 20 minutes)

(Refer to question on page 107 of textbook.)

1. What are the five numbers missing from the variance analysis? **(5)**

	January			February		
	B	**A**	**V**	**B**	**A**	**V**
Sales Revenue	140	150	10	180	175	**(5)**
Materials	70	80	(10)	90	95	**(5)**
Other direct costs	30	35	(5)	40	40	0
Overheads	20	20	0	25	22	3
Profit	20	15	(5)	**25**	18	**(7)**

Answers in bold

2. Examine one financial strength and two weaknesses in this data, from the company's viewpoint. **(9)**

Apply this grid three times:

	Knowledge 1 mark	Application 2 marks
Level 2		**2 marks** Candidate applied knowledge effectively to the data presented.
Level 1	**1 mark** Candidate identifies relevant point.	**1 mark** Candidate attempts to apply knowledge to data.

- Strength

  - Good overhead control – January saw zero variance and February saw a favourable variance.

- Weaknesses

  - Adverse raw materials variance in February – if sales were lower than expected it may be considered a surprise that they spent more, not less on materials, unless the lower revenue figure was due to a steep price cut that boosted the volume, but not value of sales.

  - Adverse profit variances in both months are a key initial indicator of possible problems with general financial control.

3. How might a manager set about improving the accuracy of a sales budget? **(6)**

	Knowledge 3 marks	Application 3 marks
Level 3	**3 marks** Candidate shows good understanding of sales budgets **and** identifies one relevant point **or** identifies two points and shows limited understanding of sales budgets.	**3 marks** Good quality analysis of how to improve accuracy of sales budget
Level 2	**2 marks** Candidate shows good understanding of sales budgets **or** identifies two relevant points.	**2 marks** Sound analysis of how to improve accuracy of sales budget.
Level 1	**1 mark** Candidate shows some understanding of sales budgets **or** identifies one relevant point	**1 mark** Limited analysis of how to improve accuracy of sales budget.

- more or better market research

- look more closely at past trends and patterns

- consult more fully with local manager

B2 Data response

(25 marks; 25 minutes)

(Refer to question on page 107 of textbook.)

1. Use the data to explain why February's profits were worse than expected. **(5)**

	Knowledge 2 marks		Application 3 marks
Level 2	2 marks Candidate shows good understanding of profit **or** identifies two relevant points.		3 marks Candidate applies knowledge effectively to data.
Level 1	1 mark Candidate shows some understanding of profit **or** identifies one relevant point.		2-1 marks Candidate attempts to apply knowledge to data.

- Sales revenue was worse than expected, by 13%.

- Overheads were higher than budgeted.

- Although variable costs were lower than budgeted (materials by 8%, others by 10%), the proportional fall in sales revenue was greater than that of costs.

- Therefore profit was reduced.

2. Why might Clinton & Collins Ltd have chosen to set monthly budgets? **(5)**

One mark per point identified up to a maximum of three, plus up to two marks for explanation of each point.

- Prevents overspending by giving managers targets within which to stick.

- Provides a yardstick against which to measure performance giving staff a chance to work towards a measurable objective.

- Allows delegation of spending power, increasing motivation of budget holders as they feel empowered.

3. Explain how the firm might have set these budgets. **(4)**

One mark per point identified, second mark for brief explanation.

- Based on last year's figures, perhaps adjusted by the plans for the coming period.

• Zero-based budgeting, expecting budget holders to justify every pound allocated.

4. The directors of Clinton & Collins Ltd knew that the recession was causing problems for the firm but were unsure as to whether things were improving or worsening. To what extent does the data suggest an improvement? (11)

	Knowledge 2 marks	Application 3 marks	Analysis 3 marks	Evaluation 3 marks
Level 3			3 marks Good quality analysis of data.	3 marks Candidate offers judgement plus full justification.
Level 2	2 marks Candidate identifies two relevant points.	3 marks Candidate applies knowledge effectively to data provided.	2 marks Sound analysis of data.	2 marks Candidate offers judgement plus limited justification.
Level 1	1 mark Candidate identifies one relevant point.	2-1 marks Candidate attempts to apply knowledge to data provided.	1 mark Limited analysis of data.	1 mark Candidate offers undeveloped judgement based on evidence.

Month	Sales variance	Profit variance
January	(16)	(10)
February	(24)	(16)
March	(40)	(38)
April	(52)	(48)

• The variances are getting worse as time goes by – suggesting something other than the recession.

• Lack of economic data prevents certainty since the recession may be deepening.

• The rate of worsening seems to be slowing.

• Overall, the chances are that problems appear to be down to more than just the recession.

Improving Cashflow

18.1 Introduction

In this unit students needs to understand how cash flow problems can develop and what actions can be taken to rectify any problems. In the previous Specification, good cash flow was treated as being synonymous with healthy working capital; the new AS Spec makes no mention of working capital and it is sensible to follow this approach in your own teaching. Quite simply, references to working capital can, and should, be erased from your AS vocabulary.

The key is to focus on the techniques that can be used to improve cash flow. They should be taught with an understanding of the context of the particular business, i.e. the skill of application. It is also important to encourage students to think beyond the finance department. They should see these issues as whole-business problems and learn to think about the ways in which different parts of the business can contribute to improving cash flow.

18.2 Further reading and resources

Title and price	Author	Publisher and ISBN	Brief account
From Acorns: How to Build a Brilliant Business 2nd Edition £9.99	Woods, C.	Prentice Hall 2007 978 0 273 71252 7	Super five pages (148–52) on 'Keeping Your Cash', including the inevitable dictum that Cash is King.
Starting Your Own Business: The Good, the Bad and the Unexpected £12.99	Lester, D.	Crimson Publishing 2008 978 185 458 401 4	Chapter 20 'Cash is King' gives a good idea of how to improve cash flow.
Good Finance Guide for Small Businesses £14.99		A&C Black 2007 978 0 7136 8209 0	Pages 213–15 on 'Coping in a cash flow crisis' are very good.
Business Case Studies 3rd Edition £17.99	Marcouse, I. and Lines, D.	Longman 2002 0 582 40636-6	Case Studies 17 and 18 are focused on cash flow in the context of business start-up.

Unit **18**

A Revision questions
(40 marks; 40 minutes)

1. Why is cash flow an especially important topic for small firms rather than large ones? **(4)**

   • Small firms are often starting out so may have uncertain business patterns and will find it more difficult to forecast cash needs accurately. Small firms may find it more difficult to negotiate a loan or an overdraft. Small firms have more limited sources of revenue.

2. Outline the probable cash cycle for a small sandwich shop. **(4)**

   • Purchases of raw materials for sandwiches are made. Sales are made. Cash is used to purchase more materials to make more sandwiches. Full marks for movement of cash and the idea of a cycle.

3. Explain why 'good management of cash flow starts with good forecasting'. **(3)**

   • Understanding when cash flow shortages are likely to occur enables good management of cash flow. Forecasting helps to see when cash is coming in and out and when shortfalls may occur. This enables the business to take the necessary measures to correct any possible future problems.

4. Outline two problems that might arise if a firm is operating with very poor cash flow. **(4)**

   • Two marks for each problem identified. Answers might include: inability to pay debts; suppliers might stop supplies of materials; bank or other lender may foreclose; might be unable to take on new business.

5. Why might a business be unable to get a loan or overdraft if it has cash flow difficulties? **(4)**

   • Full marks when there is an explanation of how the poor cash flow relates to the loan. Answers may include: the business could be seen as a bad risk as a poor cash flow often leads a business to fail; the poor cash flow might mean that it has poor sales so is unlikely to be profitable; the bank will be worried that it is unable to pay back the loan.

6. What impact does the length of the business process have on cash flow? **(4)**

   • A short business cycle will mean that cash flows quickly into and out of the business.

   • A long cycle will mean that cash is tied up in production or stock so more cash will be needed.

7. Getting money in from customers is a vital part of cash flow management. Outline two things a firm can do to ensure that cash is collected efficiently. **(4)**

   • Two marks for each suggestion. These might include: prompt invoicing; following up after the invoice has been sent; having systems to identify slow payment; chasing bad debts; using a factoring service.

8. How might a small producer of shelf fittings benefit from factoring? (**4**)

   • Most customers are likely to be other businesses therefore payment time could be long. Factoring will get a substantial part of the cash owed into the business sooner. It also ensures that there are no bad debts. The cash in the business can be used to generate more business.

9. Outline three ways in which a business can improve its cash flow situation. (**6**)

Two marks for each way identified:

   • Collecting from debtors sooner.

   • Delaying payment of bills.

   • Having more cash sales.

   • Holding less stock and/or materials.

   • Taking out a short-term loan to cover any period of cash shortages.

10. What internal factors could affect a firm's cash flow? (**3**)

   • speed of the production/sales process

   • efficiency of the business

   • efficiency of debt collection

B1 Data response

Credit crunch 'hits small firms'
(**30 marks; 30 minutes**)

(**Refer to question on page 112 of textbook.**)

1. What is meant by the term 'credit crunch'? (**2**)

   • A situation when credit such as loans are harder to obtain.

2. Why are banks less willing to lend to small businesses? (**6**)

Two marks for identification of reasons. Additional four marks for explanations.

   • Reasons might include:

   – Small businesses may not have any assets to offer as collateral.

   – They have limited revenue so may be unable to repay the loans.

   – Small business particularly if they are new may be more risky so the bank will be unwilling to take the risk.

3. What is the rate of interest that small businesses are likely to be paying? (**2**)

   • 11–12% from the text

Improving Cashflow

4. On a £10,000 loan with an interest rate of 12%, how much will the interest charges be for the first year of the loan? (**4**)

• £1200

Marks can be given for part calculations.

5. Why will a lack of available credit stop small businesses from expanding? (**8**)

	Knowledge 4 marks	Application 4 marks
Level 2	**4-3 marks** Understanding of the sources of credit and the reasons why small businesses might find it difficult to obtain credit.	**4-3 marks** Good explanation of how lack of credit affects small business expansion.
Level 1	**2-1 marks** Some understanding of credit or the difficulties of obtaining credit.	**2-1 marks** Some analysis of the effect of lack of credit.

• Sources of credit for small businesses include: loans, overdrafts, trade credit.

• Difficulties may be faced because of: lack of credit history, considered to be higher risk, no track record, lack of assets to offer as collateral.

• Expansion will be stopped because: cash is not available to buy additional materials or assets; there may be insufficient cash to take on more employees. Most businesses need investment to expand before they generate profits. Retained profit may be insufficient to enable expansion.

6. Explain how a lack of easy credit for larger firms may affect smaller businesses. (**8**)

	Knowledge 4 marks	Application 4 marks
Level 2	**4-3 marks** Understanding of credit for large firms shown and its effect on smaller firms.	**4-3 marks** Good analysis of effect of lack of credit for large businesses on smaller businesses.
Level 1	**2-1 marks** Understanding of credit shown.	**2-1 marks** Some analysis of the effects.

• Answer should show some understanding of how small firms often depend on larger firms. If large firms are hit by a credit squeeze the whole economy could be slowed down which would affect smaller firms. If credit is tight for larger firms with better credit rating then it will be even harder for smaller firms.

Improving Cashflow

B2 Case study

Hatta Lighting

(35 marks; 40 minutes)

(Refer to question on page 113 of textbook.)

1. What might be the reasons for the increase in the stock of finished goods and materials? **(6)**

    • A reduction of sales would lead to an increase in stock.

    • Overproduction.

	Knowledge 2 marks	Application 4 marks
Level 2	**2 marks** Reason for increase in stock of goods and materials identified.	**4-3 marks** Analysis of the reason for increases in both stocks of finished goods and materials.
Level 1	**1 mark** Reason given for either increase in stock of finished goods or materials.	**2-1 marks** Explanation of the reasons for increase in stocks of either finished goods or materials.

2. Consider what suggestions the production director might make. Explain your reasoning. **(7)**

    • The director might introduce lean production in order to reduce costs.

    • He might reduce the number of employees in production in order to reduce costs and quantity of production.

	Knowledge 2 marks	Application and Analysis 3 marks	Evaluation 2 marks
Level 2	**2 marks** Suggestions explained.	**3 marks** Good analysis of the suggestions.	**2 marks** Good judgement shown perhaps indicating the best suggestion.
Level 1	**1 mark** Suggestions made.	**2-1 marks** Some analysis of the suggestions or answer limited to one suggestion.	**1 mark** Some judgement shown.

3. The finance director sees slow payment as his major problem. Examine the ways in which the firm might tackle this problem. **(6)**

    • Factoring.

    • Demanding payment by letter or phone.

• Threatening legal action if necessary.

• Introducing cash discounts in order to prevent the problem from occurring in the future.

	Knowledge 2 marks	Application 2 marks	Analysis 2 marks
Level 2	**2 marks** More than one way of tackling the problem identified.	**2 marks** Explanation of why ways of tackling the problem are relevant to this business.	**2 marks** Good analysis of ways of tackling the problem.
Level 1	**1 mark** One way of tackling the problem identified.	**1 mark** Some reference to case.	**1 mark** Limited analysis of ways of tackling the problem or only one way discussed.

4. Outline the contribution the marketing department might make to help improve the cash flow situation. (**6**)

• Increase sales in order to improve cash in.

• If necessary reduce the price of the product in order to increase demand (as stock is piling up).

• Devise innovative and cost-effective marketing techniques to increase sales.

	Knowledge 2 marks	Application 2 marks	Analysis 2 marks
Level 2	**2 marks** Identification of marketing actions.	**2 marks** Connection between marketing and cash flow fully understood.	**2 marks** The effect of marketing actions on cash flow fully explained.
Level 1	**1 mark** One marketing action identified.	**1 mark** Some connection made between marketing and cash flow.	**1 mark** Limited explanation of effect of marketing action/s.

5. Apart from tackling the issue of slow payment, consider what other short term measures the firm might take to overcome the immediate cash crisis. (**10**)

• Get an overdraft so as they can pay the debt.

Improving Cashflow

• Speak to the firms they owe the £500,000 to and explain the situation and try to negotiate delaying the payments further.

	Knowledge 2 marks	Application 2 marks	Analysis 4 marks	Evaluation 2 marks
Level 2	2 marks Measures identified.	2 marks Measures selected are appropriate to the business.	4-3 marks Measures explained or one measure explained fully.	2 marks Judgement shown and answer related to short term.
Level 1	1 mark Only one measure identified.	1 mark Measure selected is appropriate to the business.	2-1 marks One measure explained.	1 mark Some judgement shown.

Section 4 Finance

Measuring and Increasing Profit

Unit 19

19.1 Introduction

The key with this section is not to get too distracted by the curious addition of 'return on capital' to the AS course. We will return to this below.

The heart of the section is 'measuring performance' and 'methods of improving profits'. These will generate the high-mark questions. They have terrific potential to achieve two desirable outcomes: to test effectively the student's skill of application; and to test whether they have an integrated grasp of the subject. Question 7 on the Workbook Exercise B2, for instance, will give you a clear understanding of your students' strengths and weaknesses of exam technique.

The chapter also covers the more technical issues of profit margins and 'return on capital'. The only margin referred to in the Spec is the net profit margin; it is wise to stick with that. It may seem helpful to explain the gross margin, but there is so much analytic scope within the net margin that it is not advisable.

With return on capital, the key will be to resist the temptation to explain to students the potential for confusion between ROC and ROCE. As they are blissfully unaware of capital employed, keep their focus on Return on Capital (Invested), making it seem what it is – a simple, back-of-the-envelope way to assess whether an investment is profitable enough to be worthwhile. (From a teacher's point of view, this version of ROC has more in common with ARR than ROCE.)

To use this chapter effectively, Table 19.1 is very useful, perhaps to discuss a) Why Ted Baker's margins are 20 times those of Woolworths and b) What can Woolworths do to boost its margins? (*Ed: give extra evaluation marks to any student who says 'Nothing. Close it down'*). For homework, Section A plus exercise B2 are recommended.

19.2 Further reading and resources

Title and price	Author	Publisher and ISBN	Brief account
From Acorns: How to Build a Brilliant Business 2nd Edition £9.99	Woods, C.	Prentice Hall 2007 978 0 273 71252 7	Pages 100-7 cover pricing and 136-9 cover customer loyalty; both give insights into how best to boost profitability.
FT Guide to Business Start Up 2008 £19.99	Williams, S.	Prentice Hall 2007 978 0273 14873	Several sections that are helpful; this book is full of insights.
Starting Your Own Business: The Good, the Bad and the Unexpected £12.99	Lester, D.	Crimson Publishing 2008 978 185 458 401 4	Pages 223-9 are full of insights into how to make a small business a success, e.g. 'Back your winners' and 'Stop activities that are losing money'.

126

© Hodder Education 2008

Measuring and Increasing Profit

A-Z AS Business Studies Worksheets – photocopiable pack plus VLE £95.00	Marcouse, I.	A-Z Business Training Ltd* 2008	Worksheet 70 focuses on profit, 71 on profit margins and 27 on the difference between cash and profit. *To order, go to www.a-zbusinesstraining.com

19. 3 Answers to workbook questions

A Revision questions

(25 marks; 20 minutes)

1. What is meant by 'net profit'? **(2)**

   • profit after taking away all variable and fixed operating costs

2. What is meant by 'revenue'? **(2)**

   • the value of sales made over a period of time, e.g. six months

3. Does an increase in price necessarily increase revenue? **(3)**

   • No, because the volume of sales might fall so sharply that the percentage increase in price is outweighed by the percentage fall in demand.

4. How can revenue increase without an increase in cash inflows? **(3)**

   • If sales are made, they will be recorded as an increase in revenue; but if the sales were made on credit, there will be no cash in yet.

5. Is profitability measured in pounds or percentages? **(1)**

   • The term 'profitability' suggests percentages not pounds. In other words it is profit in relation to something else, e.g. profit as a percentage of sales revenue.

6. What is the equation for the net profit margin? **(2)**

   • $\dfrac{\text{Net profit}}{\text{Revenue}} \times 100$

7. How can the profit margin increase and yet the return on capital fall? **(4)**

   • A price increase would boost the profit margin, but if sales fell sharply, the total profit could end up lower than before, therefore (probably) cutting the return on capital.

8. Explain two ways of increasing profits. **(6)**

   • Cut back on inessential costs such as Business Class air travel.

   • Add value to the product so that a price increase has little effect on demand.

9. Why might cutting costs end up reducing profits? (**3**)

• Lower costs might lead to a customer perception of lower quality; this could lead to a sales decline which might cut revenue by more than the decline in revenue.

10. In what ways do the different functions of a business affect its profits? (**4**)

• Marketing can hope to boost revenue.

• Operations can try to cut operating costs.

• The Finance Department can damage profits if it arranges an overpriced, risky loan.

• The Personnel Department could be invaluable if it can help motivate staff to work harder and with more enthusiasm.

B1 Data response

(30 marks; 30 minutes)

(Refer to question on page 118 of textbook.)

1. Distinguish between revenue, costs and net profit. (**3**)

One mark each for:

• revenue = value of sales

• costs = The bills generated in running the business

• net profit = The amount left after deducting all operating costs from revenue.

2. Explain why a fall in price might not have led to an increase in revenue (**5**)

	Knowledge 1 mark	Application 2 marks	Analysis 2 marks
Level 2		**2 marks** Answer is applied effectively to the specific case.	**2 marks** Build-up of argument, making use of relevant business concepts.
Level 1	**1 mark** Shows some understanding of the subject content.	**1 mark** Some relationship to the scenario (perhaps indirectly).	**1 mark** Some build-up of argument, showing grasp of cause and effect.

Possible answers include:

• Rivals may have cut their prices in response to SOFA-SOGOOD's price cut.

- The whole furniture market may have been down, as in 2008 in response to the housing crisis.

- The higher interest rates being suffered by SOFA-SOGOOD would also have hit consumers.

3. Apart from the methods mentioned in the text, analyse two other actions SOFA-SOGOOD might take to improve its profitability. **(8)**

	Knowledge 2 marks	Application 3 marks	Analysis 3 marks
Level 2	**2 marks** Shows clear understanding of the subject content.	**3 marks** Answer is applied effectively to the specific case.	**3 marks** Build-up of argument, making use of relevant business concepts.
Level 1	**1 mark** Shows some understanding of the subject content.	**2-1 marks** Some relationship to the scenario (perhaps indirectly).	**2-1 marks** Some build-up of argument, showing grasp of cause and effect.

Possible answers include:

- Retail chains have successful and less successful outlets; sometimes they even have two stores in the same town; it may be time to cut back on the under-performers, thereby cutting back the operating costs of the business; this would be especially effective if the business had an e-commerce, online division that could serve anyone at too great a distance from the new store line-up.

- It should carry out a customer survey to try to identify whether the problems are temporary or whether the brand itself has real problems; if the brand has slipped in popularity it would be better to tackle that than take decisions with only a short-term effect.

Measuring and Increasing Profit

4. Discuss the advantages and disadvantages to the business of the staffing cost-saving actions taken by Renis. **(14)**

	Knowledge 2 marks	Application 3 marks	Analysis 4 marks	Evaluation 5 marks
Level 2	**2 marks** Good understanding of the subject content; or two answers identified.	**3 marks** Answer is applied effectively to the specific case.	**4-3 marks** Build-up of argument, making use of relevant business concepts.	**5-3 marks** Shows judgement in drawing conclusions from own argument.
Level 1	**1 mark** Some understanding of the subject content; or one answer identified.	**2-1 marks** Some relationship to the scenario (perhaps indirectly).	**2-1 marks** Some build-up of argument, showing grasp of cause and effect.	**2-1 marks** Some judgement shown in argument or weighting of language.

- Advantages:

  - It's a way to cut the salary bill without causing the disruption to team spirit and harmony that's implied by redundancies (but team spirit is only worth preserving if it was good before).

  - A pay freeze for everyone is a way to share the pain; staff will be happy to accept that, but perhaps only for a year; after that, better staff will get jobs elsewhere.

- Disadvantages:

  - When times are tough it is possible to carry staff with you in making unpleasant decisions; every business has departments that add little value and staff that are weak; now might be the ideal time to get them out of the business, leaving it stronger to face the long-term future.

  - The suggestions can stop staff costs rising, but may do too little to cut staff costs back; therefore it may be an inadequate response to a tough time.

Measuring and Increasing Profit

B2 Data response

Farmoor College
(40 marks; 40 minutes)

(Refer to question on pages 118–19 of textbook.)

1. Calculate the likely net profits for the college this year. **(3)**

   • £15,000 × 200 × 12% = £360,000

2. Calculate the college's likely return on capital this year. Comment on your findings **(4)**

   • £360,000/£15m × 100 = 2.4%

   This is far below any interest rate seen in the UK for many years, so it represents a very poor return on the money invested in the college.

3. Outline two costs the college is likely to have. **(4)**

   • staffing costs, which probably account for a high proportion of the total costs

   • equipment, e.g. interactive whiteboards.

4. Explain one factor that might cause a change in demand for the college. **(4)**

   • A sharp recession might encourage parents to question whether the value to the student is worth the short-term hardship for the family of struggling with fees of £15,000 a year.

5. Explain how the net profit of the college might be used. **(5)**

   • To reinvest in college improvement, e.g. a new Drama studio or something with direct impact on A-level results, e.g. a state-of-the-art online revision programme.

   • It might be used to give the landlord of the premises more income and therefore wealth.

6. Analyse how you might measure the performance of the college apart from its looking at its financial results. **(8)**

	Knowledge 2 marks	Application 3 marks	Analysis 3 marks
Level 2	2 marks Shows clear understanding of the subject content.	3 marks Answer is applied effectively to the specific case.	3 marks Build-up of argument, making use of relevant business concepts.
Level 1	1 mark Shows some understanding of the subject content.	2-1 marks Some relationship to the scenario (perhaps indirectly).	2-1 marks Some build-up of argument, showing grasp of cause and effect.

Possible answers include:

- Exam results, perhaps in comparison with other private colleges, or by comparison with the students' achievements before joining the college (their GCSEs or even their SATs).

- Even more important might be to measure the satisfaction of students and parents with the quality and value for money of the college experience, perhaps as an annual survey; it could also include the key questions: 'Would you recommend the college to others?' And (to parents) 'Would you send other children to Farmoor College?'

7. Discuss the ways in which the college might increase its profits. **(12)**

	Knowledge 2 marks	Application 2 marks	Analysis 4 marks	Evaluation 4 marks
Level 2	2 marks Good understanding of the subject content; or two answers identified.	2 marks Answer is applied effectively to the specific case.	4-3 marks Build-up of argument, making use of relevant business concepts.	4-3 marks Shows judgement in drawing conclusions from own argument.
Level 1	1 mark Some understanding of the subject content; or one answer identified.	1 mark Some relationship to the scenario (perhaps indirectly).	2-1 marks Some build-up of argument, showing grasp of cause and effect.	2-1 marks Some judgement shown in argument or weighting of language.

Possible answers include:

- Fundamentally it has two choices: either aim to maximise its profits from within the existing capacity (200 students), or adopt a strategy of growth in capacity. To help it decide, it needs to be confident of growing demand in future, for which the market research outlined in the answer to Question 6 is all-important. Even if the demand seems to be there, the managers of the college must be sure that they can find the financial and staffing resources to make growth a success.

- If the decision is to stay within the current capacity (perhaps because a poor economic situation makes future demand too uncertain) the only options are to either increase the revenue per student (by increasing prices or by adding extra options such as Holiday Schools) or to cut costs, possibly by having larger class sizes and therefore needing fewer teachers – though the college's pride in its small classes makes this seem a very undesirable option.

- If the decision is to grow, then the management can either increase capacity at the current site, or look for further sites in different parts of the country or in different countries.

Cashflow v Profit

20.1 Introduction

This is one of the toughest topics in the subject (AS or A2) and may therefore best be left until fairly shortly before the summer exams. There are two keys to successful teaching of cash v profit: firstly to introduce it through an accessible example and secondly to accept that even if students have 'got it', few will keep it for long. Soon they'll be back to seeing the terms as interchangeable. It is a topic that must be returned to, time after time.

If you do not have an accessible example of cash v profit, try case 20 in *Business Case Studies*, Third Edition by Longman.

Within the chapter, it would be worthwhile to get students to read Sections 20.1 and 20.2 and then ask them some questions:

1. Why was revenue higher than cash inflow at the clothes shop last Saturday?

2. Why may it be a problem for firms to have high sales but low cash inflow?

3. Briefly explain three of the six financial items in Table 20.1, i.e. explain why they have been given the ticks and crosses shown in the table.

For homework, the revision questions plus B2 are especially worthwhile.

20.2 Further reading and resources

Title and price	Author	Publisher and ISBN	Brief account
From Acorns: How to Build a Brilliant Business 2nd Edition £9.99	Woods, C.	Prentice Hall 2007 978 0 273 71252 7	Super five pages (148-152) on 'Keeping Your Cash', including the inevitable dictum that Cash is King.
Starting Your Own Business: The Good, the Bad and the Unexpected £12.99	Lester, D.	Crimson Publishing 2008 978 185 458 401 4	Chapter 6 'How Much Money Will You Need?' gives a good account of the difference between cash and profit.
Business Case Studies 3rd Edition £17.99	Marcouse, I. and Lines, D.	Longman 2002 0 582 40636-6	Case Study 20 'The Furniture Shop' is a terrific way to illustrate the difference between cash flow and profit.

A-Z AS Business Studies Worksheets – photocopiable pack plus VLE £95.00	Marcouse, I.	A-Z Business Training Ltd* 2008	Four worksheets are devoted to cash flow: 15 (Difficulties), 16 (Forecasts), 17 (Management) and 27 (Difference between cash and profit) *To order, go to www.a-z businesstraining.com

20.3 Answers to workbook questions

A Revision questions

(20 marks; 25 minutes)

1. Explain in your own words why cash inflow is not the same thing as revenue. (**3**)

   • Revenue is the value of sales made (whether or not the cash has yet arrived). Cash inflow is the arrival of cash, whether from any source, e.g. a bank loan or the investment of some new share capital.

2. Look again at Table 20.1. Explain why taking out a £20,000 bank loan generates cash inflow but not revenue. (**3**)

   • Money comes in, but it is only borrowing that must eventually be repaid; it isn't revenue (the value of sales).

3. Give two reasons why a profitable business might run out of cash when it expands too rapidly. (**2**)

   • It may keep running out of capacity, forcing managers to keep spending cash on new buildings.

   • Rapid growth puts pressure on cash flow because (in most businesses) cash has to be spent on costs before income arrives from customers.

4. Look again at Table 20.2. Explain why 'purchases from suppliers on credit' is treated as a cost, yet not as a cash outflow. (**3**)

   • Purchases are a cost and will eventually be a cash outflow, but if suppliers have provided credit the cash outflow hasn't occurred yet.

5. Identify and briefly explain whether each of the following business start-ups would be cash-rich or cash-poor in the early years of the business.

   (**a**) a pension fund, in which people save money in return for later pay-outs (**2**)

      • cash-rich

(b) building a hotel (**2**)

- cash-poor

(c) starting a vineyard (grapes only pickable after three to five years) (**2**)

- (very) cash-poor

6. Look again at Table 20.3. Use it and the accompanying text to explain why the cash flow of the beauty salon is different from its profit. (**4**)

- One reason is that it takes many months for the sales to build up to what appears to be the normal level; so the monthly net cash flow only turns positive from month 6.

- The fact that it takes three months to complete the £60,000 of start-up work cuts three months out of the income-earning equation; so the expected profit of £80,000 a year is not possible because there are only nine months of income earning in the year.

7. Why is it important for a small business to look both at profit and cash flow? (**4**)

- Because cash flow provides the essential information about the bank balance in the near future …

- … while profit shows the longer term impact of a financial decision.

B1 Data response

(15 marks; 20 minutes)

(Refer to question on page 124 of textbook.)

1. Outline three groups of people (stakeholders) who would have lost out in the collapse of Independent Insurance. (**6**)

- The shareholders would have been hard hit; some, such as Michael Bright, would have known about the operational problems and may share some blame for mistakes; others would have been entirely innocent investors, trying to find a profitable home for their pension savings.

- Staff have been hit worse still, as they have lost their whole income, together with the social and psychological strengths that come from a job.

- Customers have also been hurt because their insurance premiums are no longer valid, i.e. if they need to make a claim there will be no way to make payments to them.

Cashflow v Profit

2. Explain how a fast-growing insurance business could be cash-rich, yet unprofitable. (9)

	Knowledge 2 marks	Application 3 marks	Analysis 4 marks
Level 2	2 marks Good understanding of the subject content; or two answers identified.	3 marks Answer is applied effectively to the specific case.	4-3 marks Build-up of argument, making use of relevant business concepts.
Level 1	1 mark Some understanding of the subject content.	2-1 marks Some relationship to the scenario (perhaps indirectly).	2-1 marks Some build-up of argument, showing grasp of cause and effect.

Possible answers include:

- The 'premiums' are collected from customers at the outset, and it may be many years before they need to be paid out; in the meantime the business can be earning interest from a bank account.

- With the costs not yet due to be paid, the business may kid itself that it is making lots of profit, and therefore allow business expenses to creep up higher than necessary.

B2 Data response

Investment dragon Peter Jones on cash and profit
(20 marks; 25 minutes)

(Refer to question on pages 124–5 of textbook.)

1. Explain why, in the first paragraph, Peter Jones seems to be suggesting that cash flow is more important than profit for a small business. (4)

	Knowledge 1 mark	Application 3 marks
Level 2		3 marks Answer is applied effectively to the specific case (of small business).
Level 1	1 mark Shows understanding of the subject content.	2-1 marks Some relationship to the scenario (perhaps indirectly).

Possible answers include:

- Whereas a big firm such as Honda can wait 10 years to make a profit from its Swindon UK factory, small firms must generate the cash today to pay the wages tomorrow.

- Banks are always nervous about lending to small firms; as overdrafts are on 24-hour recall, a slip with cash flow can make the bank worried enough to insist on overdraft repayment – which will be sufficient to put many small firms out of business.

2. By 'run-rate' Peter Jones means the revenue generated by the business once it is up and running. Why does he think an entrepreneur should wait before spending at this rate? (5)

	Knowledge 2 marks	Application 3 marks
Level 2	2 marks Shows clear understanding of the subject content.	3 marks Answer is applied effectively to the specific case (of small business).
Level 1	1 mark Shows understanding of the subject content.	2-1 marks Some relationship to the scenario (perhaps indirectly).

Possible answers include:

- Because the 'run rate' cannot be known for certain until a year or two's business has been completed (many firms have seasonally tough times); therefore it is unwise to start spending on fixed costs until you really know what the run-rate is.

- The run-rate may not reflect the cash flows within the business, e.g. you may see a rate of sale of £30,000 a month, yet find later on that only £25,000 turns up as client payments (the rest disappears as bad debts or demands for discounts).

3. Growing 'organically' means from within, i.e. not rushing to buy up other businesses). Organic growth is usually at a slow enough pace to cope with cash flow pressures. Examine why rapid growth can cause big cash flow problems. (6)

	Knowledge 2 marks	Application 2 marks	Analysis 2 marks
Level 2	2 marks Good understanding of the subject content; or two answers identified.	2 marks Answer is applied effectively to the specific case.	2 marks Build-up of argument, making use of relevant business concepts.
Level 1	1 mark Some understanding of the subject content.	1 mark Some relationship to the scenario (perhaps indirectly).	1 mark Some build-up of argument, showing grasp of cause and effect.

Possible answers include:

- Rapid growth means that today's cash outflows are always high, because they're dealing with today's highest-ever level of demand; the cash inflow, though, is based on the (lower) sales made two months ago; as cash in always lags behind cash out, this is a permanent problem.

Cashflow v Profit

- Rapid growth means that, regularly, the business runs out of capacity; every increase in capacity means a huge extra chunk of cash outflow, e.g. to buy a new lease, new machinery and recruit and train new staff.

4. Explain why it's 'better to overestimate expenditure and time and underestimate revenue'? (5)

	Knowledge 1 mark	Application 2 marks	Analysis 2 marks
Level 2		**2 marks** Answer is applied effectively to the specific case.	**2 marks** Build-up of argument, making use of relevant business concepts.
Level 1	**1 mark** Shows some understanding of the subject content.	**1 mark** Some relationship to the scenario (perhaps indirectly).	**1 mark** Some build-up of argument, showing grasp of cause and effect.

Possible answers include:

- It is never possible to be consistently right about the future; the key is to be wrong in the right way. If revenue proves higher than expected, that's great! And if costs prove lower than planned for, fantastic!

- So clever entrepreneurs 'overestimate expenditure' (costs), so that surprises are nice ones and they also underestimate revenue.

Integrated Finance

Unit **21**

21.1 Introduction

Given the imperatives of Schemes of Work, it is easy to ignore the Integrated chapters in this book. When you look at the text, you'll see why that would be a pity. It is absolutely worthwhile within the teaching programme, but perhaps even more valuable as part of the students' revision. All the material is worthwhile, but the most obviously valuable are Sections 21.5 and 'Issues for Analysis'.

If students are using this chapter for revision, it might be sensible to copy these answers and hand them out. They can judge the qualities of their own answers, especially for the Section A questions.

21.2 Further reading and resources

Title and price	Author	Publisher and ISBN	Brief account
From Acorns: How to Build a Brilliant Business 2nd Edition £9.99	Woods, C.	Prentice Hall 2007 978 0 273 71252 7	The key chapter in this book is 19: keeping hold of your cash.
FT Guide to Business Start Up 2008 £19.99	Williams, S.	Prentice Hall 2007 978 0273 14873	Worth dipping into various parts of this excellent book.
How to Fund Your Business: The Essential Guide to Raising Finance to Start and Grow Your Business £14.99	Parks, S.	Prentice Hall 2006 978 0273 70624 3	Worth dipping into various parts of this excellent book.
Starting Your Own Business: The Good, the Bad and the Unexpected £12.99	Lester, D.	Crimson Publishing 2008 978 185 458 401 4	Read Chapter 21: 'Is it working?' – it's broader than just finance, but gives a good insight into key financial questions.
Entrepreneurship and Small Business £34.99 (!)	Burns P.	Palgrave 2007 978 140 394 7338	For teachers only, but a gem of a book (and, at that price, it should be).

Integrated Finance

21.3 Answers to workbook questions

A Revision questions

(50 marks; 50 minutes)

1. List three ways in which decisions by the finance department can affect other functions of the business such as marketing, people or operations. **(3)**

   • A decision to cut costs might affect staff recruitment and training.

   • An increase in budgets might allow a business to advertise on TV for the first time.

   • Deciding to increase the time taken to pay suppliers (to improve short-term cash flow) may make it harder for operations to buy in high quality supplies.

2. What is meant by profit? **(2)**

   • The amount left after all costs are deducted from revenues.

3. Why is profit important to a business? **(2)**

   • It provides the regular injection of extra capital that enables a business to grow without getting into debt.

4. What is the difference between profit and cash flow? **(2)**

   • Cash flow is a short-term measurement of what's happening to the bank balance; profit looks at the longer-term effects of a financial transaction.

5. How is the concept of 'contribution' used in break-even analysis? **(2)**

   • Fixed costs are divided by contribution per unit to find the break-even point.

6. Explain what is meant by budgeting. **(2)**

   • Setting or agreeing limits on future spending and targets for minimum sales.

7. Why do firms produce cash flow forecasts? **(4)**

   • To see whether future cash inflows will be able to cover cash outflows, month by month.

   • To give the business time to adjust if there is a period of forecast negative cash flow (e.g. arrange a bank overdraft).

8. What is the difference between profits and profitability? **(2)**

   • Profits are measured in pounds, i.e. as a total; profitability is measured in percentages, i.e. in relation to something else, e.g. as a percentage of sales.

9. List the two most likely sources of finance for a new business. **(2)**

  • the entrepreneur's own capital

  • bank finance, e.g. a loan or overdraft

10. Explain two possible benefits of budgeting. **(4)**

  • Minimises the likelihood of directors being shocked by underperformance at the end of a year.

  • Should act to limit the costs incurred by the business.

11. What is meant by a return on capital? **(2)**

  • The net profit as a percentage of the sum invested in the business.

12. What is meant by an increase in the profit margin? Why might profits fall as a result? **(4)**

  • A higher margin means a greater percentage gap between revenue and costs.

  • If this has been achieved by a price increase, sales may fall by a high enough percentage to mean that total profits end up falling.

13. Explain two ways a firm might improve its cash flow. **(4)**

  • Cutting stock levels, perhaps by cutting orders with suppliers (and therefore cutting cash outflows).

  • Using factoring as a way to bring cash in more quickly from customers.

14. Distinguish between fixed and variable costs. **(3)**

  • Fixed costs are not affected by changes in the level of demand faced by the business (e.g. rent) whereas variable costs are (e.g. raw materials).

15. What is the effect of an increase in the variable cost per unit on the breakeven output? **(2)**

  • It will increase the break-even point.

16. Why might introducing budgets motivate some staff? **(3)**

  • Most people like to know how their success (or failure) will be measured; a sales target gives a reason to work harder – until the target has been met.

17. How can variance analysis help a manager to make decisions? **(3)**

  • It can point to underperforming departments or retail stores (e.g. Woolworths deciding in 2008 to close down some of its bigger shops).

  • Persistent failure to meet targets may point to such a poor underlying position that major staff cutbacks are needed.

18. In 2007 customers queued to get their money out of Northern Rock bank. They feared that the bank's poor cash flow would make the bank unable to allow customers to withdraw their cash. Outline two possible effects of this upon the bank. **(4)**

• The bank might have had to cease trading (as it was, the government stepped in to prevent this).

• Even if the bank pulled through the short-term crisis, future potential customers might not trust the bank with their money.

B1 Data response

DeDeLicious Ltd
(30 marks; 35 minutes)

(Refer to question on page 130 of textbook.)

1. What is meant by an overdraft? **(2)**

   • A flexible way to borrow from within an agreed 'facility'.

   • Borrowing that is useful for short-term financial needs, e.g. stockbuilding for Christmas.

2. Excluding the possibility of factoring, calculate the company's expected profits for this year. **(3)**

   • Revenue × profit margin = profit **(1)**

   £400,000 × 12% **(1)** = £48,000 **(1)**

3. Explain one way in which the company might increase its profits **(4)**

	Knowledge 2 marks	Application 2 marks
Level 2	**2 marks** One way explained briefly but accurately.	**2 marks** Relevant points applied in detail to the case.
Level 1	**1 mark** One way explained, but showing limited understanding.	**1 mark** Limited attempt to apply points to the case.

Relevant answers might include:

• A price increase that covers the company's cost increases in milk and staff pay, to restore margins to 20%; as the product is luxury chocolates the wealthy customers may not be too price sensitive.

• It may be necessary to cut costs, perhaps by not replacing any staff who leave in the near future; unless the business has growth plans, it may not need as many admin or marketing people as it has at present.

4. Analyse two ways in which DeDeLicious might improve its cashflow. **(7)**

	Knowledge 2 marks	Application 2 marks	Analysis 3 marks
Level 2	**2 marks** Good understanding of the subject content.	**2 marks** Answer is applied effectively to the specific case.	**3 marks** Build-up of argument, making use of relevant business concepts.
Level 1	**1 mark** Shows some understanding of the subject content.	**1 mark** Some relationship to the scenario (perhaps indirectly).	**2-1 marks** Some build-up of argument, showing grasp of cause and effect.

Possible answers include:

- Jojo should make a visit personally to the main customers to discuss payment terms, agreeing a credit period that they are happy with, but making it clear that it must be stuck to; this would inevitably have a big impact.

- The use of a factoring service should not be ignored, as Jojo needs to consider whether using a factor would allow her to make do with one or two fewer members of staff in her accounts department; lower staff costs may make up for the 6% charge.

5. Should improving its cashflow be more important for DeDeLicious than improving its profit margin? Justify your answer (**14**)

	Knowledge 3 marks	Application 3 marks	Analysis 4 marks	Evaluation 4 marks
Level 2	**3 marks** Good understanding of the subject content; or two answers identified.	**3 marks** Answer is applied effectively to the specific case.	**4-3 marks** Build-up of argument, making use of relevant business concepts.	**4-3 marks** Shows judgement in drawing conclusions from own argument.
Level 1	**2-1 marks** Some understanding of the subject content; or one answer identified.	**2-1 marks** Some relationship to the scenario (perhaps indirectly).	**2-1 marks** Some build-up of argument, showing grasp of cause and effect.	**2-1 marks** Some judgement shown in argument or weighting of language.

Cash flow more important because:

- Poor cash flow and a big overdraft are giving Jojo sleepless nights, which implies that she sees this as a threat to the survival of the business; running out of cash would mean she'd be unable to pay her staff or suppliers, which would be humiliating and very bad for her reputation.

- Profit margin issues can be dealt with in the future, whereas cash flow problems have to be addressed immediately.

- Profit margins are nevertheless important because:

  - In the long term the business can only survive (or, preferably, thrive) if it makes enough profit to cover the need for reinvestment and business improvement.

  - So as soon as the cash flow problem is sorted, some serious work is needed on the profit margins, e.g. does the business really need to be located in the centre of Oxford, which sounds expensive.

B2 Data response

Cleaning up
(45 marks; 50 minutes)

(Refer to question on page 131 of textbook.)

1. What was the return on capital in Maria's first year of trading? Comment on your finding. (5)

   - Return on capital was £1000 as a percentage of £30,000, i.e. 3.33%

   This figure would be poor for an established business (lower than bank interest rates) ... but is perfectly satisfactory for the first year.

2. Explain two possible reasons why Maria's budgets proved inaccurate (6)

	Knowledge 3 marks	Application 3 marks
Level 2	3 marks Good understanding of the subject content; or two answers identified.	3 marks Answer is applied effectively to the specific case.
Level 1	2-1 marks Shows understanding of the subject content.	2-1 marks Some relationship to the scenario (perhaps indirectly).

Possible answers include:

- Perhaps the 10% positive revenue variance occurred because Maria's fantastic attitude to customers has created even more growth in demand than she had forecast (which would suggest that a 5% price rise may indeed be sensible).

Integrated Finance

- Perhaps the very rapid growth of the business is making it hard to control costs, especially now that there are five middle managers between Maria and the 50 'shopfloor' cleaners.

3. Analyse the possible benefits to the business of examining the costs and revenue variances. (9)

	Knowledge 2 marks	Application 3 marks	Analysis 4 marks
Level 2	2 marks Good understanding of the subject content.	3 marks Answer is applied effectively to the specific case.	4-3 marks Build-up of argument, making use of relevant business concepts.
Level 1	1 mark Shows some understanding of the subject content.	2-1 marks Some relationship to the scenario (perhaps indirectly).	2-1 marks Some build-up of argument, showing grasp of cause and effect.

Possible answers include:

- With such a rapidly growing business, constant monitoring of costs and revenues makes sense as it can be a fine line between controlled and uncontrolled growth – and the latter can easily lead to financial collapse.

- By analysing her revenue variances Maria may be able to make a better decision on pricing her service; underpricing is a sure-fire way to disrupt a business (too much work; too many costs and not enough profit to make it worthwhile).

- Cost controls will be important, especially the salary bill now that she has 50 workers and five managers.

4. Do you think that increasing her prices will increase the net profit margin and the net profits of the business? (10)

	Knowledge 2 marks	Application 2 marks	Analysis 3 marks	Evaluation 3 marks
Level 2	2 marks Good understanding of the subject content; or two answers identified.	2 marks Answer is applied effectively to the specific case.	3 marks Build-up of argument, making use of relevant business concepts.	3 marks Shows judgement in drawing conclusions from own argument.
Level 1	1 mark Some understanding of the subject content; or one answer identified.	1 mark Some relationship to the scenario (perhaps indirectly).	2-1 marks Some build-up of argument, showing grasp of cause and effect.	2-1 marks Some judgement shown in argument or weighting of language.

Possible responses include:

- It is possible that a price rise will cause a sharp fall in sales, leaving the profits worse off as a consequence.

- In this case, though, this seems very unlikely, as Maria is offering a Rolls Royce cleaning service which is likely to lead to a high level of customer loyalty; her only concern should be whether her own attitude to standards is shared by all her staff. Is the quality consistent?

- As long as she is sure that her business does deliver the quality she wants, she should feel comfortable that increased prices will lead to increased margins and profits.

5. Instead of increasing prices do you think it would be better for Maria to cut costs in the following year to boost the company's profits? (15)

	Knowledge 3 marks	Application 3 marks	Analysis 4 marks	Evaluation 5 marks
Level 2	3 marks Good understanding of the subject content; or two answers identified.	3 marks Answer is applied effectively to the specific case.	4-3 marks Build-up of argument, making use of relevant business concepts.	5-3 marks Shows judgement in drawing conclusions from own argument.
Level 1	2-1 marks Some understanding of the subject content; or one answer identified.	2-1 marks Some relationship to the scenario (perhaps indirectly).	2-1 marks Some build-up of argument, showing grasp of cause and effect.	2-1 marks Some judgement shown in argument or weighting of language.

Possible responses include:

- Yes, cut costs if there is evidence that they can be cut without affecting the customer service, e.g. by cutting the number of supervisors; perhaps Maria could find a financial incentive to get the cleaners self-checking, with just Maria and an assistant phoning or visiting customers from time to time to make sure that the right standards are being maintained.

- If, however, the cost-cutting was at the expense of the service quality, it would be a foolish policy; better by far to push prices up and maintain the reputation of the business; people would expect to pay a premium price for a top quality service.

Productivity and Performance

22.1 Introduction

Student answers to 'people' questions can be very woolly, so it is helpful to start with a hard-edged concept such as productivity. It can be used effectively to add an analytic dimension to answers to questions about recruitment or training. Even better is when a student can see that higher productivity leads to lower unit costs. As the phrase 'competitive advantage' has entered the AQA Specification, productivity again can be brought into play.

Productivity is an absolutely crucial concept when it comes to discussing a firm's costs and competitiveness. It can form the basis of some very valuable discussions focusing on issues such as: Why does productivity matter? Why may one firm's productivity be lower than another? How can it be increased?

Students' understanding of this topic can often be rather inexact. It is important to stress the difference between productivity and output and to highlight the link between productivity and unit costs. In many cases students believe the key to higher productivity lies simply in more motivation – a more motivated workforce is seen as automatically more productive. It is important to stress that motivation is only one influence upon productivity. Students also need to take account of factors such as technology, capital investment and ability.

22.2 Further reading and resources

Title and price	Author	Publisher and ISBN	Brief account
Business Case Studies 3rd Edition £17.99	Marcouse, I. and Lines, D.	Longman 2002 0 582 40636-6	Case Study 52 'The New Laser Scanning System' remains surprisingly up-to-date on productivity. Use with questions 1, 3 and 4.
The Machine That Changed the World £12.99	Womack, J., Jones, D. and Roos, D.	Simon & Schuster 2007 edition (but really written in 1990) 978 184737 0556	Not specifically on productivity but an absolute must if you want to read about the Japanese approach to production. Old, but a classic.
The Truth About Managing People 2nd Edition £10.99	Robbins, S.	Pearson Books 2007 978 0 13 234603 0	Short, sharp insights into people management. Several useful chapters.
Business Review		Philip Allan Updates	November 2007: 'Productivity Matters'.

Productivity and Performance

Unit**22**

22.3 Answers to workbook questions

A Revision questions

(40 marks; 40 minutes)

1. What is meant by the term 'productivity'? **(3)**

    • Output/input, e.g. labour productivity is output per worker.

2. Why may it be hard to measure the productivity of staff who work in service industries? **(4)**

    • No tangible output, e.g. how to measure the productivity of a teacher, doctor or receptionist?

3. How does productivity relate to labour costs per unit? **(4)**

    • Higher productivity should reduce the labour cost per unit (all other things equal, e.g. no wage increases) because less labour input is needed per unit of ouput.

4. Explain how a firm might be able to increase its employees' productivity. **(4)**

    • Easiest way to four marks would be two points, each with some explanation; also allow one point very well developed. Answers from: training; improved technology; better capital equipment; increased motivation.

5. How can increased investment in machinery help to boost productivity? **(3)**

    • Working with better machines should enable faster production and so more output per worker per day; may be less down time and less time to change over from producing one product to another.

6. Identify two factors which help and two factors which limit your productivity as a student. **(4)**

    • Possible help: good teaching; good time management.

    • Possible constraints: working conditions, e.g. whether you have space and quiet to work in; whether you can motivate yourself.

7. Outline the likely effect of increased motivation on the productivity of a teacher. **(5)**

    • Could lead to more effective teaching: better preparation, better relations with students; better results.

8. Look at the table below and calculate the change in productivity at BDQ Co since last year. **(4)**

	Output	Number of staff
Last year	32,000	50
This year	30,000	40

    Last year: 640 units; This year: 750 units

9. Explain how motivation and productivity might be linked. (**4**)

   • Greater motivation may lead to more motivation – more effort and commitment BUT other factors are also important, e.g. training.

10. Explain how productivity can be linked to unit labour costs. (**5**)

   • Higher productivity should reduce unit labour costs; if each worker makes more units the cost of labour per unit falls. However the impact on unit costs overall depends on how significant the labour input is.

B1 Case study

(60 marks; 75 minutes)

(Refer to question on pages 136–7 of textbook.)

1a FS Ltd employs 50 pot makers while Frandon Ltd employs 30 people in production. Calculate the total output for each of the two companies. (**4**)

   • FS Ltd Total output: $160 \times 50 = 8000$ pots

   • Frandon Ltd Total output: $30 \times 280 = 8400$ pots

1b With reference to FS Ltd and Frandon Ltd explain the difference between 'total output' and 'productivity'. (**6**)

   • Output is the total amount produced, e.g. 8000 pots at FS.

   • Productivity is the output per worker, e.g. 160 pots at FS.

   • Although there are fewer workers at Frandon their productivity is so much higher that the total output is higher than at FS Ltd.

2a Calculate the average labour cost per pot at FS Ltd if employees are paid £8 an hour and their daily output is 160 pots each. (**4**)

   • Average output per hour $= 160/8 = 20$ pots

   • Labour cost per pot $= £8/20 = 40$p each

2b What is the wage cost per pot at Frandon? (assume an eight-hour day) (**3**)

   • Average output per day $= 280/8 = 35$ pots

   • Labour cost per pot $= £10/35 = 28.57$p each

2c Analyse the short- and long-term benefits to Frandon of its lower labour costs per unit. (**12**)

	Knowledge 4 marks	Application 4 marks	Analysis 4 marks
Level 2	**4-3 marks** Good understanding of the subject content.	**4-3 marks** Answer is applied effectively to the specific case.	**4-3 marks** Build-up of argument, making use of relevant business concepts.
Level 1	**2-1 marks** Shows some understanding of the subject content.	**2-1 marks** Some relationship to the scenario (perhaps indirectly).	**2-1 marks** Some build-up of argument, showing grasp of cause and effect.

Possible answers include:

- Could mean more profit per item (if sell at the same price as their competitors).

- Could mean they could lower their prices and possibly gain market share.

- Long-term gains could include more funds for investment or rewards for owners.

2d Jeff Battersby claims that if the employees at FS Ltd were paid £10 an hour their productivity would increase 50%. What would the unit wage cost be then? **(5)**

- Average output per hour $= 20 + 50\% = 30$ pots

- Average labour cost $= £10/30 = 33.33$p each (still higher than Frandon)

3. Would you recommend Farah increases the pay of her employees to £10 an hour? Justify your answer. **(12)**

	Knowledge 3 marks	Application 3 marks	Analysis 3 marks	Evaluation 3 marks
Level 2	**3 marks** Good understanding of the subject content; or two answers identified.	**3 marks** Answer is applied effectively to the specific case.	**3 marks** Build-up of argument, making use of relevant business concepts.	**3 marks** Shows judgement in drawing conclusions from own argument.
Level 1	**2-1 marks** Some understanding of the subject content; or one answer identified.	**2-1 marks** Some relationship to the scenario (perhaps indirectly).	**2-1 marks** Some build-up of argument, showing grasp of cause and effect.	**2-1 marks** Some judgement shown in argument or weighting of language.

Possible answers include:

- One needs to know whether Frandon is nearby; is there a risk that good staff will leave?

- How serious is the problem of poor equipment? If the equipment *is* poor, then even paying £10 an hour is unlikely to mean productivity matches Frandon's.

- If industrial relations have been poor in recent years, the problem should be tackled. A pay rise might be a good signal of a willingness to change; but given the firm's poor finances, it would be wiser to offer a bonus scheme linked to extra productivity.

4. Discuss the possible gains from involving employees in discussions about how to improve productivity. (14)

	Knowledge 3 marks	Application 3 marks	Analysis 4 marks	Evaluation 4 marks
Level 2	3 marks Good understanding of the subject content; or two answers identified.	3 marks Answer is applied effectively to the specific case.	4-3 marks Build-up of argument, making use of relevant business concepts.	4-3 marks Shows judgement in drawing conclusions from own argument.
Level 1	2-1 marks Some understanding of the subject content; or one answer identified.	2-1 marks Some relationship to the scenario (perhaps indirectly).	2-1 marks Some build-up of argument, showing grasp of cause and effect.	2-1 marks Some judgement shown in argument or weighting of language.

Possible answers include:

- Improved sense of involvement helps meet social needs.

- Discussions could provide an outlet for creativity or analytic reasoning, helping to fulfil self-actualisation needs.

- Should help break down barriers between Farah and her staff.

- BUT unless demand is high enough, discussions will founder on the consequences of productivity increases: job losses.

Organisational Structure

23.1 Introduction

Although the chapters of this book follow the sequence of the AQA Spec, there is a strong case for delivering this topic after covering motivation. Then issues such as span of control and delegation can be analysed in relation to an area the students find both clear and engaging.

Compared with the previous Spec, the 2008 one places more emphasis on job roles and relationships, i.e. the mechanics within the structure rather than the theory. Perhaps as a result, both consultation and delayering have been dropped and have therefore been excluded from the chapter.

Over many years, span of control has been an examiner's mainstay. It gives huge scope for writing intelligently and precisely about the management structure and the level of empowerment among the workforce. The 2008 Specification makes it still more important, both because of the elimination of the classic consultation/delegation counterpoint and because leadership styles are not mentioned at AS level.

Nevertheless the chapter contains plenty of challenging material, supplemented by some worthwhile exercises. For homework, exercises A 1-9 and B2 would probably be the most useful.

23.2 Further reading and resources

Title and price	Author	Publisher and ISBN	Brief account
The Truth About Managing People 2nd Edition £10.99	Robbins, S.	Pearson Books 2007 978 0 13 234603 0	Short, sharp insights into people management. Strong on issues such as delegation and decentralisation.
A-Z AS Business Studies Worksheets – photocopiable pack plus VLE £95.00	Marcouse, I.	A-Z Business Training Ltd* 2008	AQA Worksheets 57, 58 and 96 will be useful for this section of the course. They'll provide a wide variety of suitable AS questions (and answers). *To order, go to www.a-zbusinesstraining. com
Business Case Studies 3rd Edition £17.99	Marcouse, I. and Lines, D.	Longman 2002 0 582 40636-6	Case Study 48 'Management Structure' is a nicely accessible case study for AS, covering issues such as span of control and hierarchy.

23.3 Answers to workbook questions

A Revision questions

(30 marks; 30 minutes)

1. What is meant by the chain of command? **(2)**

   • It is the line of authority from the top to bottom of the organisation.

2. Define span of control. **(2)**

   • the number of people directly answerable to each manager

3. Some theorists believe that the ideal span of control is between three and six. To what extent do you agree with this? **(5)**

   • It all depends. Six might be too high in an organisation with a lot of new young staff each carrying out important jobs; it might also be too low in a business where staff have jobs with clear responsibilities and can monitor their own progress, e.g. teachers.

4. Explain two implications of a firm having too wide a span of control. **(4)**

   • Initiatives taken by individual staff members may clash with those taken by others.

   • Inconsistency may affect customers, e.g. a burger made by A may be bigger and better than one made by B.

5. Explain what an organisational chart shows. **(4)**

   • How the organisation is arranged into different departments or functions.

   • Who is responsible to whom.

6. Why is it important for a growing firm to think carefully about its organisational structure? **(4)**

   • Growth means more staff; more staff means constant changes to spans of control and/or the number of layers of hierarchy.

   • New staff may need a tighter span of control than existing staff.

7. State three possible problems for a business with many levels of hierarchy. **(3)**

   • slow, ineffective vertical communications

   • a them-and-us split between 'them directors' and 'us staff'

   • may be very bureaucratic, with every decision taking ages

8. What is meant by the term 'accountable'? **(2)**

   • To have to answer to someone, typically a superior, if you make a mistake (or have a great success).

9. What do you think would be the right organisational structure for a hospital? Explain your answer. **(4)**

  • Sufficiently narrow span of control to feel that staff are being supervised in how well they treat patients.

  • Sufficiently wide span to mean that staff feel they are trusted to do their job, and can make decisions quickly.

B1 Data Response

These questions are based on the organisation structure of Crazy Beetles featured in this chapter.

(25 marks; 30 minutes)

(Refer to question on page 143 of textbook.)

1. Describe the chain of command that Sara would use if she needed to discuss overtime with Pete. **(3)**

  • Sara would probably talk first to Luke, Pete's line manager, perhaps also letting Martin and Steve know what's been done.

2. What symptoms would indicate that James' span of control was too wide? **(5)**

  • Increasing difficulties with day-to-day issues such as having the right number of vans in the right place at the right time.

  • Dissatisfaction among Luke, Martin and Steve with the amount of input they are able to provide into the management decision making.

3. Explain the usefulness of this chart for a new member of staff **(2)**

  • Helps identify who they are answerable to (and who their boss's boss is, in case of a need to complain, e.g. about bullying in the workplace).

4. How might Crazy Beetles use a matrix management approach? **(5)**

Knowledge 2 marks		Application 3 marks
Level 2	2 marks Good understanding of the subject content.	3 marks Answer is applied effectively to the specific case.
Level 1	1 mark Shows some understanding of the subject content.	2-1 marks Some relationship to the scenario (perhaps indirectly).

Possible answers include:

  • Could organise a project using staff from marketing, finance and operations, perhaps headed up by James (who has no direct responsibility for any of the departments).

• The project team could include people from different management levels, e.g. Jon or Will as well as shop floor staff and supervisors.

5. To what extent would Sara benefit if she introduced a more decentralised approach? (10)

	Knowledge 2 marks	Application 2 marks	Analysis 3 marks	Evaluation 3 marks
Level 2	**2 marks** Good understanding of the subject content; or two answers identified.	**2 marks** Answer is applied effectively to the specific case.	**3 marks** Build-up of argument, making use of relevant business concepts.	**3 marks** Shows judgement in drawing conclusions from own argument.
Level 1	**1 mark** Some understanding of the subject content; or one answer identified.	**1 mark** Some relationship to the scenario (perhaps indirectly).	**2-1 marks** Some build-up of argument, showing grasp of cause and effect.	**2-1 marks** Some judgement shown in argument or weighting of language.

Possible answers include:

• Luke and Martha have expertise, so it might be worthwhile for Sara and James to delegate more extensively on the operations and marketing tasks; James might find it hard to let go of operational decision making, as that is what he's skilled in, but successful businesses thrive on decentralising and therefore empowering staff.

• As the business is growing, it would make an increasing amount of sense to delegate and therefore encourage a new breed of managers capable of becoming tomorrow's directors.

B2 Data response

Chicken Little

(25 marks; 30 minutes)

(Refer to question on pages 143–4 of textbook.)

1a What is the Managing Director's span of control? (**1**)

• Answer = 3

1b Comment on the strength and weaknesses of this organisational structure. (**6**)

Organisational Structure

	Knowledge 3 marks	Application 3 marks
Level 2	**3 marks** Good understanding of the subject content.	**3 marks** Answer is applied effectively to the specific case.
Level 1	**2-1 marks** Shows understanding of the subject content.	**2-1 marks** Some relationship to the scenario (perhaps indirectly).

- Possible strengths include:

  - Clear structure, with a general plan of a span of control of three (excluding the HR manager).

  - The Marketing department should be able to operate highly effectively with a small team of managers with clear responsibilities.

- Possible weaknesses:

  - Surely the stock controller should come under the factory manager, not alongside?

  - The HR manager is positioned alongside two directors, but clearly a manager will not have as much sway as a director; so the relatively junior role of HR is being masked by the diagram.

  - Doesn't include staff below manager level.

1c How important does Human Resources seem within this business? **(3)**

  - Lacks importance because there's no HR director.

  - Also lacks importance because the HR manager appears to have no staff.

2. Explain why vertical communications may not be as effective today as they used to be in the past at Chicken Little. **(5)**

	Knowledge 2 marks	Application 3 marks
Level 2	**2 marks** Good understanding of the subject content.	**3 marks** Answer is applied effectively to the specific case.
Level 1	**1 mark** Shows understanding of the subject content.	**2-1 marks** Some relationship to the scenario (perhaps indirectly).

Possible responses include:

- The growth of the business has left the boss quite cut off from ordinary staff; there are at least two intermediaries between the quality manager's five staff and the MD.

Organisational Structure

• It may be that the middle managers are trying to keep staff views from Peter because they may not be favourable about the way the business is being run ('communication like treacle' may be deliberate).

• Peter may be at fault for only being interested in vertical communications when it suits him.

3. Discuss the ways in which the Factory Manager might benefit or suffer from the organisational structure shown in the diagram. (10)

	Knowledge 2 marks	Application 2 marks	Analysis 3 marks	Evaluation 3 marks
Level 2	2 marks Good understanding of the subject content; or two answers identified.	2 marks Answer is applied effectively to the specific case.	3 marks Build-up of argument, making use of relevant business concepts.	3 marks Shows judgement in drawing conclusions from own argument.
Level 1	1 mark Some understanding of the subject content; or one answer identified.	1 mark Some relationship to the scenario (perhaps indirectly).	2-1 marks Some build-up of argument, showing grasp of cause and effect.	2-1 marks Some judgement shown in argument or weighting of language.

Possible answers include:

• Quality and stock are fundamental aspects of a successful factory, yet the Quality Manager and the Stock Controller are answerable to the Operations Director, not the Factory Manager; that seems increasingly odd the more one thinks about it; is the Factory Manager not trusted enough? What happens when quality is poor and the Factory Manager is unhappy? Does the Quality Manager tell the Factory Manager to mind his/her own business? Surely not.

• The Factory Manager seems to be on the same level as the New Product Manager, ensuring that operational issues are taken seriously by marketing, e.g. how long it takes to turn a new product idea into a production process.

Measuring the Effectiveness of The Workforce

24.1 Introduction

As with many of the numerical parts of the course, there is a real danger that students will spend a disproportionate amount of time learning the 'sums' whilst neglecting the real issues. Performance measurement ought to focus on the interpretation and analysis of figures as an aid to management decision making.

In particular, a set of performance measurement data tells the student much more than whether or not the firm has a problem, or is especially good, in one area or another. Better students can take these figures and identify likely relationships of cause and effect, or even the knock-on effect of changes they may propose. Too often students will leave their 'analysis' as a statement of the answers.

For homework, a good combination is Section A plus B2.

24.2 Further reading and resources

Title and price	Author	Publisher and ISBN	Brief account
The Machine That Changed the World £12.99	Womack, J., Jones, D. and Roos, D.	Simon & Schuster 2007 edition (but really written in 1990) 978 184737 0556	Not specifically on productivity but an absolute must if you want to read about the Japanese approach to production. Old, but a classic.
Business Case Studies 3rd Edition £17.99	Marcouse, I. and Lines, D.	Longman 2002 0 582 40636-6	Case Study 52 'The New Laser Scanning System' remains surprisingly up-to-date on productivity. Use with questions 1, 3 and 4.
Performance Management Pocket Book £7.99	Jones, P.	Management Pocket Books 2008 978 18704 71657	Remarkably good background resource.
Business Review		Philip Allan Updates	Nov 2006: 'Recent Research on Labour Turnover'. Nov 2007: 'Productivity Matters'.
The Truth About Managing People 2nd Edition £10.99	Robbins, S.	Pearson Books 2007 978 0 13 234603 0	Short, sharp insights into people management. Chapter 52: 'Employee Turnover Can Be Good'.

Measuring the Effectiveness of The Workforce

24.3 Answers to workbook questions

A Revision questions
(20 marks; 20 minutes)

1. Define the following terms:

    (a) labour productivity

    (b) labour turnover **(4)**

    • Labour productivity is the firm's output in relation to the number of employees.

    • Labour turnover is the rate of change in the workforce.

2. Why might an increase in labour productivity help a firm to reduce its costs per unit? **(3)**

    • Extra labour productivity reduces labour costs per unit …

    … which are often a major part of total costs per unit.

3. In what ways might a hotel business benefit if labour turnover rose from 2% to 15% per year? **(4)**

    • Fresh ideas from new staff.

    • If the overall wage bill needs to be reduced, this is an effective way to do it.

    • When selecting new staff, you can recruit the right type of person, e.g. friendly and dedicated.

4. Some fast food outlets have labour turnover as high as 100% per year. What might be the effects of this on the firm? **(4)**

    • a risk that few staff know enough to cope when something unusual happens

    • high cost of recruitment and training

    • may be hard to establish effective teamworking

5. How might a firm know if its personnel strategy was working effectively? **(5)**

    • By considering these measures in comparison with the past, other firms and/or targets.

Measuring the Effectiveness of The Workforce

B1 Data response

(15 marks; 15 minutes)

(Refer to question on page 148 of textbook.)

1. Calculate the following ratios for both years:

   (a) labour productivity

   (b) labour turnover **(5)**

		Year 1	Year 2
Labour productivity	$\dfrac{\text{Output}}{\text{No. of workers}}$	$\dfrac{50{,}000}{250}=200$	$\dfrac{55{,}000}{220}=250$
Labour turnover	$\dfrac{\text{Staff leaving}}{\text{Average no. of staff}} \times 100$	$\dfrac{12}{250}\times100=4.8\%$	$\dfrac{8}{220}\times100=3.6\%$

2. Explain what questions these figures might raise in the minds of the firm's management. **(10)**

One mark for each question raised, with up to four marks for explaining why the question might be asked.

Possible questions could be:

- Why have the figures changed?
- Are the positive changes reflected in other areas of the firm, such as the firm's profit, its market position, etc.?
- How do they compare with competitors?
- How can the firm ensure the favourable changes continue into the future?

Measuring the Effectiveness of The Workforce

B2 Data response

Monitoring personnel performance at Best Motors

(25 marks; 30 minutes)

(Refer to question on pages 148–9 of textbook.)

1. Calculate labour turnover and labour productivity at Best Motor for all five years. **(10)**

	Labour turnover	Productivity
4 years ago	13.04%	33.91 cars
3 years ago	8.00%	32.12 cars
2 years ago	16.00%	32.20 cars
1 year ago	25.00%	32.92 cars
this year	26.92%	31.19 cars

2. Using your results, evaluate the effectiveness of Best Motors' personnel management. **(8)**

	Knowledge 2 marks	Application 2 marks	Analysis 2 marks	Evaluation 2 marks
Level 2	2 marks Good understanding of the subject content; or two answers identified.	2 marks Answer is applied effectively to the specific case.	2 marks Build-up of argument, making use of relevant business concepts.	2 marks Shows judgement in drawing conclusions from own argument.
Level 1	1 mark Some understanding of the subject content; or one answer identified.	1 mark Some relationship to the scenario (perhaps indirectly).	1 mark Some build-up of argument, showing grasp of cause and effect.	1 mark Some judgement shown in argument or weighting of language.

Possible issues could be:

- labour turnover (and absenteeism) increasing

- productivity is falling slightly

- no signs of long-term improvements in the firm's human relations

3. What additional information would you seek to help James gain a better understanding of how staff have been managed at Best Motors? Explain your reasoning. **(7)**

Measuring the Effectiveness of The Workforce

One mark for each issue raised, with up to two extra marks for an explanation.

- other data could be: labour satisfaction surveys

- quality of output data, e.g. number of defects per car, waste levels

- data on wage rates and bonus levels

B3 Case study

(30 marks; 45 minutes)

(Refer to question on page 149 of textbook.)

Workforce performance data per shop			
	Grayton Road	St John's Precinct	Lark Hill
Staff (full-time)	8	6	7
Labour turnover	25%	150%	0
Absence rate	5%	12%	1%
Sales per employee (£000s)	14	15	18

1. Briefly outline your observations on each of the three shops in terms of their personnel management. **(12)**

Four marks for each shop. Up to two marks for observations, and up to three marks for discussing them.

- Grayton Road: moderate throughout, but low sales.

- St. John's: high turnover and absence – fair sales per employee.

- Lark Hill: best performing – stable staff, low absences and high sales per employee.

2. Give possible reasons for the factors you described in question 1. **(9)**

Up to three marks for each shop.

- Grayton Road: two new staff – perhaps staff left following absence and poor sales per employee.

- St. John's: high turnover – possibly temporary staff, but possibly poor management.

- Lark Hill: staff staying, loyal and working well.

3. Taking the business as a whole, make justified recommendations as to how any problems could be tackled by the management. **(9)**

	Knowledge 2 marks	Application 2 marks	Analysis 2 marks	Evaluation 3 marks
Level 2	**2 marks** Good understanding of the subject content; or two answers identified.	**2 marks** Answer is applied effectively to the specific case.	**2 marks** Build-up of argument, making use of relevant business concepts.	**3 marks** Shows judgement in drawing conclusions from own argument.
Level 1	**1 mark** Some understanding of the subject content; or one answer identified.	**1 mark** Some relationship to the scenario (perhaps indirectly).	**1 mark** Some build-up of argument, showing grasp of cause and effect.	**2-1 marks** Some judgement shown in argument or weighting of language.

Possible answers include:

- Look at Lark Hill and see if lessons can be applied at the other two sites.

- Grayton Road needs to improve sales – look at motivation and/or organisation.

- Stabilise labour situation at St. John's; it is worth getting a manager to go into the St John's branch to discuss how personnel issues are usually handled. Is the management style rather too tough?

Recruitment and Training

25.1 Introduction

This topic can be interesting, if you approach it from the students' perspective. For them, this is potentially one of the most useful parts of the A Level! It makes sense to keep your eyes open for a recent episode of *The Apprentice* – possibly the penultimate (in most series) in which the semi-finalists are grilled by some of Alan Sugar's meanest mates.

The fact is that the importance of recruitment is underestimated by students. Their exam focus on motivation could helpfully be switched to the realisation that successful motivation, teamwork and communications all hinge on recruiting the right people, and then inducting them effectively into the workplace. 'Truth 8' in *The Truth About Managing People* covers this issue superbly.

The ideal homework would combine the Section A questions with Case Study 53, as mentioned in the further reading below.

25.2 Further reading and resources

The following books should provide helpful supplementary reading for staff and enthusiastic students.

Title and price	Author	Publisher and ISBN	Brief account
The Truth About Managing People 2nd Edition £10.99	Robbins, S.	Pearson Books 2007 978 0 13 234603 0	'Truth 8' is an intelligent insight into induction, called 'Manage the socialisation of employees'.
The Truth About Hiring the Best £10.99	Fyock, C.	Pearson 2007 978 0 273 71533 7	Lots of useful, three-page snippets on recruitment, e.g. 'Truth 8' on the advantages of internal recruitment.
Understanding Organisations 4th Edition	Handy, C.	Penguin 1993 978 0140 15603 4	More for staff than students; Chapter 8 'On the People of Organisations and their Development' has some thought-provoking material on training.
Business Review		Philip Allan Updates	September 2008: The article on Alex Wotherspoon is worth a look, as it focuses on his extended job interview (*The Apprentice*).
Business Case Studies 3rd Edition £17.99	Marcouse, I. and Lines, D.	Longman 2002 0 582 40636-6	Case Study 53 focuses on recruitment, and includes some thought-provoking questions that could be used for group work in class.

Recruitment and Training

In addition, the following web site addresses may be helpful:

Site	Web address	Brief account
Chartered Institute of Personnel Development	www.cipd.co.uk	Contains a large bank of very useful fact sheets on all the key HR topics.
People Management	www.peoplemanagement.co.uk	The magazine of the CIPD – contains regularly updated articles on HR issues – a good source of case studies.
HRM Guide	www.hrmguide.co.uk	Publishes news releases and articles on human resources research and surveys.
Human Resources	www.hrmagazine.co.uk	More regularly updated articles on relevant HR issues – another good source of case studies.

25.3 Answers to workbook questions

A Revision questions

(40 marks; 40 minutes)

1. Outline two reasons why a business might need to recruit new employees. **(4)**

    • to cope with excessive workload/growth

    • to replace staff who have left through natural wastage

2. Briefly explain the difference between a job description and a person specification. **(4)**

    • Job description is about the job itself, e.g. duties and tasks, while the person specification is about the type of person to fill it, e.g. character and qualities.

3. Outline two factors that would influence the method of recruitment used by a business. **(4)**

    • the type of job, e.g. whether it's for a senior manager or a new trainee

    • whether staff of this type are in short supply or not

4. Suggest two reasons why internal recruitment may not be a suitable means of filling vacancies for a rapidly expanding business. **(2)**

    • No one can be spared from their existing jobs.

    • The need is for more people in total as well as a new person for a specific job.

5. Outline one advantage and one disadvantage of external recruitment. **(4)**

   • The newcomer can bring fresh ideas and perhaps fresh insights into their rival's strengths and weaknesses (if hired from a rival)

   • but the outsider may struggle to fit into the culture of the new workplace.

6. Examine one suitable method for recruiting applicants to the following job roles:

   (a) caretaker for a local school **(3)**

   • advertising in the local paper would probably provide a wide enough range of suitable applicants

   (b) a temporary sales assistant for a high street retailer over the Christmas period. **(3)**

   • asking local schools and colleges to put recruitment posters up during the autumn

   (c) a marketing director for a multi-national company. **(3)**

   • hire an executive search consultant to track down a suitable person and sound them out on a move

7. Examine one advantage and one disadvantage of using interviewing as a method of selecting candidates for a job vacancy. **(4)**

   • allows a wide range of information to be obtained by both sides....

   ... but is susceptible to conscious or unconscious bias on the part of the interviewer/s ('I never trust anyone with a tattoo')

8. Suggest two methods that a firm could use to evaluate the effectiveness of its recruitment and selection procedure. **(2)**

   • measure how many new recruits last for more than 6 months

   • carry out an interview with those who accept and those that reject a job offer

9. Outline two reasons why a firm should provide induction training for newly recruited employees. **(2)**

   • to make newcomers feel welcome and to lessen their feeling of being an outsider

   • to ensure that new staff understand the objectives and ethos of the business

10. Briefly explain why market failure might lead to a skills gap in the UK labour market. **(5)**

    • In a normal market, the supply of something should match the demand. With training, though, private sector firms want well-trained staff, but hate to spend a lot of money training someone who could then get 'poached' by a rival firm. So firms don't train as much as they 'should'.

Recruitment and Training

B1 Data response

Performance-based recruitment at O2

(25 marks; 30 minutes)

(Refer to question on page 156 of textbook.)

1. Outline three 'tactical' skills that an employee would need to successfully carry out the role of a customer services adviser at O_2. **(6)**

	Knowledge 3 marks	Application 3 marks
Level 2	**3 marks** Good understanding of the subject content.	**3 marks** Answer is applied effectively to the specific case.
Level 1	**2-1 marks** Shows some understanding of the subject content.	**2-1 marks** Some relationship to the scenario (perhaps indirectly).

Possible answers include:

- The ability to keep calm in response to an angry customer.

- The ability to keep cheerful and positive when feeling lousy (Monday morning, perhaps).

- The ability to recognise (and empathise with) the customer viewpoint.

2. Analyse two ways in which O_2 could assess the effectiveness of the new recruitment model. **(8)**

	Knowledge 2 marks	Application 3 marks	Analysis 3 marks
Level 2	**2 marks** Good understanding of the subject content.	**3 marks** Answer is applied effectively to the specific case.	**3 marks** Build-up of argument, making use of relevant business concepts.
Level 1	**1 mark** Shows some understanding of the subject content.	**2-1 marks** Some relationship to the context (perhaps indirectly).	**2-1 marks** Some build-up of argument, showing grasp of cause and effect.

Possible answers include:

- Conduct customer surveys before and after the introduction of the new model; as long as the questions are unbiased and the sample size is high enough, this should help in the assessment.

- It could use standard quantitative measures such as labour turnover, level of customer complaints, level of staff absence and so on.

3. Assess the importance of effective recruitment and selection for a company like O$_2$. (11)

	Knowledge 2 marks	Application 3 marks	Analysis 3 marks	Evaluation 3 marks
Level 2	2 marks Good understanding of the subject content; or two answers identified.	3 marks Answer is applied effectively to the specific case.	3 marks Build-up of argument, making use of relevant business concepts.	3 marks Shows judgement in drawing conclusions from own argument.
Level 1	1 mark Some understanding of the subject content; or one answer identified.	2-1 marks Some relationship to the scenario (perhaps indirectly).	2-1 marks Some build-up of argument, showing grasp of cause and effect.	2-1 marks Some judgement shown in argument or weighting of language.

Possible answers include:

- May be crucial in such a competitive market as mobile phones ... though so many people have low expectations of customer service that they might not switch to another network supplier.

- Years ago O$_2$ spent billions on licences for mobile phone networks; but today the main operating cost for running a mobile network will be the amount spent on staff; ineffective recruitment and selection hits costs and undermines sales – a double whammy.

B2 Data response

Solving skills shortages at Mulberry
(25 marks; 30 minutes)

(Refer to question on page 157 of textbook.)

1. Briefly explain, using examples, the difference between 'on-the-job' and 'off-the-job' training. (4)

   - On the job means training on the shop floor, e.g. trained on a live customer till with a supervisor standing by

   - Off the job training is away from the floor, e.g. learning about a new software system at a staff college or outside University.

2. Analyse one benefit and one drawback to a company such as Mulberry of its new apprenticeship scheme. (8)

Recruitment and Training

	Knowledge 3 marks	Application 3 marks	Analysis 3 marks
Level 2	**2 marks** Good understanding of the subject content.	**3 marks** Answer is applied effectively to the specific case.	**3 marks** Build-up of argument, making use of relevant business concepts.
Level 1	**1 mark** Shows some understanding of the subject content.	**2-1 marks** Some relationship to the context (perhaps indirectly).	**2-1 marks** Some build-up of argument, showing grasp of cause and effect.

Possible answers include:

- The benefit is that the staff will be trained to work in the 'Mulberry way', which will make them very useful from the day the apprenticeship ends.

- But better educated staff may be unwilling to come to Mulberry, if the qualification is one recognised in Somerset, but nowhere else.

3. To what extent do you agree that the reputation, and therefore success, of UK manufacturers like Mulberry depends on maintaining a highly skilled workforce? **(13)**

	Knowledge 3 marks	Application 3 marks	Analysis 3 marks	Evaluation 4 marks
Level 2	**3 marks** Good understanding of the subject content; or two answers identified.	**3 marks** Answer is applied effectively to the specific case.	**3 marks** Build-up of argument, making use of relevant business concepts.	**4-3 marks** Shows judgement in drawing conclusions from own argument.
Level 1	**2-1 marks** Some understanding of the subject content; or one answer identified.	**2-1 marks** Some relationship to the scenario (perhaps indirectly).	**2-1 marks** Some build-up of argument, showing grasp of cause and effect.	**2-1 marks** Some judgement shown in argument or weighting of language.

Possible answers include:

- If 'manufacturers like Mulberry' means producers of luxury goods, then yes. A highly skilled workforce is the only way to keep the brand seen as classy and worth the (high) price.

Recruitment and Training

- Today everything can be produced in the Far East at a fraction of the UK cost, so quality is the only valid way to compete.

- For a manufacturer such as Mulberry, success depends entirely on reputation, which in turn depends on very high quality and a skilled workforce.

Motivation in Theory

26.1 Introduction

Written in 1989, the introduction to the first edition of this Teachers' Guide said: 'Some teachers and examiners have become rather blasé about motivation theory. It is assumed to be rather old hat in the modern era of 'gurus' such as Peters or Handy. In fact the mid-Century theorists we study still provide wonderful, timeless tools of analysis. They make it easy to analyse David Blunkett's top-down approach to education, Julian Richer's approach to people management, or the absurdity of performance related pay.'

In 2008 this looks to have been pretty sound. Tom Peters is now a peripheral figure, the New Labour project has foundered on its top-down approach to everything and performance-related pay has been a key element in the credit crunch. Motivation theory remains poorly understood in the wider world and much underrated, even among some teachers of A level Business Studies.

This unit is based upon the original writing of the theorists concerned, to ensure accuracy and authority. In particular, it examines Herzberg in more detail than in most texts. It is to be hoped that this provides the substantial platform that his theory deserves.

For up-to-date research on job satisfaction, see *Topical Cases* February 2008, A-Z Business Training Ltd, www.a-zbusinesstraining.com.

26.2 Further reading and resources

Title and price	Author	Publisher and ISBN	Brief account
Maslow on Management £23.99	Maslow, Abraham	John Wiley 1998 0 471 24780 4	This compilation of the great man's thoughts is a delight. Includes gems such as his 'Notes on Leadership' and 'Notes on Synergy'.
The Truth About Managing People 2nd Edition £10.99	Robbins, S.	Pearson 2007 978 0 273 71532 0	'Truth 15' (You Get What You Reward) provides intelligent coverage of the risks of using incentives. Could be used for Chapter 27, but also useful in relation to Herzberg or Taylor.
Writers on Organizations, 5th Edition £12.99	Pugh, D.S. and Hickson, D.J.	Penguin 1996 0 14 025023 9	Charles Handy finally makes it, alongside Taylor, Mayo, McGregor and Herzberg. Wonderfully brief, intelligent summaries of the life and thoughts of over 30 greats.

Motivation in Theory

Organisation Theory 4th Edition £12.99	Pugh, D.S.	Penguin 1997 0 14 02 5024 7	Some excellent readings including Taylor, Mayo, Herzberg, Handy, Senge and Kantner. The Herzberg is the celebrated *Harvard Business Review* article.
The One Best Way £18.95	Kanigel, R.	Abacus 2000 0 349 110379	Why would anyone want to read 650 pages on F.W. Taylor? Because it's a fascinating study of a man who still seems to be in the genes of many managers.
Understanding Organisations 4th Edition	Handy, C.	Penguin 1993 978 0140 15603 4	More for staff than students; Chapter 2 'On the Motivation to Work' gives a brilliant overview of the topic, for you or perhaps a very bright student.

26.3 Answers to workbook questions

A Revision questions

(35 marks; 35 minutes)

1. Which features of the organisation of a McDonald's could be described as Taylorite? (**3**)

    • High division of labour; high degree of mechanisation; deskilled jobs.

2. Explain the meaning of the term 'economic man'. (**3**)

    • Man is focused upon financial self-interest, not the social good.

3. Explain how workers in a bakery might be affected by a change from salary to piece rate. (**3**)

    • Might make them work harder to achieve a better overall income.

    • Might make them work harder at getting bread made, but much less willing to clear up around them, train newcomers in how to make bread and any other task that is not part of the payment system.

4. Give a brief outline of Mayo's research methods at the Hawthorne plant. (**4**)

    • In the Relay Assembly Test Mayo found six volunteers who tried out a new way of working every twelve weeks. These included individual versus group bonuses, different work layouts and so on. Before and after every change there was detailed consultation with the women. Productivity stayed consistently high.

Motivation in Theory

5. How may 'group norms' affect productivity at a workplace? (3)

    · May be 'social loafing', i.e. common pattern of low level of effort; or there may be a positive culture of effort and suggestions for improvement.

6. Explain the meaning of the term 'the Hawthorne effect'. (2)

    • The effect on worker morale and motivation of a manager taking an interest in what they do.

7. Which two levels of Maslow's hierarchy could be called 'the lower-order needs'? (2)

    • physical and safety needs

8. Describe in your own words why Maslow organised the needs into a hierarchy. (3)

    • To emphasise the underpinning role of the lower order needs.

    • To show that the fulfillment of a set of needs would mean they cease to motivate.

    • To show how a threat to lower needs would mean they become of supreme importance once more.

9. State three business implications of Maslow's work on human needs. (3)

    • Importance of job security; the importance of status; the need for continual challenges to keep the brightest interested.

10. Herzberg believes pay does not motivate, but it is important. Why? (3)

    • To avoid dissatisfaction; to avoid a feeling of being exploited (avoid a remembered pain); important as a signal of recognition for achievement.

11. How do motivators differ from hygiene factors? (3)

    • Motivators can cause upward motivation, hygiene factors can only prevent dissatisfaction.

12. What is job enrichment? How is it achieved? (3)

    • Job enrichment is a programme to give staff the opportunity to use their ability. It is achieved by providing a complete unit of work and automatic feedback on achievement.

Motivation in Theory

B1 Data response

(20 marks; 25 minutes)

(Refer to question on page 165 of textbook.)

1. Which of the factors had the least effect on satisfaction or dissatisfaction? **(1)**

   • security

2. One of Herzberg's objectives was to question whether good human relations were as important in job satisfaction as claimed by Elton Mayo. Do you think he succeeded? **(6)**

	Knowledge 3 marks	Application 3 marks
Level 2	3 marks Good understanding of the subject content.	3 marks Answer is applied effectively to the specific case.
Level 1	2-1 marks Shows understanding of the subject content.	2-1 marks Some relationship to the scenario (perhaps indirectly).

Possible answers include:

- The graph (Figure 26.2) shows human relations factors such as *Relationship with supervisor*, *Relationship with peers*, *Relationship with subordinates* and *Status*. None of these cause large responses as causes of satisfaction or dissatisfaction. Therefore Herzberg's research did suggest that human relations were of less importance than in Mayo's theory.

- Despite this, people today talk about teamwork as an important feature of a successful workplace, so Herzberg did not succeed in his mission.

3. Responsibility had the longest-lasting effects on job satisfaction. Why may this be the case? **(5)**

	Knowledge 3 marks	Application 2 marks
Level 2	3 marks Good understanding of the subject content.	2 marks Answer is applied effectively to the specific case.
Level 1	2-1 marks Shows understanding of the subject content.	1 mark Some relationship to the scenario (perhaps indirectly).

Possible answers include:

- Because of the permanent boost to self-esteem/ego.

- Because responsibility may imply empowerment over one's whole working life, not just one task or issue.

- Because responsibility provides scope for achieving many of the other motivators, such as achievement, recognition and personal growth.

4. Discuss which of the factors is the most important motivator. **(8)**

	Knowledge 2 marks	Application 2 marks	Analysis 2 marks	Evaluation 2 marks
Level 2	**2 marks** Good understanding of the subject content; or two answers identified.	**2 marks** Answer is applied effectively to the specific case.	**2 marks** Build-up of argument, making use of relevant business concepts.	**2 marks** Shows judgement in drawing conclusions from own argument.
Level 1	**1 mark** Some understanding of the subject content; or one answer identified.	**1 mark** Some relationship to the scenario (perhaps indirectly).	**1 mark** Some build-up of argument, showing grasp of cause and effect.	**1 mark** Some judgement shown in argument or weighting of language.

Possible answers include:

- achievement is the one quoted most often…

  …but responsibility is the longest lasting herefore the answer lies between the two

- achievement can arise even if the person has **not** been given responsibility (success in a task, even if someone else is responsible for the action/department); this is why it is more numerous…

- … but if responsibility has a longer lasting effect, managers should view it as the more important of the two, and seek to provide it.

Motivation in Theory

Unit**26**

B2 Case study

(25 marks; 30 minutes)

(Refer to question on pages 165–6 of textbook.)

1. Analyse the working lives of the shift workers at the bakery, using Herzberg's two factor theory. **(8)**

	Knowledge 2 marks	Application 2 marks	Analysis 4 marks
Level 2	2 marks Good understanding of the subject content; or two answers identified.	2 marks Answer is applied effectively to the specific case.	4-3 marks Build-up of argument, making use of relevant business concepts.
Level 1	1 mark Shows some understanding of the subject content.	1 mark Some relationship to the scenario (perhaps indirectly).	2-1 marks Some build-up of argument, showing grasp of cause and effect.

Possible answers include:

- Hygiene factors: pay, working conditions (no break between 18.00 and 22.00), 'discomfort', work relationships.

- Motivators: none relating to the work itself; only motivation is towards subversion, such as dough fights and joking about the managers; the tedious job and 'very simple task' explain the low motivation, as shown by cheering when machines break down.

2. If a managerial follower of Taylor's methods came into the factory, how might s/he try to improve the productivity level? **(7)**

	Knowledge 2 marks	Application 2 marks	Analysis 3 marks
Level 2	2 marks Good understanding of the subject content; or two answers identified.	2 marks Answer is applied effectively to the specific case.	3 marks Build-up of argument, making use of relevant business concepts.
Level 1	1 mark Shows some understanding of the subject content.	1 mark Some relationship to the scenario (perhaps indirectly).	2-1 marks Some build-up of argument, showing grasp of cause and effect.

Possible answers include:

- Time and motion study to decide on the 'one best way'.

- Financial incentives such as differential piece rate to stimulate greater effort (and self-regulation).

- A system of penalties put in place, such as that throwing dough would result in instant dismissal.

3. Later on in this (true) story, Tania read in the local paper that the factory was closing. The reason given was 'lower labour productivity than at our other bakeries'. The newspaper grumbled about the poor attitudes of local workers. Consider the extent to which there is some justification in this view. (**10**)

	Knowledge 2 marks	Application 2 marks	Analysis 3 marks	Evaluation 3 marks
Level 2	**2 marks** Good understanding of the subject content; or two answers identified.	**2 marks** Answer is applied effectively to the specific case.	**3 marks** Build-up of argument, making use of relevant business concepts.	**3 marks** Shows judgement in drawing conclusions from own argument.
Level 1	**1 mark** Some understanding of the subject content; or one answer identified.	**1 mark** Some relationship to the scenario (perhaps indirectly).	**2-1 marks** Some build-up of argument, showing grasp of cause and effect.	**2-1 marks** Some judgement shown in argument or weighting of language.

Possible answers include:

- Workers are behaving childishly, perhaps even dangerously. The workplace culture seems unproductive. But is this because of a poor example from unofficial leaders …

- …. or is it an inevitable result of what appears to be incompetent management?

- To what extent: very largely the managers' fault. The staff should have little or no blame attached to them (on the basis of the evidence provided. Of course there may be other points of view/ evidence).

Motivation in Practice

27.1 Introduction

Motivation theory has its conceptual elegance, but it leaves many students with the question: but what happens in practice? Of course, the reality of many a workplace is that incredibly little happens that fits into any motivation theory. Simply because no one is thinking about it. This unit explains what can be done, how best to do it and provides some *A-grade application* examples of the real world.

An important teaching point is to try to get students to critically assess the many newspaper articles that cover this ground. Are these articles journalism or public relations? How often have we read an article about a brilliant new teamworking scheme that has transformed productivity – only to read a year later that the firm is in a state of uncompetitive crisis?

27.2 Further reading and resources

The following books should provide helpful supplementary reading for staff and enthusiastic students.

Title and price	Author	Publisher and ISBN	Brief account
The Truth About Managing People 2nd Edition £10.99	Robbins, S.	Pearson 2007 978 0 273 71532 0	'Truth 15' (You Get What You Reward) provides intelligent coverage of the risks of using incentives. Teamwork is covered well in Truth 33 (What Makes Teams Work) and 34 on the possible downside risks. 'Truth 43' is on Job Design, including four actions that will make staff more productive.
The Truth About Getting the Best from People £10.99	Finney, M.	Pearson 2008 978 0 273 71808 6	Lots of useful, three-page 'Truths', e.g. Truth 3 'It's Not Money That Motivates' or Truth 29 on performance appraisal.
Understanding Organisations 4th Edition	Handy, C.	Penguin 1993 978 0140 15603 4	More for staff than students; Chapter 3 'On the Workings of Groups' and Chapter 8 on training and appraisal – but there's lots to dip into.
Business Case Studies 3rd Edition £17.99	Marcouse, I. and Lines, D.	Longman 2002 0 582 40636-6	Case Study 49 'BMW at 23' remains a terrific way to assess student understanding of Mayo and Maslow. Tell them to ignore Q2, which is on leadership. Case 47 on 'Money and Motivation' is timeless, and Q4 is worded exactly in line with the 2008 AQA Spec.

Motivation in Practice

In addition, the following web site addresses may be helpful:

Site	Web address	Brief account
Chartered Institute of Personnel Development	www.cipd.co.uk	Contains a large bank of very useful fact sheets on all the key HR topics.
People Management	www.peoplemanagement.co.uk	The magazine of the CIPD – contains regularly updated articles on HR issues – a good source of case studies.
HRM Guide	www.hrmguide.co.uk	Publishes news releases and articles on human resources research and surveys.
Human Resources	www.hrmagazine.co.uk	More regularly updated articles on relevant HR issues – another good source of case studies.

27.3 Answers to workbook questions

A Revision questions

(40 marks; 40 minutes)

1. 'Job design is the key to motivation'. Outline one reason why this might be true, and one reason why it might not. **(4)**

   • Might be true because without a well-considered job design there's a huge risk that talented people will become frustrated and leave the employer.

   • Might not be true because there are many other factors, e.g. the status given by the job; if the hygiene factors aren't in place, motivation is undermined, according to Professor Herzberg.

2. Look at the famous saying by Lee Iacocca on page 167. Explain in your own words what he meant by this. **(3)**

   • The most important things are probably 'motivation is everything' and the notion that it's about inspiring the people under you. The point about 'you can't be two people' means that however hard you work, you can't have the number of ideas that you plus one other person could have.

3. How *should* a manager deal with a mistake made by a junior employee? **(4)**

   • Discuss its possible effects, and how to minimise them. Then discuss its causes with a view to making sure that the mistake isn't repeated. All this should be done in a positive spirit.

4. State three reasons why job enrichment should improve staff motivation. (**3**)

    • More interesting work should generate enthusiasm.

    • More varied work should reduce boredom.

    • Direct feedback should help provide a sense of achievement.

5. Distinguish between job rotation and job enrichment. (**4**)

    • Job rotation means swapping jobs of comparable difficulty and responsibility.

    • Job enrichment means increasing the scope of a job, providing a range of activities *and* responsibilities.

6. How does 'empowerment' differ from 'delegation'? (**4**)

    • 'The empowered worker not only has the authority to manage a task, but also some scope to decide what that task should be.' Whereas delegation only means passing authority down the hierarchy.

7. Identify three advantages to an employee of working in a team. (**3**)

    • more social interaction

    • more variety

    • more of a chance to discuss ideas

8. State two advantages and two disadvantages of offering staff performance-related pay. (**4**)

    • Pros: may encourage greater effort; may prevent a sense of unfairness if great efforts gain no extra reward.

    • Cons: performance is hard to measure – it is often subjective, and therefore gives scope for bias and

    • disharmony; risk of distorting behaviour – staff only doing what they think is being measured.

9. What might be the implications of providing a profit share to senior managers but not to the workforce generally? (**5**)

    • Profit shares give scope for high rewards at zero risk to the receiver. If the cause of a high profit is the excellent management, other staff might not mind. The real problem is when profits rise for other reasons (perhaps a wave of redundancies) meaning the gains by the managers can seem undeserved and unfair to ordinary staff.

10. What problems might result from a manager bullying staff to 'motivate' them? (**6**)

    • Bullying in the workplace (as in schools) is a serious issue. It happens. It is bound to lead to a bad atmosphere which would encourage good young staff to go elsewhere. Bullying can also lead to overwork and stress, which may cause increased absenteeism or even a nervous breakdown.

Motivation in Practice

B1 Data response

Gambling on people
(30 marks; 35 minutes)

(Refer to question on page 173 of textbook.)

1. How might motivation be affected by 'taking away the rule book'? (**6**)

   • 'Taking away the rule book' forces staff to make their own minds up when faced with a decision or a new situation. This might be worrying but should also be empowering and therefore motivating. One of Herzberg's key motivators is responsibility. Removing a rule book forces people to take more responsibility for themselves.

2. Explain the importance to staff motivation of freely flowing, accurate communication. (**6**)

	Knowledge 3 marks	Application 3 marks
Level 2	**3 marks** Good understanding of subject content.	**3 marks** Answer is applied effectively to the specific case.
Level 1	**2-1 marks** Shows understanding of the subject content.	**2-1 marks** Some relationship to the scenario (perhaps indirectly).

Possible answers include:

   • Free flowing information is necessary to provide feedback on achievement ....

   • ... and it can be a way of democratising the workplace and encouraging greater trust between staff and management.

   • Accurate communication is also necessary for successful delegation; you cannot hold someone responsible for a task, if they don't know all the relevant facts.

3. Explain how the views of McGregor were put into practice by P&G's Dave Swanson. (**8**)

	Knowledge 2 marks	Application 2 marks	Analysis 4 marks
Level 2	**2 marks** Good understanding of the subject content.	**2 marks** Answer is applied effectively to the specific case.	**4-3 marks** Build-up of argument, making use of relevant business concepts.
Level 1	**1 mark** Shows some understanding of the subject content.	**1 mark** Some relationship to the scenario (perhaps indirectly).	**2-1 marks** Some build-up of argument, showing grasp of cause and effect.

Possible answers include:

- McGregor disapproved of 'command and control management', which is why Swanson advocated empowerment.

- He rejected the mistrust of staff implied by restricting information. He believed that communication should be open and free to all.

- Swanson shared with McGregor the belief that good training will pay dividends.

4. In this case, high motivation boosted productivity by 30%. Discuss whether increased motivation need always result in increased productivity. (10)

	Knowledge 2 marks	Application 2 marks	Analysis 3 marks	Evaluation 3 marks
Level 2	2 marks Good understanding of the subject content; or two answers identified.	2 marks Answer is applied effectively to the specific case.	3 marks Build-up of argument, making use of relevant business concepts.	3 marks Shows judgement in drawing conclusions from own argument.
Level 1	1 mark Some understanding of the subject content; or one answer identified.	1 mark Some relationship to the scenario (perhaps indirectly).	2-1 marks Some build-up of argument, showing grasp of cause and effect.	2-1 marks Some judgement shown in argument or weighting of language.

Possible answers include:

- Increased motivation should result in falling absence, labour turnover and industrial action.

- These points, plus increased levels of effort, could be expected to boost output per person.

- It will depend, though, on the focus of the extra motivation; a more motivated painter/decorator might take longer to complete a task because of a greater commitment to quality.

- It would be risky to assume, therefore, that motivation up *always* means productivity up.

B2 Activity

(Refer to question on page 174 of textbook.)

There is no reason to mark this exercise rigidly to a content-based mark scheme. Your students will be helped, though, if you give them some feedback on the skills they have (or haven't) shown. Assuming a mark out of 20:

Motivation in Practice

	Knowledge 5 marks	Application 5 marks	Analysis 5 marks	Evaluation 5 marks
Level 2	5-3 marks Good understanding of the subject content; or two answers identified.	5-3 marks Answer is applied effectively to the specific case.	5-3 marks Build-up of argument, making use of relevant business concepts.	5-3 marks Shows judgement in drawing conclusions from own argument.
Level 1	2-1 marks Some understanding of the subject content; or one answer identified.	2-1 marks Some relationship to the scenario (perhaps indirectly).	2-1 marks Some build-up of argument, showing grasp of cause and effect.	2-1 marks Some judgement shown in argument or weighting of language.

Integrated People in Organisations

28.1 Introduction

Managing people is a key element in the success of any business, regardless of size. The topics within this area range from the essentially practical issues of when and how to recruit more staff to the more theoretical areas of motivation, communication and organisational structure. Most students are able to acquaint themselves with the necessary content and develop a reasonable understanding of the theories and concepts. However, far fewer appear to be able to apply their knowledge effectively. Teaching needs to focus, therefore, on helping students to develop the skills needed to analyse the particular human resources issues faced by different businesses, and to make considered judgements as to deal with them effectively.

28.2 Further reading and resources

Title and price	Author	Publisher and ISBN	Brief account
The Truth About Managing People 2nd Edition £10.99	Robbins, S.	Pearson 2007 978 0 273 71532 0	Nicely thought through, with a series of punchy, readable 'Truths' about people management – some sceptical, many positive – all interesting.
The Truth About Getting the Best from People £10.99	Finney, M.	Pearson 2008 978 0 273 71808 6	Good sections on motivation, communication, teamwork and employee performance.
Understanding Organisations 4th Edition	Handy, C.	Penguin 1993 978 0140 15603 4	More for staff than students, but worth having around to stretch the more able.
Business Case Studies 3rd Edition £17.99	Marcouse, I. and Lines, D.	Longman 2002 0 582 40636-6	Case Studies 47, 48, 51, 52, 53, 59 and 60 are all worth using – so if you haven't used any of these by now, give them your consideration.

In addition, the following web site addresses may be helpful:

Site	Web address	Brief account
Chartered Institute of Personnel Development	www.cipd.co.uk	Contains a large bank of very useful fact sheets on all the key HR topics.
People Management	www.peoplemanagement.co.uk	The magazine of the CIPD – contains regularly updated articles on HR issues – a good source of case studies.
HRM Guide	www.hrmguide.co.uk	Publishes news releases and articles on human resources research and surveys.
Human Resources	www.hrmagazine.co.uk	More regularly updated articles on relevant HR issues – another good source of case studies.

28.3 Answers to workbook questions

A Revision questions
(60 marks; 60 minutes)

1. Identify two reasons why a business might use an organisational chart. (2)

    • To show the levels of hierarchy within a business.

    • To illustrate lines of accountability and responsibility.

    • To show likely lines of communication between levels and departments.

2. Explain what is meant by a narrow span of control. (3)

    • A narrow span of control exists when a manager is responsible for a relatively small number of subordinates. Narrow spans of control tend to lead to relatively tall hierarchies.

3. Describe one benefit and one drawback for a business of reducing the levels within its hierarchy. (4)

    • Possible benefits include:

    – A reduction in overhead costs as the number of management or supervisory roles are reduced.

    – A likely improvement in the speed and accuracy of vertical communication, i.e., from the top of the organisation to the bottom and vice versa, and decision-making.

Integrated People in Organisations Unit **28**

- Possible drawbacks include:

  - Greater responsibility may mean that staff become overstretched and stressed, especially if they do not receive appropriate training.

  - Reduced opportunities for promotion, as the move from layer to layer becomes a much bigger and increasingly competitive step, which may lead to demotivation.

4. Outline two elements required for successful delegation. (**4**)

   - Training – subordinates need to have the skills required to carry out delegated tasks.

   - Mutual willingness and trust – both manager and subordinate must be willing to delegate and believe in the ability of the subordinate.

5. Give one example of internal communication and one example of external communication. (**2**)

   - Internal: emails, telephone calls, meetings, etc. between employees within an organisation.

   - External: advertising and other promotional efforts to customers, as well as emails, telephone calls and meetings with suppliers, investors, etc.

6. Explain two reasons why good communications can improve the performance of a firm. (**4**)

   - Can improve performance by ensuring employees know what to do, so reducing mistakes.

   - Can improve decision-making by providing feedback on the impact of actions taken.

7. Outline two potential barriers to communication within a firm. (**4**)

   - Ineffective communication skills, leading to messages being misunderstood.

   - Inappropriate channels of communication, leading to messages being missed.

   - Communication overload, leading to messages being ignored.

8. Briefly distinguish between labour productivity and labour turnover. (**3**)

   - Labour productivity measures output per worker for a given period, calculated by the formula: Output per period/number of employees.

   - Labour turnover measures the proportion of the workforce leaving a firm over a given period, calculated by the formula: number of staff leaving per year/average number of staff $\times$ 100.

9. Outline one positive and one negative effect of an increase in labour turnover on a firm's performance. (**4**)

   - Positive effects include bringing new ideas and skills into the business.

   - Negative effects include disruption to production and working relationships between staff and increased costs of recruitment and training.

10. Suggest two ways that a business can reduce its level of labour absenteeism. **(2)**

    • Improve employees' conditions of work, e.g., pay, working conditions.

    • Improve motivation by giving workers more varied or challenging tasks, creating opportunities for promotion, etc.

11. State two reasons why a business might choose to recruit internally rather than externally. **(2)**

    • Likely to be more cost-effective by avoiding the use of external agencies or the need to pay to advertise.

    • The performance and attitudes to work of existing staff are already known, making suitability easier to judge.

12. Identify three methods of recruiting staff from outside the business. **(3)**

    • media advertising, e.g. in newspapers and on the radio

    • government-funded job centres

    • executive search consultants or 'head-hunters'

    • using existing employees or business contacts

13. Explain the difference between on-the-job and off-the-job training. **(3)**

    • On the job training involves employees acquiring or developing skills without leaving their usual workplace, perhaps by being guided through an activity by a more experienced member of staff.

    • Off the job training involves employees leaving their normal place of work in order to receive instruction, either within the firm or by using an external organisation such as a college or university.

14. State two benefits to a firm of training its workers. **(2)**

    • an increase in the level and range of staff skills

    • an increase in the degree of flexibility within a business

    • a more motivated workforce

15. Briefly explain what is meant by motivation. **(3)**

    • Motivation, according to Herzberg, is the will to work for the enjoyment of work itself. Other definitions would take into account any factors that encourage or maintain the desire to work, including pay or recognition.

16. Suggest two reasons why employee motivation is important to a business. **(2)**

    • High levels of motivation may lead to increased labour productivity.

    • High levels of motivation help reduce absenteeism and labour turnover.

17. Give two examples of hygiene factors and two examples of motivators. **(4)**

   • Hygiene factors include salary, working conditions, company policies and supervision.

   • Motivators include personal achievement and recognition of this, responsibility and opportunities for development and promotion.

18. Identify three key characteristics of a meaningful and well-designed job. **(3)**

   • workers are given clear and challenging goals

   • workers carry out tasks that lead to a definite end product

   • opportunities for planning and checking the work carried out

19. State three ways in which employers can reward staff financially. **(3)**

   • competitive salaries/wages

   • fringe benefits, e.g., company cars, private health insurance

   • performance-related pay and bonuses; profit sharing; share options

20. Briefly explain the difference between job enlargement and job enrichment. **(3)**

   • Job enlargement increases the number of tasks involved in carrying out a job. These tasks tend to be similar in terms of the degree of complexity and responsibility.

   • Job enrichment occurs when employees are given tasks that vary in terms of their level of responsibility and complexity.

B1 Data response

Training is the key choice for graduates
(25 marks; 25 minutes)

(Refer to question on pages 177–8 of textbook.)

1. Describe two costs associated with training employees. **(3)**

   • The cost of the administration time needed to set up and evaluate the training course.

   • The fees paid to external training agencies.

   • The loss of production as a result of staff absence.

2. Using a suitable theory, examine the link between training and worker motivation. **(8)**

	Knowledge 2 marks	Application 3 marks	Analysis 3 marks
Level 2	**2 marks** Good understanding of the subject content.	**3 marks** Answer is applied to the specific case, e.g. the poll of young employees.	**3 marks** Build-up of argument, making use of relevant business concepts.
Level 1	**1 mark** Shows some understanding of the subject content.	**2-1 marks** Some relationship to the context (perhaps indirectly).	**2-1 marks** Some build-up of argument, showing grasp of cause and effect.

Possible answers include:

- Herzberg – according to him, personal achievement, growth and advancement acts as motivator – training allows workers to gain new skills or develop existing ones, allowing them to become more competent and gain promotion into more senior jobs.

- Maslow – according to him – esteem is one of the 'higher' order needs – training would increase opportunities for greater recognition and achievement by improving workers' skills.

3. To what extent do you believe that the research carried out for Ernst & Young confirms the view that money does not motivate? Explain your answer **(14)**

	Knowledge 3 marks	Application 3 marks	Analysis 4 marks	Evaluation 4 marks
Level 2	**3 marks** Good understanding of the subject content; or two answers identified.	**3 marks** Answer is applied effectively to the specific case.	**4-3 marks** Build-up of argument, making use of relevant business concepts.	**4-3 marks** Shows judgement in drawing conclusions from own argument.
Level 1	**2-1 marks** Some understanding of the subject content; or one answer identified.	**2-1 marks** Some relationship to the scenario (perhaps indirectly).	**2-1 marks** Some build-up of argument, showing grasp of cause and effect.	**2-1 marks** Some judgement shown in argument or weighting of language.

Possible answers include:

- A number of motivational theorists claim that money may not be an effective motivator – this appears to be supported by the research findings.

- Many motivational theorists claim that other factors, such as the opportunity for personal development, are more important, especially among more highly qualified employees, such as graduates.

However:

- Although money may not motivate, theorists such as Herzberg would still accept that unsatisfactory levels of pay can lead to demotivation (a hygiene factor).

- The survey results may be misleading – job recruits may wish to create a favourable impression by not focusing on the financial aspects of a job.

B2 Data response

HRM and social networking
(25 marks; 30 minutes)

(Refer to question on page 178 of textbook.)

1. Suggest two methods, other than the Internet, that a small business could use to recruit candidates for a job vacancy. (**4**)

	Knowledge 2 marks	Application 2 marks
Level 2	2 marks Suitable methods explained showing good understanding.	2 marks Relevant points applied in detail to the case.
Level 1	1 mark Suitable methods identified, showing some understanding.	1 mark Limited attempt to apply points to the case.

Possible suggestions could include:

- Local newspaper – relatively cheap method and unlikely to need to advertise to a national pool of recruits.

- Job centre – offers a free service – a small business is likely to have very limited funds to spend on recruitment.

- Networking via existing employees or other business contacts – another cost-effective means of attracting recruits initially.

2. Analyse the main advantages for a small business of using the Internet to recruit new staff. (9)

	Knowledge 2 marks	Application 3 marks	Analysis 4 marks
Level 2	**2 marks** One or more relevant advantage(s) explained.	**2 marks** Relevant points consistently applied to the case.	**4-3 marks** Good analysis of identified advantage(s).
Level 1	**1 mark** One or more relevant advantage(s) identified.	**1 mark** Some attempt to apply point(s) to the case.	**2-1 marks** Limited analysis of identified advantage(s).

Relevant points might include:

- The Internet provides a relatively cheap means of accessing a national (and, indeed, international) audience, without having to resort to more expensive methods of recruitment, such as employment agencies.

- Access to a larger pool of recruits could improve the chances of appointing staff with the skills needed – this should improve the performance of the business, leading to growth and greater profits.

3. To what extent do you agree with the view that, in the future, recruitment is more likely to take place via computer than by using more traditional methods? (12)

	Knowledge 3 marks	Application 3 marks	Analysis 3 marks	Evaluation 3 marks
Level 2	**3 marks** Good understanding of the subject content; or two answers identified.	**3 marks** Answer is applied effectively to the specific case.	**3 marks** Build-up of argument, making use of relevant business concepts.	**3 marks** Shows judgement in drawing conclusions from own argument.
Level 1	**2-1 marks** Some understanding of the subject content; or one answer identified.	**2-1 marks** Some relationship to the scenario (perhaps indirectly).	**2-1 marks** Some build-up of argument, showing grasp of cause and effect.	**2-1 marks** Some judgement shown in argument or weighting of language.

Possible answers include:

- The Internet is an increasingly popular channel of communication, especially for younger employees, who are more likely to search for job vacancies online.

- The Internet can provide a relatively cost-effective means of recruiting on a national and international scale – firms can interact with a large pool of applicants via 'virtual' job fairs and interviews, without the expense of actually meeting up – particularly useful in the early stages of recruitment.

However:

- It may be easier to create a misleading 'virtual' personality, i.e., one that emphasises positive qualities.

- It may be harder to judge applicants' 'soft skills', e.g., teamwork, communication, in a virtual environment.

B3 Case study

Managing staff at Innocent
(25 marks; 30 minutes)

(Refer to question on pages 178–9 of textbook.)

1. Identify two benefits to Innocent from using its own website to recruit new employees. **(4)**

	Knowledge 2 marks	Application 2 marks
Level 2	2 marks Two relevant benefits given showing good understanding.	2 marks Relevant points applied in detail to the case.
Level 1	1 mark One benefit given showing some understanding.	1 mark Limited attempt to apply points to the case.

Relevant answers might include:

- It avoids the costs of using alternative methods, e.g., recruitment agency fees – so that Innocent can spend more time and money assessing and selecting candidates.

- It allows them to communicate information in a style that reflects the company's image, attracting candidates who are more likely to fit in with the company's culture.

- It gives the company more control of the initial recruitment process, preventing time being wasted on unsuitable candidates.

2. Examine one advantage and one disadvantage to Innocent of using in-house training to develop its staff. **(9)**

	Knowledge 2 marks	Application 3 marks	Analysis 4 marks
Level 2	**2 marks** One or more relevant benefit(s) explained.	**3 marks** Relevant points consistently applied to the case.	**4-3 marks** Good analysis of identified benefit(s).
Level 1	**1 mark** One or more relevant benefit(s) identified.	**2-1 marks** Some attempt to apply point(s) to the case.	**2-1 marks** Limited analysis of identified benefit(s).

- In-house or internal training is carried out by staff employed by an organisation, either on-the-job or off-the-job.

Relevant points might include:

- Advantages

  - Training is more likely to be more relevant – in this case, the Innocent Academy should be able to pass on information and develop skills needed by the company to operate more effectively in the soft drinks market.

  - Staff may feel more comfortable training with other colleagues in their usual working environment, leading to more effective training.

- Disadvantages

  - The cost of providing in-house trainers and facilities – external training agencies may be cheaper – the cost savings would free up finance to spend on new product development or advertising to increase sales further.

  - Access to the skills or information needed might be limited – unless the trainers are experts on the soft drinks industry, Innocent may fail to keep up with changes in the market and lose its competitive edge.

3. Evaluate the effectiveness of Innocent's approach to managing the company's 'human element' in helping it to achieve its long-term objectives. (12)

	Knowledge 3 marks	Application 3 marks	Analysis 3 marks	Evaluation 3 marks
Level 2	**3 marks** Good understanding of the subject content; or two answers identified.	**3 marks** Answer is applied effectively to the specific case.	**3 marks** Build-up of argument, making use of relevant business concepts.	**3 marks** Shows judgement in drawing conclusions from own argument.
Level 1	**2-1 marks** Some understanding of the subject content; or one answer identified.	**2-1 marks** Some relationship to the scenario (perhaps indirectly).	**2-1 marks** Some build-up of argument, showing grasp of cause and effect.	**2-1 marks** Some judgement shown in argument or weighting of language.

Possible answers include:

- Innocent's success so far has been built around its ability to create a humorous and laid-back image that differentiates it from the competition – to what extent is maintaining this culture vital to future success?

- Innocent's success so far has focused on the creativity of its employees – recruitment, training and staff motivation should help to maintain the quality and productivity of its workforce.

- Innocent appears to recognise the importance of being 'talent rich' – the link between effective human resources management and the company's vision is obvious.

However:

- Innocent needs to respond to its market – customers and competitors – to what extent can a company with a premium priced product continue to increase sales in an increasingly competitive market?

29.1 Introduction

The most striking aspect to the AQA 2008 AS Operations Management specification is the virtual elimination of any aspect of 'production'. The focus on service operations is almost total. This creates a bit of a problem, because it means that issues such as quality control and quality assurance lack a context.

It is also true to say that the Spec seems to have only one operations topic that is truly challenging – capacity utilisation. Topics such as quality, customer service and working with suppliers are too easily reduced to a mush of common sense and weak analysis. Although the Spec does not demand it (and, regrettably, this book does not cover it), there is a case for beefing up the content by introducing business ethics in the context of 'working with suppliers'. A careful look at topics such as Fairtrade and the use of low-wage labour could provide better students with the ability to develop their answers beyond common sense.

These issues are covered regularly by the press and TV; watch out especially for any repeat of the BBC's wonderful series *Blood, Sweat and T-shirts.*

29.2 Further reading and resources

Title and price	Author	Publisher and ISBN	Brief account
Schaum's Outlines: Operations Management £9.99	Monks, J.	McGraw-Hill 1996 0 07 0427 64 X	Far too advanced mathematically, but contains some great stuff, e.g. the illustration of a production system on page 8 and the Fishbone diagram of customer services on page15.
Key Concepts in Operations Management £14.95	Sutherland, J. and Canwell, D.	Palgrave Macmillan 2004 9 781 4039 1529 0	Not great, but it's helpful to have an alphabetically organised book specialising on Ops. Good entries on TQM, quality control and the quality framework – worth buying one copy.
A-Z AS Business Studies Worksheets – photocopiable pack plus VLE £95.00	Marcouse, I.	A-Z Business Training Ltd* 2008	Four worksheets arc devoted to cash flow: 14 (Customer Service), 25 (Capacity Utilisation), 50 (Matching Production to Demand) and 74 (Quality Management) and 55 (Revision for Operations Management) *To order, go to www. a-zbusinesstraining.com

Introduction to Operations Management

29.3 Answers to workbook questions

A Revision questions

(25 marks; 25 minutes)

1. Why may the quality of product design be less important for some businesses than others? **(3)**

   • Some businesses face little competition, therefore they can get away with poor design (e.g. Heathrow airport).

   • Some businesses make products entirely to customer order, therefore manufacturing skill is more important than design, e.g. 'make me a wedding dress just like Danni's'.

2. Explain two key elements of operations management for:

   (a) A children's shoe shop **(4)**

      • Making sure that staff are trained properly in measuring children's feet.

      • Making sure that a full range of shoe sizes is always in stock.

   (b) A new, all-business-class airline **(4)**

      • Working with suppliers to ensure a very high quality service, e.g. top notch food.

      • Managing quality effectively, e.g. a very comfortable seat.

3. Choose one of the examples in Table 29.1 and outline one strength and one weakness of that business idea. **(4)**

   • Strength of family car:

      – Good focus on the comfort and entertainment of the kid passengers (making life more pleasant for the driver)

   • Weakness:

      – An expensive solution to the perceived problem (might it be better to give away two Sony PSPs plus games with each car!)

4. Identify three ways in which staff might be at fault in production line errors that cause wastage. **(3)**

   • lack of care and concentration

   • absenteeism (causing too much pressure on the staff who've turned up)

   • simple human error

5. Examine the possible effects on a firm such as Coca-Cola of being unreliable in delivering to a big customer such as Waitrose. **(5)**

- Waitrose may demand compensation, e.g. for lost sales due to empty shelves.

- Waitrose may decide to start stocking a strong branded alternative, e.g. Pepsi.

- Waitrose might consider 'delisting' (stop stocking) Coke; in fact this is very unlikely for Coke, but less powerful suppliers would face a serious risk of being dropped.

6. Outline one possible benefit to a business from 'delighting' rather than 'satisfying' its customers. (2)

- Customers will remember this supplier and make sure to return, therefore becoming a loyal customer (who may be willing to pay a small price premium for the service).

B1 Data response

Lean, green, efficient operations
(30 marks; 35 minutes)

(Refer to question on page 184 of textbook.)

1a Outline two features of the C-Cactus that might prove appealing to car buyers. (**6**)

	Knowledge 3 marks	Application 3 marks
Level 2	3 marks Clear explanation of both terms showing good understanding.	3 marks Relevant points applied in detail to the case.
Level 1	2-1 marks Some explanation of both terms, or clear explanation of one term, showing some understanding.	2-1 marks Limited attempt to apply points to the case.

Relevant answers might include:

- The C-Cactus will 'drink less fuel'.

- It will cost less than a Prius because it has far fewer parts.

1b Outline one reason why buyers of large family cars may not buy the C-Cactus. (**4**)

	Knowledge 2 marks	Application 2 marks
Level 2	2 marks Clear explanation of both terms showing good understanding.	2 marks Relevant points applied in detail to the case.
Level 1	1 mark Some explanation of both terms, or clear explanation of one term, showing some understanding.	1 mark Limited attempt to apply points to the case.

Relevant answers might include:

- It won't have the luxury touches some car buyers expect, especially those of large cars.

- It will have a very different look and feel, which might make some drivers worry whether it is as safe to drive as other cars.

2a On average, Prius cars have sold for £12,000. How much revenue, therefore, has the brand generated for Toyota? (**3**)

- Revenue = Sales volume × Price (**1**)

  Revenue = 1 million × £12,000 = £12 (**1**) billion (**1**)

2b Product development on the Prius took 8 years and cost an estimated £850 million. Was it worth it? Explain your answer. (**5**)

	Knowledge 2 marks	Application 3 marks
Level 2	**2 marks** Clear explanation of both terms showing good understanding.	**3 marks** Relevant points applied in detail to the case.
Level 1	**1 mark** Some explanation of both terms, or clear explanation of one term, showing some understanding.	**2-1 marks** Limited attempt to apply points to the case.

Relevant answers might include:

- It isn't possible to relate the £850 million cost to the £12 billion of revenue, because we do not know how much profit is being generated from the revenue.

- But the brand has clearly been worth a huge amount because it has 'made the Toyota brand stand out in a crowded market'.

3. The unit set out five important elements of operations management. Discuss which one of the five proved the most important in the development of the C-Cactus. (**12**)

	Knowledge 3 marks	Application 3 marks	Analysis 3 marks	Evaluation 3 marks
Level 2	**3 marks** Good understanding of the subject content; or two answers identified.	**3 marks** Answer is applied effectively to the specific case.	**3 marks** Build-up of argument, making use of relevant business concepts.	**3 marks** Shows judgement in drawing conclusions from own argument.

Introduction to Operations Management

Level 1	2-1 marks Some understanding of the subject content; or one answer identified.	2-1 marks Some relationship to the scenario (perhaps indirectly).	2-1 marks Some build-up of argument, showing grasp of cause and effect.	2-1 marks Some judgement shown in argument or weighting of language.

Possible answers include:

- Design: because the key to the C-Cactus is exactly as described in the unit: 'The process starts by designing a product or service to meet the needs or desires of a particular type of customer'. Has Citroen really managed to identify customers with a specific need?

- Supply chain: the company needed to see how the supply chain (including its own factories) could produce the new car effectively (with far fewer component parts).

- Working with suppliers: would be critical, as they will have to meet Citroen's brand new specifications for every single car part.

- Managing quality: is always important in car production; there doesn't seem to be a reason why it's more important in this case than others.

- Using technology efficiently: may be critical to get costs down to the level where the price of the Prius can be undercut significantly.

Of all these, the first – design – seems the most important, as it has to be related to whether Citroen has the right understanding of what customers really want from a modern car.

Customer Service

30.1 Introduction

This new addition to the AS Level will present a very particular teaching challenge. Student understanding of the concept should be straightforward, given their already wide experiences of being on the end of customer service. Yet somehow we will want to find a way to differentiate our own students from other people's.

In some cases, the key will be to use the experiences of worker-students; their part-time jobs must yield many customer service experiences. So too will the training they are being given. Best of all might be students who work part-time in call centres, perhaps in the holidays.

Yet we all have to be careful of taking a woolly approach to the topic. Anecdotes may bring the topic to life, but successful students will be those who familiarise themselves with the basic bones behind the topic:

- Definition
- How customer service is provided
- The process of meeting customer expectations
- Customer service and quality
- Benefits of offering good customer service

This is a topic where students should find it easy to gain application marks by tailoring their answer to suit the business context being tackled. Class exercises, such as those offered at the end of the unit, should be designed to provide students with helpful contexts that allow them to develop this skill. The Section A questions are especially testing of application.

30.2 Further reading and resources

Title and price	Author	Publisher and ISBN	Brief account
The Economist Guide to Management Ideas and Gurus £20.00	Hindle, T.	Profile Books 2008 978 1 84668 108 0	Three hundred pages of 1-2 page accounts that help to fill in holes, e.g. Customer Relationship Marketing (CRM).
50 Management Ideas you really need to know £8.99	Russell-Walling, E.	Quercus Publishing plc 2008 978 1 84724 009 5	Two hundred pages, so again it's two pages per topic; some are the same as the Economist book, but many are

Customer Service

			different. Here, the 'Value Chain' is worth reading (in relation to competitive advantage) and 'Loyalty' gives a clear idea of the relationship between customer loyalty and staff loyalty.
The Customer Service Pocketbook	Newby, T. and McManus, S.	Management Pocketbooks Ltd 2002 1 903 776 007	A practical guide to customer service aimed at practitioners, containing a number of useful exercises, checklists and quizzes.

30.3 Answers to workbook questions

A Revision questions

(35 marks; 35 minutes)

1. List three methods of meeting customer expectations (**3**)

    • clearly identify expectations using market research

    • train customer service staff

    • quality management systems monitoring the customer service function

2. Explain how the use of a mystery shopper can help to maintain standards of customer service. (**4**)

    • A mystery shopper can provide clear feedback on 'where the firm is now', spotting weaknesses and strengths for management to work on.

    • The mystery element helps to keep all staff on their toes at all times.

3. Briefly explain how the following businesses might benefit from providing excellent customer service. (**9**)

    (**a**) a café

    • Regular custom at a café may mean daily visits from loyal customers. This assists in building the customer base that is so crucial to success.

(b) a manufacturer of washing machines

- Manufacturers of white goods such as washing machines live or die by their reputation. Good customer service is likely to enhance a firm's reputation, through word of mouth recommendations to friends – priceless promotion linked probably with reduced second phase costs.

(c) a bank.

- Banks now offer a broad range of financial services. Happy customers who have experienced good customer service may prefer to stick with the same supplier for all their financial service needs, boosting the bank's revenue per customer.

4. For a business that you use regularly where you feel customer service could be better, briefly explain: **(9)**

(a) your own customer expectations

- Sensible criteria for different firms will vary widely by type. Better answers will be clearly applied to the context of the chosen business.

(b) how the business could identify what your expectations are

- A variety of market research methods are available, but again a good answer here will show clear application to context.

(c) how the business could try to meet your expectations.

- Answers here may be innovative (best), predictable but applied (OK), or generic and not clearly applied to the business (weak).

5. Explain why a small local plumber might benefit from offering better customer service than all her local rivals. **(4)**

- Word of mouth is absolutely crucial for most tradesmen. Good customer service may be the most effective way of attracting new customers. Meanwhile happy customers, notoriously suspicious of 'cowboys' will be loyal.

6. Explain two benefits that an electricity supplier such as npower might find as a result of gaining a customer service quality standard such as the Charter Mark. **(6)**

- With increased shopping around for utility supplies, competitive advantage is vital. Price may not be the only route to an advantage with many customers concerned about levels of service. A standard such as the Charter Mark can therefore feature strongly in promotional material.

- Assuming that gaining the standard has improved customer service there may well be reduced 'second phase costs' for the company, such as fewer customer complaint phone lines.

Customer Service

B1 Data response

The chiropracter
(20 marks; 25 minutes)

(Refer to question on page 189 of textbook.)

1a Briefly explain how Brian's business seeks to identify customer expectations. **(2)**

- The customer satisfaction survey should allow Brian to identify customer expectations – and identify any changes in their wishes, by a twice-yearly survey.

1b Explain two features of Brian's business that you consider may be vital elements of good customer service for medical practitioners. **(4)**

	Knowledge 2 marks	Application 2 marks
Level 2	2 marks Good understanding of the subject content.	2 marks Answer is applied effectively to the specific case.
Level 1	1 mark Shows some understanding of the subject content.	1 mark Some relationship to the scenario (perhaps indirectly).

Possible answers include:

- Highly skilled staff are surely a must for a medical practitioner.

- A calming waiting area can help to settle any nerves customers may have before they meet the chiropractor.

2. Explain how Brian's business attempts to monitor and improve customer service levels within the business. **(6)**

	Knowledge 3 marks	Application 3 marks
Level 2	3 marks Good understanding of the subject content.	3 marks Answer is applied effectively to the specific case.
Level 1	2-1 marks Shows some understanding of the subject content.	2-1 marks Some relationship to the scenario (perhaps indirectly).

Possible answers include:

- Monitoring will be down to the customer satisfaction survey, although other methods not mentioned in the case could be used, such as focus groups, mystery patients or informal conversations with patients.

- Improvement can come through the careful recruitment of staff mentioned in the case, the training offered to staff, especially with its focus on meeting customers' expectations whilst the systems implemented in order to gain the ISO quality standard for customer complaints will also be aimed at continually improving customer service levels.

3. Analyse two possible benefits to Brian of providing the highest levels of customer service. (8)

	Knowledge 2 marks	Application 3 marks	Analysis 3 marks
Level 2	2 marks Good understanding of the subject content.	3 marks Answer is applied effectively to the specific case.	3 marks Build-up of argument, making use of relevant business concepts.
Level 1	1 mark Shows some understanding of the subject content.	2-1 marks Some relationship to the scenario (perhaps indirectly).	2-1 marks Some build-up of argument, showing grasp of cause and effect.

Possible answers include:

- Word of mouth in the form of customer recommendations leading to a growing business along with reduced marketing costs.

- Loyalty of existing customers means less need to continually attract new customers – an expensive business. In addition, customer loyalty may increase willingness of customers to take part in the survey, creating a virtuous circle.

Customer Service

B2 Data response

Twinkle.com

(30 marks; 35 minutes)

(Refer to question on page 190 of textbook.)

1. Briefly explain how the table shows evidence of poor customer service. (3)

	Knowledge 1 mark	Application 2 marks
Level 2		**2 marks** Answer is applied effectively to the specific case.
Level 1	**1 mark** Shows some understanding of the subject content.	**1 mark** Some relationship to the scenario (perhaps indirectly).

Possible answers include:

- an increased number of customer complaints

- a falling customer service rating

2. Identify and explain a possible cause of poor customer service performance suggested by the table. (4)

	Knowledge 2 marks	Application 2 marks
Level 2	**2 marks** Good understanding of the subject content.	**2 marks** Answer is applied effectively to the specific case.
Level 1	**1 mark** Shows some understanding of the subject content.	**1 mark** Some relationship to the scenario (perhaps indirectly).

Possible answers include:

- Increased customer numbers in the first half of the year may have led to over-stretched customer service staff struggling to deal with problems, but this is perhaps contradicted by having more problems being dealt with within 24 hours. The reduced training expenditure does not appear to be a cause.

Customer Service

Unit 30

3. Analyse two other possible causes of poor customer service within the business. (6)

	Knowledge 2 marks	Application 2 marks	Analysis 2 marks
Level 2	2 marks Good understanding of the subject content.	2 marks Answer is applied effectively to the specific case.	2 marks Build-up of argument, making use of relevant business concepts.
Level 1	1 mark Shows some understanding of the subject content.	1 mark Some relationship to the scenario (perhaps indirectly).	1 mark Some build-up of argument, showing grasp of cause and effect.

Possible answers include:

- Failure to identify customer expectations. Without knowing what the customer wants it is hard to satisfy them; this can harm Twinkle's reputation – a huge issue for a firm aiming at the top end of the market.

- Growth in customer numbers causes stresses on the whole operations function of a business – offering customers a poor product or in this case internet connection is a sure way to increase complaints, placing added pressure on already stretched customer service staff.

4. Analyse the reasons why customer service may be especially important for an ISP (Internet Service Provider) (8)

	Knowledge 2 marks	Application 3 marks	Analysis 3 marks
Level 2	2 marks Good understanding of the subject content.	3 marks Answer is applied effectively to the specific case.	3 marks Build-up of argument, making use of relevant business concepts.
Level 1	1 mark Shows some understanding of the subject content.	2-1 marks Some relationship to the scenario (perhaps indirectly).	2-1 marks Some build-up of argument, showing grasp of cause and effect.

Possible answers include:

- competitive market

- reliability of service is a key factor

- fairly easy to switch between suppliers

- new customers are hard (and expensive) to get, so it's vital to hang on to current ones

5. To what extent can an external consultant help to improve the customer service levels offered by a firm such as Twinkle.com? **(9)**

	Knowledge 2 marks	Application 2 marks	Analysis 2 marks	Evaluation 3 marks
Level 2	**2 marks** Good understanding of the subject content; or two answers identified.	**2 marks** Answer is applied effectively to the specific case.	**2 marks** Build-up of argument, making use of relevant business concepts.	**3 marks** Shows judgement in drawing conclusions from own argument.
Level 1	**1 mark** Some understanding of the subject content; or one answer identified.	**1 mark** Some relationship to the scenario (perhaps indirectly).	**1 mark** Some build-up of argument, showing grasp of cause and effect.	**2-1 marks** Some judgement shown in argument or weighting of language.

- Yes, they can help because:
  - They bring a new set of eyes to spot previously overlooked problems.
  - Staff may be more willing to open up to an outsider if there are internal problems.
  - The consultant is likely to be an expert in their field.
- No, they may not be able to help because:
  - They don't know the ins and outs of this particular organisation.
  - Will the consultant's fee reduce the share of budget available for other activities?
  - Will management listen to and act on the consultant's recommendations?
- Overall – perhaps the managers have taken their eye off the ball during this period of expansion, so the consultant may be useful, but can any external consultant really understand a business in such a short space of time? The consulting industry certainly thinks so, and on the whole, in this case the consultant may be able to help.

Effective Quality Management

31.1 Introduction

The teaching of quality management has changed in line with the shift in the UK economy from manufacturing to services. Instead of production issues such as numerical process control, there is more of an overlap with HR management, e.g. the emphasis within TQM upon the whole business working together. Quality management is now seen as an aspect of the business culture. It is now the concern of the whole business not just the production department.

From a teaching view this makes quality a very useful vehicle for integrating business issues. People are an essential part of any quality issue. The balance between the cost of a quality initiative and the cost of lost business from poor quality must be considered. As quality issues have moved away from the production department the importance of quality as a marketing issue has also grown.

It is important to remind students that the new quality approaches are not a universal panacea for business success. They have not been without problems. Quality initiatives can become bogged down in bureaucracy. Some businesses have found that changing cultures is not easy. Resistance from workers and management has often caused problems. Like many other aspects of running a business quality management is about balancing the benefits of implementing an initiative with the costs of not doing it.

For homework, Section A questions plus B2 look likely to be the best bet.

31.2 Further reading and resources

Title and price	Author	Publisher and ISBN	Brief account
The Economist Guide to Management Ideas and Gurus £20.00	Hindle, T.	Profile Books 2008 978 1 84668 108 0	Three hundred pages of 1-2 page accounts that help to fill in holes, e.g. the ideas of W.E. Deming and Joseph Juran (QC) plus TQM, Six Sigma, Kaizen and planned obsolescence.
50 Management Ideas you Really Need to Know £8.99	Russell-Walling, E.	Quercus Publishing plc 2008 978 1 84724 009 5	Two hundred pages, so again it's 2 pages per topic; some are the same as the Economist book, but still have a different take, e.g. TQM and Six Sigma. Also worth a look at Japanese Management.
The Toyota Way £16.99	Liker, J.K.	McGraw-Hill 2004 0 07 139231 9	Masses on quality, especially Chapter 11: 'Build a culture of stopping to fix problems to get quality right the first time'; Chapter 5 on the development of the Lexus is also useful.

Effective Quality Management

Business Case Studies 3rd Edition £17.99	Marcouse, I. and Lines, D.	Longman 2002 0 582 40636-6	Case Study 34 'Bring in Quality Circles' is a good lead into TQM and the idea of a quality culture (to contrast it with QC or QA systems. Also, if you haven't used it, there's Case 51 on Herzberg, which again points to quality as an intrinsic issue.

31.3 Answers to workbook questions

A Revision questions
(35 marks; 35 minutes)

1. State two reasons why quality management is important. (2)

   • To ensure customer satisfaction

   • To keep down costs of quality problems.

2. How important is quality to the consumer? (3)

   • To keep down costs of quality problems.

   • How important quality is to the consumer depends on the situation. A manufacturer buying components will have the need for 100% reliability. Customers consider quality as part of the buying decision. This will be offset by other factors such as price. The customer may trade in some aspects of quality for a lower price.

3. Suggest two criteria customers might use to judge quality at:

   (a) a budget-priced hotel chain (2)

      • cleanliness, satellite TV

   (b) a Tesco supermarket (2)

      • good displays of fresh produce, helpful staff

   (c) a McDonald's (2)

      • quick service, fresh food.

4. Why has there been an increase in awareness of the importance of improving the quality of products? (3)

   • Increased customer awareness of quality as part of the buying decision.

- Realisation of the costs involved in poor quality.

- Competitors (in particular Japanese firms) have made quality an issue.

5. Give two marketing advantages that come from a quality reputation. **(2)**

- A quality reputation generates repeat sales.

- It allows the firm to charge a price premium.

6. What costs are involved if the firm has quality problems? **(3)**

- scrapping of unsuitable goods

- reworking of defective goods

- lower prices for goods classed as seconds.

7. Explain what is meant by the Gucci slogan shown among the Quality quotes on page 193. **(4)**

- You pay a price to buy something, but three weeks later it is the quality or style that matters to you (and you keep being reminded of) rather than the price, which you may start to forget. So, for repeat custom, quality matters most.

8. What is total quality management? **(4)**

- Total quality management is a philosophy of commitment to quality that operates throughout the entire organisation.

9. Outline two benefits of adopting quality circles to a clothing chain such as Topshop. **(4)**

Two marks for each benefit

Answers might include:

- better control of quality of clothing on sale

- feedback from different parts of the business

- identification of problems

- greater job satisfaction for members of quality circle

- better communication between management and shop floor workers

10. Outline two additional costs that might be incurred in order to improve quality. **(4)**

Answers might include:

- equipment costs

- material costs

- training costs

- inspection costs

- costs of changes to production methods

- direct costs of the initiative such as quality circles.

B1 Data response

Trac Parts

(25 marks; 30 minutes)

(Refer to question on page 198 of textbook.)

1. What is ISO 9000? **(3)**

    • An internationally recognised quality accreditation system. Firms who are registered have to document their business procedures, prepare a quality manual and assess their quality management systems.

2. Why might a business want to become ISO 9000 approved? **(4)**

    • To improve quality. Gaining the award focuses effort on quality issues. Customers may insist on the firm having the award. (Two marks for explaining each reasonable suggestion to a maximum of four marks.)

3. Examine the benefits to Trac Parts of the performance improvements identified in the text. **(6)**

    Up to three marks for each benefit identified and developed.

    • Answers include:

    – increased customer satisfaction so increased sales

    – lower costs from errors and possibility of reduced staff costs

    – increase in turnover will reduce stock storage

4. In order to be accepted by ISO 9000, the firm will have had to introduce procedures to ensure that levels of quality control are maintained. Using the four stages of quality control (prevention, detection, correction and improvement) examine the actions it might have taken. **(12)**

    For each stage up to three marks. One mark for a simple suggestion or up to three marks for a well developed suggestion.

    • **Prevention:** this will try to avoid problems occurring.

    – ensuring that the design allows for quality production, e.g. building in features that minimise production errors.

    – using good quality materials

    – maintaining machinery at most efficient level

    – training staff

    – ensuring that quality is maintained by suppliers

    • **Detection:**

    – statistical analysis

- sampling of products and testing for quality

- employee awareness

- analysis of customer feedback

• **Correction:**

- ensuring that problems once discovered are corrected

- analysis of reasons for problems

• **Improvement:**

- continually looking at the processes in the business to see where improvements could be made

- analysis of customer feedback to detect where improvement could be made

B2 Case study

Manufacturing defects – producer comparisons: PcNow
(40 marks; 50 minutes)

(Refer to question on pages 198–9 of textbook.)

1a What does the chart show? (**2**)

• Both Japanese and US manufacturers have significantly lower levels of defects. The European level is slightly lower. PcNow are the worst performers. One mark for each acceptable point.

1b What further data would help to make the bar chart more useful? (**4**)

• The source of the information (the firms themselves or an independent benchmarking consultant?).

• The date the information was collected (all recently, or is some quite old?).

2. From the case study identify two reasons for the quality problems experienced by PcNow. (**2**)

• poor quality components

• inefficient production facilities

3. What are the marketing implications for PcNow of the data in the bar chart? **(8)**

	Knowledge 2 marks	Application 3 marks	Analysis 3 marks
Level 2	**2 marks** Good understanding of the subject content; or two answers identified.	**3 marks** Answer is applied effectively to the specific case.	**3 marks** Build-up of argument, making use of relevant business concepts.
Level 1	**1 mark** Shows some understanding of the subject content.	**2-1 marks** Some relationship to the scenario (perhaps indirectly).	**2-1 marks** Some build-up of argument, showing grasp of cause and effect.

Possible answers include:

- Loss of customer satisfaction which will lead to loss of sales and may therefore necessitate price cuts.

- Distributors may be less willing to take the goods.

- Costs involved in defects will raise production costs and may mean the price is higher than competitors'.

4. Outline the advantages PcNow might get from the discussion group formed to discuss the quality problems. **(8)**

	Knowledge 2 marks	Application 3 marks	Analysis 3 marks
Level 2	**2 marks** Good understanding of the subject content; or two answers identified.	**3 marks** Answer is applied effectively to the specific case.	**3 marks** Build-up of argument, making use of relevant business concepts.
Level 1	**1 mark** Shows some understanding of the subject content.	**2-1 marks** Some relationship to the scenario (perhaps indirectly).	**2-1 marks** Some build-up of argument, showing grasp of cause and effect.

Possible answers include:

- Workers' knowledge will help to identify problems and possibly solutions.

- Increased productivity, as workers feel involved in the manufacturing process.

- Increased communication as the managers discuss issues with workers.

- Discussion groups will be expensive – time off work, etc., they may not work; they could turn into a forum for other discussions.

5. How might Cara convince the firm's management to change the layout of the production facilities? **(6)**

	Knowledge 2 marks	Application 2 marks	Analysis 2 marks
Level 2	**2 marks** Good understanding of the subject content; or two answers identified.	**2 marks** Answer is applied effectively to the specific case.	**2 marks** Build-up of argument, making use of relevant business concepts.
Level 1	**1 mark** Shows some understanding of the subject content.	**1 mark** Some relationship to the scenario (perhaps indirectly).	**1 mark** Some build-up of argument, showing grasp of cause and effect.

Possible answers include:

• She needs to prepare a balanced report showing the advantages of the new system compared to the costs.

• Detailed analysis of the changes and the benefits expected.

• Costs of implementing the idea need to be compared with the cost of not taking the measures.

6. Once these changes have been made, the firm needs to ensure that quality is maintained and improved. Discuss the implications for the firm of implementing a total quality management initiative. **(10)**

	Knowledge 2 marks	Application 2 marks	Analysis 3 marks	Evaluation 3 marks
Level 2	**2 marks** Good understanding of the subject content; or two answers identified.	**2 marks** Answer is applied effectively to the specific case.	**3 marks** Build-up of argument, making use of relevant business concepts.	**3 marks** Shows judgement in drawing conclusions from own argument.
Level 1	**1 mark** Some understanding of the subject content; or one answer identified.	**1 mark** Some relationship to the scenario (perhaps indirectly).	**2-1 marks** Some build-up of argument, showing grasp of cause and effect.	**2-1 marks** Some judgement shown in argument or weighting of language.

Effective Quality Management

• Positive implications:

- Initiative based on changing attitudes is time-consuming and expensive; a great many training courses will be needed and a lot of support from senior managers; if this is budgeted for, the results can transform the business.

- The initiative will force a rethink of all production and service systems; this should uncover some inefficiencies that can be changed in a way that boosts productivity.

• Negative implications:

- If the culture isn't right, the initiative may be dismissed by staff as a management fad ('flavour of the month').

- Have senior managers made the necessary adjustments to seeing quality as a top priority; if they're not willing to make sacrifices in a trade-off between quantity and quality, word will soon spread and the initiative will be undermined.

Working with Suppliers

32.1 Introduction

On the face of it, this topic should be straightforward. Initial work needs to focus on the factors that firms will consider when choosing between suppliers. Here it is important to strike a balance between competing factors. Students may find this topic allows them to develop evaluative skills, by weighing up the relative importance of the different factors for different types of business.

There is plenty of scope here for class exercises where students are asked to rank the importance of the factors for a range of different types of business. Students may need some guidance on the relative importance of cost. Most will start thinking cost is the most important factor for all firms. Then, once you have worked through the other factors with them, there is a danger they might underestimate the importance of cost. Perhaps it is worth finishing the topic by re-stressing the importance of cost to any business.

The frustration will be that the topic cries out for JIT, but it's not in the AS Spec. Probably this will be a topic to consider reintroducing – after the first year is out of the way and you are in a better position to judge whether there is enough time to spare.

Once students have a sound understanding of the different factors considered when choosing a supplier, the unit moves on to consider the benefits of building a long-term relationship with suppliers. Particularly relevant here is the second data response question at the end of the unit.

32.2 Further reading and resources

Title and price	Author	Publisher and ISBN	Brief account
The Economist Guide to Management Ideas and Gurus £20.00	Hindle, T.	Profile Books 2008 978 1 84668 108 0	Three hundred pages of 1-2 page accounts that help to fill in holes, e.g. enterprise resource planning; JIT; offshoring; outsourcing; supply chain management and the value chain.
50 Management Ideas you Really Need to Know £8.99	Russell-Walling. E.	Quercus Publishing plc 2008 978 1 84724 009 5	Two hundred pages, so again it's 2 pages per topic; some are the same as the Economist book, but still have a different take, e.g. outsourcing, supply chain management and value chain. Also worth a look at Porter's 5 Forces.

Working with Suppliers

The Toyota Way £16.99	Liker, J.K.	McGraw-Hill 2004 0 07 139231 9	Chapter 17 covers: Challenge suppliers and help them improve: about 20 pages on the topic. Use Figure 17.1 in the classroom – it shows a hierarchy of needs in relation to suppliers.
Business Case Studies 3rd Edition £17.99	Marcouse, I. and Lines, D.	Longman 2002 0 582 40636-6	Case Study 43 'JIT Production' is a bit long, but hasn't dated, and gives a lot of insight into the Toyota/Japanese way of dealing with suppliers.

32.3 Answers to workbook questions

A Revision questions

(30 marks; 30 minutes)

1. Explain why the cheapest supplier may not always be the best choice. **(4)**

   • There is probably a reason they are cheapest, perhaps due to poor quality or a lack of reliability.

2. Identify two businesses for which daily deliveries may be absolutely crucial. **(2)**

   • sandwich shop

   • Toyota uses JIT and may therefore need hourly deliveries

3. Briefly explain two problems that may arise when a firm uses a supplier with poor levels of quality. **(4)**

   • customer complaints

   • machinery breakdowns

   • increased guarantee claims

   • damage to reputation

4. Describe why attractive credit terms from a supplier will be particularly useful for a new business. **(4)**

   • Cash flow is notoriously tight for new businesses. Credit terms for a supplier may mean the firm is able to sell the supplies and gain the cash inflow, before they need to pay (cash outflow) for those supplies.

5. Outline two reasons why a firm might choose to change its supplier of an existing component. **(4)**

  • The firm may be dissatisfied with one aspect of the current supplier - perhaps price, quality or reliability.

  • Alternatively the company's needs may have changed, if they have redesigned their product.

6. Examine one benefit a mobile phone shop might receive from encouraging several suppliers to compete with each other for every month's order of components. **(4)**

  • Cheaper supplies may be gained by encouraging suppliers to compete with each other on a regular basis. This would reduce costs for the shop allowing them to either increase profit margins or cut selling prices.

7. What benefits might the mobile phone shop miss out on by not building a long-term relationship with its suppliers? **(4)**

  • Suppliers may be unwilling to help out in an emergency, perhaps by rushing along new stocks of a popular item, or delivering at odd times. Meanwhile, firms that have developed a long-term relationship may benefit by including suppliers in the process of new product development – something the shop would not be able to do.

8. Describe how a car manufacturer such as Ford might benefit from including its component suppliers in the development process when designing a new car. **(4)**

  • Suppliers may have advice on the properties of their products that would enable Ford's designers to maximise the potential of each component.

  • Suppliers would develop a commitment to the success of the new model which should make them more helpful once production is underway.

B1 Data response

Doll's Choice

(20 marks; 25 minutes)

(Refer to question on page 204 of textbook.)

1. Which supplier offers the best:

   (a) quality

   (b) lead time

   (c) credit terms **(3)**

      (a) C

      (b) B

      (c) B

2. Explain why lead time is important. **(5)**

	Knowledge 3 marks	Application 2 marks
Level 3	**3 marks** Candidate shows good understanding of lead time **and** identifies one relevant point **or** identifies two points and shows limited understanding of lead time.	
Level 2	**2 marks** Candidate shows good understanding of lead time **or** identifies two relevant points.	**2 marks** Candidate applies knowledge effectively to context.
Level 1	**1 mark** Candidate shows some understanding of lead time **or** identifies one relevant point	**1 mark** Candidate attempts to apply knowledge to context.

• Lead time is the time lag between ordering and receiving supplies.

• Shorter lead times allow greater manufacturing flexibility.

• As this firm is operating in a highly seasonal, probably unpredictable market, this flexibility could be crucial.

3. Which supplier should the firm choose, and why? **(12)**

	Knowledge 2 marks	Application 3 marks	Analysis 3 marks	Evaluation 4 marks
Level 2	**2 marks** Good understanding of the subject content.	**3 marks** Answer is applied effectively to the specific case.	**3 marks** Build-up of argument, making use of relevant business concepts.	**4-3 marks** Shows judgement in drawing conclusions from own argument.
Level 1	**1 mark** Some understanding of the subject content.	**2-1 marks** Some relationship to the scenario (perhaps indirectly).	**2-1 marks** Some build-up of argument, showing grasp of cause and effect.	**2-1 marks** Some judgement shown in argument or weighting of language.

Positive implications:

- Small firm – best credit terms may be useful – company B. B also offers the shortest lead time, which may be useful for a firm focused on coping with a Christmas rush.

- Company C offers the benefit of the lowest reject rate – something that may have longer-term benefits for the firm's reputation with customers.

- Company A is the cheapest supplier and the importance of this factor should not be underestimated.

- The best judgements will be those that are well argued rather than specifically coming down in favour of any particular company.

B2 Data response

Crepe Heaven
(30 marks; 35 minutes)

(Refer to question on pages 204–5 of textbook.)

1. Explain why Carla tended to under-order ingredient supplies in the early days of the business. **(5)**

	Knowledge 2 marks		Application 3 marks
Level 2	**2 marks** Candidate identifies two relevant points.		**3 marks** Candidate applies knowledge effectively to context.
Level 1	**1 mark** Candidate identifies relevant point.		**2-1 marks** Candidate attempts to apply knowledge to context.

- Carla's ingredients are perishable – throwing ingredients away at the end of the day must seem a terrible waste.

- As a new business start-up, Carla must be concerned about cash flow and therefore would be keen to avoid any unnecessary expenditure, such as over-ordering stock.

- Crepes may be an impulse purchase which may lead to wide variations in demand from day to day.

2. Explain which two factors may have been most important to Carla when originally choosing her ingredient supplier. (6)

	Knowledge 2 marks	Application 2 marks	Analysis 2 marks
Level 2	**2 marks** Good understanding of the subject content; or two answers identified.	**2 marks** Answer is applied effectively to the specific case.	**2 marks** Build-up of argument, making use of relevant business concepts.
Level 1	**1 mark** Shows some understanding of the subject content.	**1 mark** Some relationship to the scenario (perhaps indirectly).	**1 mark** Some build-up of argument, showing grasp of cause and effect.

Possible answers include:

- Price must have been important with Carla potentially concerned with ensuring she breaks even as soon as possible, a higher contribution per unit would make break-even lower.

- Any credit terms offered would have been extremely useful when starting up a small firm.

3. Analyse the benefits to Carla of choosing the American supplier for her second crepe machine. (8)

	Knowledge 2 marks	Application 3 marks	Analysis 3 marks
Level 2	**2 marks** Good understanding of the subject content; or two answers identified.	**3 marks** Answer is applied effectively to the specific case.	**3 marks** Build-up of argument, making use of relevant business concepts.
Level 1	**1 mark** Shows some understanding of the subject content.	**2-1 marks** Some relationship to the scenario (perhaps indirectly).	**2-1 marks** Some build-up of argument, showing grasp of cause and effect.

Possible answers include:

- The quicker delivery time means that Carla could increase capacity sooner, therefore start earning extra revenue to pay back the cost of the machine quicker.

- The credit terms would have been a great aid to cash flow for a small firm.

4. To what extent does the case study support the view that building a long-term relationship with a supplier is a better approach than shopping around for 'the best deal'? **(11)**

	Knowledge 2 marks	Application 3 marks	Analysis 3 marks	Evaluation 3 marks
Level 2	**2 marks** Good understanding of the subject content.	**3 marks** Answer is applied effectively to the specific case.	**3 marks** Build-up of argument, making use of relevant business concepts.	**3 marks** Shows judgement in drawing conclusions from own argument.
Level 1	**1 mark** Some understanding of the subject content.	**2-1 marks** Some relationship to the scenario (perhaps indirectly).	**2-1 marks** Some build-up of argument, showing grasp of cause and effect.	**2-1 marks** Some judgement shown in argument or weighting of language.

- **Supporting long-term relationship:**

  – The letter from her catering supplier came after six months, once they clearly felt Carla was a reliable customer and this relationship bore fruit as Carla got her afternoon delivery, reducing 'top-up trips' to the supermarket thus reducing running costs.

  – Shopping around for a different crepe machine supplier got her a supplier not willing to help out when she had problems, indeed, their reluctance to return her money could have driven the firm out of business.

- **Supporting shopping around:**

  – Carla got better terms from US machine supplier with both a faster delivery and crucially good credit terms.

- Overall – there seems little doubt that this case illustrates the benefits of a long-term relationship and the drawbacks of shopping around.

Capacity Utilisation

Unit **33**

33.1 Introduction

Capacity utilisation starts with the relationship between capacity use and fixed costs, but needs to move beyond this basic idea.

As an introduction, one approach is to provide real, or mental, images of different types of business operating at full capacity and then at low levels of utilisation. A football stadium or an airplane can provide accessible examples. The school/college canteen can also work as an example, before moving on to a manufacturing context.

Once the basic idea is established for students, the formula can be tackled. Try to discourage students from rote-learning a formula. It is far better if they develop sufficient understanding of the concept to be able to work out the percentage capacity utilisation for themselves. Just before their exam, relent with those who are still failing to cope.

It is necessary to use numerate examples to illustrate how fixed costs per unit fall at higher levels of utilisation. Visual examples are also necessary to help show how spreading a fixed quantity over a larger total area results in an increasingly thin layer, e.g. the fixed cost of a £2 jar of Marmite being spread on toast.

Now students can begin to consider the ways in which a firm can increase capacity utilisation. Most are happy with the concept that increased output leads to higher capacity utilisation. You may have to work harder pointing out that reducing maximum capacity will also increase capacity utilisation (try two different sized bottles to represent different maximum capacities, and a fixed quantity of water).

Within the Workbook, exercises A and B2 are likely to prove the most valuable for homework. The higher numerical content in B1 marks it out as a classroom exercise.

33.2 Further reading and resources

Title and price	Author	Publisher and ISBN	Brief account
The Economist Guide to Management Ideas and Gurus £20.00	Hindle, T.	Profile Books 2008 978 1 84668 108 0	Three hundred pages of 1–2 page accounts that help to fill in holes, e.g. JIT, lean production, downsizing and outsourcing.
50 Management Ideas you Really Need to Know £8.99	Russell-Walling, E.	Quercus Publishing plc 2008 978 1 84724 009 5	Two hundred pages, so again it's 2 pages per topic; some are the same as the Economist book, but still have a different take, e.g. outsourcing and business process re-engineering. Also worth a look at lean production.

The Toyota Way £16.99	Liker, J.K.	McGraw-Hill 2004 0 07 139231 9	Masses on quality, especially Chapter 11: 'Build a culture of stopping to fix problems to get quality right the first time'; Chapter 5 on the development of the Lexus is also useful.
Business Case Studies 3rd Edition £17.99	Marcouse, I. and Lines, D	Longman 2002 0 582 40636-6	Case Study 32 'Production and Stock Scheduling' is really focused on capacity utilisation. It's a genuinely fun task for pairs of students in class (Ed note: which I've enjoyed using for 20 years). Old but in no way dated.

33.3 Answers to workbook questions

A Revision questions

(30 marks; 30 minutes)

1. What is meant by the phrase '100% capacity utilisation'? (**3**)

   • Output is at the highest level possible given the current level of resources available.

2. At what level of capacity utilisation will fixed costs per unit be lowest for any firm? Briefly explain your answer. (**4**)

   • When capacity utilisation is 100%, fixed costs will be spread over as many units as possible, meaning that fixed costs per unit are at their lowest possible level.

3. What formula is used to calculate the capacity utilisation of a firm? (**2**)

   • $\dfrac{\text{Current level of output}}{\text{Maximum output}} \times 100 = \text{Capacity utilisation}$

4. How can a firm increase its capacity utilisation without increasing output? (**3**)

   • The firm can increase capacity utilisation by reducing maximum capacity, perhaps by renting out unused factory space. This would mean that the current output accounts for a greater proportion of full capacity, thereby increasing capacity utilisation.

5. If a firm is currently selling 11,000 units per month and this represents a capacity utilisation of 55%, what is its maximum capacity? (**4**)

   • $\dfrac{11,000}{???} \times 100 = 55\%$

So ??? must equal: $\dfrac{11{,}000}{0.55} = 20{,}000$ units

6. Use the following information to calculate profit per week at 50%, 75% and 100% capacity utilisation. **(9)**

Maximum capacity	800 units per week
Variable cost per unit	£1800
Total fixed cost per week	£1.5 million
Selling price	£4300

Capacity utilisation	50%	75%	100%
Output	400	600	800
Revenue	£1.72m	£2.58m	£3.44m
Variable cost	£720,000	£1.08m	£1.44m
Fixed cost	£1.5m	£1.5m	£1.5m
Total cost	£2.22m	£2.58m	£2.94
Profit	−£0.5m	0	£0.5m

7. Briefly explain the dangers of operating at 100% capacity utilisation for any extended period of time. **(5)**

- 100% capacity utilisation leaves no free time for important activities such as cleaning and maintenance of machinery and equipment. If this situation is sustained for any length of time, machinery breakdowns are far more likely to occur. Meanwhile, any errors in production will be nearly impossible to catch up on as there will be no slack periods at 100% utilisation.

B1 Data response

(30 marks; 35 minutes)

(Refer to question on pages 211–12 of textbook.)

1. What is the firm's current monthly profit? **(5)**

	Knowledge 1 mark	Application 4 marks
Level 2		**4-3 marks** Candidate applies knowledge effectively to the data provided.
Level 1	**1 mark** Candidate identifies an appropriate formula for calculating profit.	**2-1 marks** Candidate attempts to apply formula to data provided.

- Total contribution per month: $12{,}000 \times £5 = £60{,}000$

Total fixed costs per month:

£10,000/12 × 10 = £8,333.33
£12,000/12 × 4 = £4,000
£32,000/12 × 3 = £8,000
Plus overheads of £40,000
So total FC = £60,333.33
Therefore profit = £60,000 − £60,333.33 = loss of £333.33

2. Calculate the monthly profit that would result from each of the two options. **(10)**

Apply the mark grid from question 1 again, for each section of this question

- **Option 1**

Contribution still £60,000 per month

Fixed costs per month now:

£10,000/12 × 6 = £5,000
£12,000/12 × 2 = £2,000
£32,000/12 × 3 = £8,000
Plus overheads of £40,000
So total FC = £55,000, leaving a profit per month of £5,000

- **Option 2**

New monthly contribution = £5 × 20,000 = £100,000
Fixed costs will remain at £60,333.33 per month
So new profit per month will be £39,666.67

3. Explain the advantages and disadvantages of each option. **(10)**

	Knowledge 3 marks	Application 3 marks	Analysis 4 marks
Level 2	**3 marks** Good understanding of the subject content.	**3 marks** Answer is applied effectively to the specific case.	**4-3 marks** Build-up of argument, making use of relevant business concepts.
Level 1	**2-1 marks** Shows some understanding of the subject content.	**2-1 marks** Some relationship to the scenario (perhaps indirectly).	**2-1 marks** Some build-up of argument, showing grasp of cause and effect.

- **Option 1 (redundancies)**

Advantages may include:

– boosts level of capacity utilisation

- brings capacity down to a more realistic level

- restores profitability

Disadvantages may include:

- removes any further scope for increasing output beyond current level

- limits potential profitability

- may damage firm's reputation

• **Option 2 (new order)**

Advantages may include:

- higher level of capacity utilisation

- greater profit per month

- allows firm to avoid making redundancies

- should be a guaranteed source of income for the next four years

Disadvantages may include:

- may prompt dependency on one large customer

- removes pricing power over the next four years on a large chunk of output

- limits ability to produce other orders

- removes production planning flexibility

4. State which of the two options you would choose, and list any other information you would need before making the final decision. **(5)**

   One mark for decision, then up to two marks per point for other information which could include:

   • demand forecasts

   • seasonal fluctuations for demand

   • costs of redundancies

   • details of financial penalties

   • corporate objectives

Capacity Utilisation

B2 Data response

Out of the red and into success

(25 marks; 30 minutes)

(Refer to question on page 212 of textbook.)

1. Using the concept of capacity utilisation, analyse why Steven's business had initially failed to cover its costs. **(6)**

	Knowledge 2 marks	Application 2 marks	Analysis 2 marks
Level 2	2 marks Candidate shows good understanding of capacity utilisation.	2 marks Candidate applies knowledge effectively to the data presented.	2 marks Sound analysis of the question.
Level 1	1 mark Candidate shows some understanding of capacity utilisation.	1 mark Candidate attempts to apply knowledge to data.	1 mark Limited analysis of the question.

- With only one of three floors given over to sales, Steven was only using 33% of his capacity to generate revenue. This meant that the sales floor had to work extra hard to try to cover the cost of keeping the other two floors. Even worse was the news that many of Steven's visitors were not buying – in effect, only a tiny fraction of his selling capacity was actually generating revenue.

2a Explain why Robbie's ideas were always likely to improve Steven's profit. **(4)**

	Knowledge 2 marks	Application 2 marks
Level 2	2 marks Candidate explains relevant point(s).	2 marks Candidate applies knowledge effectively to the data presented.
Level 1	1 mark Candidate identifies relevant point(s).	1 mark Candidate attempts to apply knowledge to data.

- Both ideas are based on the principle of reducing overall capacity. Although Steven did not actually sell off his unused space, he turned both the top floor flat and the other half of the retail space into revenue generating areas – thus using more of his capacity to help cover his fixed costs. This spread his fixed costs over a broader range of revenue sources.

2b What crucial assumptions did Robbie make when offering his advice? (**3**)

Possible answers could include:

- Steven would be able to find tenants for the flat.

- Steven would be able to find another retailer to take on the new shop space.

- The building costs involved in converting both areas could be funded by Steven.

- There was no clause in the lease preventing the suggested courses of action.

3. Steven had few other options as a result of the length of his lease on the property. Use the case as a starting point to discuss why flexibility is vital in a small business start-up. (**12**)

	Knowledge 2 marks	Application 2 marks	Analysis 4 marks	Evaluation 4 marks
Level 2	**2 marks** Good understanding of the subject content.	**2 marks** Answer is applied effectively to the specific case.	**4-3 marks** Build-up of argument, making use of relevant business concepts.	**4-3 marks** Shows judgement in drawing conclusions from own argument.
Level 1	**1 mark** Some understanding of the subject content.	**1 mark** Some relationship to the scenario (perhaps indirectly).	**2-1 marks** Some build-up of argument, showing grasp of cause and effect.	**2-1 marks** Some judgement shown in argument or weighting of language.

- Business start-ups rarely go to plan.

- Flexibility allows adjustments to original plans to be made easily.

- New opportunities can emerge at any time, and a small business may need flexibility to grab those opportunities before they disappear.

- However, Steven has survived despite having such a long lease, but this was perhaps only possible as a result of the flexibility he managed to show with the uses of his premises, and the online ordering service.

Making Operational Decisions

34.1 Introduction

This unit covers a wide range of issues and is likely to form the basis of a number of high-mark exam questions. Starting with the concept of setting targets, it is sensible to focus on the three types of targets covered in the unit. Unit costs should bring echoes of work covered in the finance section of the course. Students will need help adjusting to the notion of total cost per unit consisting of an element of variable cost and an element of fixed cost. It is then time to discuss methods of reducing unit costs, but try to encourage students to consider the broader impact of their suggestions – e.g. using cheaper materials could have severe repercussions on quality, marketing and reputation. Capacity utilisation was covered in detail in the previous unit, and is therefore unlikely to need much time. Quality has also already been covered in some detail previously.

Next comes another fundamental operational issue – matching production to demand. Students must understand the purpose as well as why it may be tricky. This is the point where the skill of application should be stressed to students as they can consider particular types of firms that will find this hard for differing reasons. When discussing the 'solutions', be sure to emphasise the underlying importance of flexibility to the field of operations management.

Other operational decisions are covered later in the unit, with stock management flowing naturally from the principle of matching production to demand. Rationalisation is a follow on from the closing stages of the capacity utilisation unit, whilst non-standard orders will be a familiar topic to most teachers, many of whom will have been delivering this material to AQA A2 students. The big teaching issue is whether to teach 'special order decisions' as a numerical topic. There is no reason to assume that this will arise as an exam topic, but it could be argued that good students would find it easier to answer a qualitative question if they understood the underlying maths (golden rule – if price is above VC p.u. and doesn't generate extra fixed costs then accept the order). In the first year it seems wise to lay off this (quite confusing) use of contribution; in subsequent years you may choose to try it.

The Section A questions in the Workbook are relatively easy. Better groups should be challenged with B1 or – even better – B2. For a challenging but fun class groupwork task, try Case 32 from *Business Case Studies* 3e. (Ed note: I've used the latter for 20 years and always found it a great success.)

34.2 Further reading and resources

Title and price	Author	Publisher and ISBN	Brief account
Schaum's Outlines: Operations Management £9.99	Monks, J.	McGraw Hill 1996 0 07 0427 64 X	Far too advanced mathematically, but contains some great stuff, e.g. the illustration of a production system on p8 and the Fishbone diagram of customer services on p15.

Key Concepts in Operations Management £14.95	Sutherland, J. and Canwell, D.	Palgrave Macmillan 2004 9 781 4039 1529 0	Not great, but it's helpful to have an alphabetically organized book specialising on Ops. Good entries on TQM, quality control and the quality framework – worth buying one copy.
A-Z AS Business Studies Worksheets – photocopiable pack plus VLE £95.00	Marcouse, I.	A-Z Business Training Ltd* 2008	Four worksheets are devoted to cash flow: 14 (Customer Service), 25 (Capacity Utilisation), 50 (Matching Production to Demand) and 74 (Quality Management) and 55 (Revision for Operations Management). *To order, go to www.a-zbusinesstraining.com
Business Case Studies 3rd Edition £17.99	Marcouse, I. and Lines, D.	Longman 2002 0 582 40636-6	Case Study 32 gives a lovely overview of the problems of matching supply to demand, of capacity utilisation and of the implications for cash flow.

34.3 Answers to workbook questions

A Revision questions

(35 marks; 35 minutes)

1. Briefly explain what is meant by capacity utilisation. (**2**)

    • The proportion of maximum possible output that the firm is currently producing.

2. Explain why a high level of capacity usage makes cost per unit fall. (**2**)

    • At higher levels of capacity use, the firm's fixed costs are spread over more units of output, meaning that each unit carries less fixed costs.

3. Calculate the unit cost for a firm that manufactured 23,000 units with total costs of £11,500. (**3**)

    • £11,500/23000 = £0.50

4. Explain why quality targets may suffer if management is only concerned with meeting unit cost targets. (**4**)

    • Reducing costs may be achieved by actions that directly hurt quality of production. Cheaper materials, less maintenance of machinery, increased speed of production can all reduce costs yet clearly have a negative effect on quality.

5. Explain what is meant by the term rationalisation. (**2**)

    • Rationalisation refers to reducing maximum capacity in order to reduce fixed costs, perhaps by laying off staff or closing a factory.

6. Explain two methods that could be used to improve the level of capacity utilisation in a clothing factory. (**4**)

    • Increased sales – through a variety of measures such as price cutting, promotional offers or even manufacturing for other companies.

    • Reducing maximum capacity would also boost capacity utilisation, so renting out part of the factory space could be an option.

7. Explain two possible drawbacks to a farmer of relying on temporary staff when picking strawberries. (**4**)

    • Reliability – may be high rates of absenteeism as staff are uncommitted to the business.

    • Skill – basic training would need to be given every year, increasing costs.

8. Explain two benefits to a farmer of using temporary staff to pick strawberries. (**4**)

    • Reduced costs – temporary staff may work for less but most notably are not entitled to many of the benefits such as sick pay, that permanent staff receive.

    • Flexibility – when strawberry harvests are poor, the farmer would only need to recruit a few staff, yet in bumper years a far larger temporary workforce could be recruited.

9. Explain two reasons why a company might agree to provide a customer with a special order at a selling price lower than its average unit cost. (**4**)

    • Profit – if the firm had already broken even, any selling price above variable cost per unit would boost profit.

    • Gain a new customer – if the customer could become a long-term regular customer, a one-off special order may be the convincer needed to form a longer-term relationship.

10. Outline three possible reasons why a cake manufacturer may try to closely match production with demand in order to reduce stock levels to a minimum. (**6**)

    • Seasonality – different cake designs may be produced for different seasons. Few will buy Valentine's cakes on 15 February.

    • Perishability – cakes have a limited shelf-life. The firm would not want to carry stock that may have to be thrown out if it is not sold in time.

    • Reduced cash tied up in stock – though not especially applicable to cakes, most firms will be keen to minimise the amount of working capital they have tied up unproductively in stock.

B1 Data response

(20 marks; 20 minutes)

(Refer to question on page 218 of textbook.)

1. Explain what the table reveals about Hotel Torres's operational efficiency during the year. **(4)**

	Knowledge 1 mark	Application 3 marks
Level 2		**3 marks** Answer is applied effectively to the specific case.
Level 1	**2-1 marks** Shows understanding of the subject content.	**2-1 marks** Some relationship to the scenario (perhaps indirectly).

Possible answers include:

- **Capacity utilisation** (in the case of hotels, room occupancy rates)

  These seem to have followed a predictable seasonal pattern, yet consistently failed to reach either the targets set for the hotel or the average rate achieved across the rest of the firm.

- **Unit costs**

  These too show a poor picture, as the hotel's unit costs are above target for each quarter.

2. Use the data in the table to explain the possible link between room occupancy performance and cost per guest. **(6)**

	Knowledge 3 marks	Application 3 marks
Level 2	**3 marks** Good understanding of the subject content.	**3 marks** Answer is applied effectively to the specific case.
Level 1	**2-1 marks** Shows understanding of the subject content.	**2-1 marks** Some relationship to the scenario (perhaps indirectly).

Possible answers include:

- The table shows clearly that higher occupancy rates lead to lower costs per guest. Both in the actual figures for the hotel, and in the target figures set, there is a clear illustration of the principle that higher levels of capacity utilisation lead to lower unit costs as fixed costs are spread over more units.

3. Analyse the benefits that the hotel might gain by setting targets for occupancy rates and cost per guest. (**6**)

	Knowledge 2 marks	Application 2 marks	Analysis 2 marks
Level 2	**2 marks** Good understanding of the subject content; or two answers identified.	**2 marks** Answer is applied effectively to the specific case.	**2 marks** Build-up of argument, making use of relevant business concepts.
Level 1	**1 mark** Shows some understanding of the subject content.	**1 mark** Some relationship to the scenario (perhaps indirectly).	**1 mark** Some build-up of argument, showing grasp of cause and effect.

Possible answers include:

- Targets give managers and staff something to work towards. This allows them to feel a sense of achievement if targets are met. This is likely to be a motivating factor.

- Targets also allow judgements of performance to be made, when actual data is compared to the targets set. This means that managers can receive objective feedback on the performance of their hotel and head office can monitor the performance of each hotel fairly easily, focusing their attention on hotels that fail to meet their targets.

4. Briefly explain two possible reasons why Hotel Torres failed to meet its targets. (**4**)

	Knowledge 2 marks	Application 2 marks
Level 2	**2 marks** Shows understanding of the subject content or gives two reasons.	**2 marks** Answer is applied effectively to the specific case.
Level 1	**1 mark** Some understanding of the subject content or gives one reason.	**1 mark** Some relationship to the scenario (perhaps indirectly).

Possible answers include:

- Unit cost targets are most likely to have been missed as a direct result of poor room occupancy rates. Room occupancy rates could be below target for many reasons, with no obvious hints in the data. Suggestions such as poor weather in Barcelona, increased flight costs or cancellation of major events hosted in the city would all ring true.

• Or perhaps the hotel responded to high unit costs by putting up prices – thereby lowering the occupancy rate.

B2 Data response

(35 marks; 45 minutes)

(Refer to question on page 219 of textbook.)

1a Draw a graph to show units sold, output and maximum capacity. **(6)**

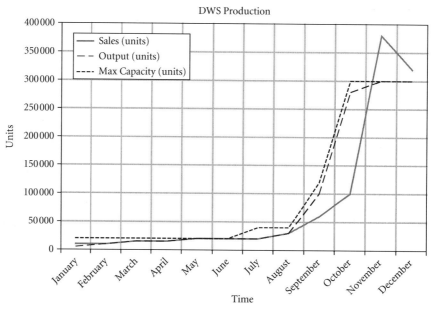

DWS Production

1b Shade the areas on the graph that represent under-use of capacity **(2)**

• The student should shade any gap between the maximum capacity (yellow) and output (pink) lines

2. Analyse the problems that DWS might experience by maintaining a consistent level of production all year round in order to avoid using overtime, temporary staff and subcontracting. **(9)**

	Knowledge 2 marks	Application 3 marks	Analysis 4 marks
Level 2	**2 marks** Good understanding of the subject content; or two answers identified.	**3 marks** Answer is applied effectively to the specific case.	**4–3 marks** Build-up of argument, making use of relevant business concepts.
Level 1	**1 mark** Shows some understanding of the subject content.	**2–1 marks** Some relationship to the scenario (perhaps indirectly).	**2–1 marks** Some build-up of argument, showing grasp of cause and effect.

Possible answers include:

Making Operational Decisions

- The storage requirements would be huge. Excluding the new order, the data in the table shows total annual sales volume of 1,000,000 units. Consistent production levels would therefore set monthly output at 1,000,000/12 = 83,333 units. Starting from January, this would lead to a stockpile, by the end of September of 550,000 units. The storage cost for this many toys would surely be prohibitive.

- Assuming a switch to consistent production levels was accompanied by a rationalisation, perhaps bringing monthly capacity down to 85,000 units, the firm may struggle to cope with unexpected surges in demand.

3. Describe the pros and cons of two possible methods of increasing maximum capacity in the three affected months. (6)

	Knowledge 3 marks	Application 3 marks
Level 2	**3 marks** Shows understanding of the subject content or gives three reasons.	**3 marks** Answer is applied effectively to the specific case.
Level 1	**2-1 marks** Shows some understanding of the subject content or gives one or two reasons.	**2-1 marks** Some relationship to the scenario (perhaps indirectly).

Possible answers include:

- Overtime

  - Pros include huge flexibility, along with trusted staff that are trained and hopefully loyal.

  - Cons include the disproportionate increase in labour costs usually caused by increased rates for overtime, along with the possible difficulty of finding staff willing to work the overtime.

- Temporary staff

  - Pros include the possibility of being able to reduce labour costs due to fewer fringe benefits for temps, along with the flexibility of only having to pay these staff when they are needed.

  - Cons include the strong chance of temps being less committed and motivated, alongside the need to provide some training.

- Subcontracting

  - Pros could include the possible eagerness of a subcontractor to reach high standards of quality and reliability, along with offering a competitive price in the hope of gaining future business.

  - Cons may include the difficulty of finding a willing subcontractor with available spare capacity at peak periods, whilst problems of maintaining quality standards could occur.

4. Discuss whether DWS should accept this special order. **(12)**

	Knowledge 2 marks	Application 3 marks	Analysis 3 marks	Evaluation 4 marks
Level 2	**2 marks** Good understanding of the subject content; or two answers identified.	**3 marks** Answer is applied effectively to the specific case.	**3 marks** Build-up of argument, making use of relevant business concepts.	**4-3 marks** Shows judgement in drawing conclusions from own argument.
Level 1	**1 mark** Some understanding of the subject content; or one answer identified.	**2-1 marks** Some relationship to the scenario (perhaps indirectly).	**2-1 marks** Some build-up of argument, showing grasp of cause and effect.	**2-1 marks** Some judgement shown in argument or weighting of language.

- Arguments in favour

    - The order would boost sales in three months when the firm is working below maximum capacity.

    - The initial order may lead to future orders from the same firm, or even its rivals.

    - Assuming DWS has already passed its break-even point and does not incur extra fixed costs as a result of the order, the 5% mark-up on variable costs would be pure profit.

- Arguments against

    - Such a narrow margin may set a dangerous precedent for DWS; if current customers find out about such a low price they may demand a lower price too.

    - Although March and January are very quiet at DWS, October is already busy in the factory, running at over 90% capacity – this could cause problems.

- Overall – if management set the terms of the contract appropriately, the order does seem attractive, boosting capacity utilisation in two especially quiet months.

Using Technology in Operations

35.1 Introduction

Interestingly, the guts of this unit have not needed to change since the first edition of the book in 1999. Technology is still about speeding up and monitoring systems that can be intelligently or unintelligently designed by humans. The only really significant change has been the Internet – especially its effect on purchasing (by businesses or consumers).

The 2008 Specification includes quite bland statements on the use of technology – all focused on its benefits. This unit tends to follow that path (on reflection, with too little of a critical eye). Successful teaching will probably require some more critical reflections, in order to provide more analytic scope for students. In particular it would be useful to reflect on: voicemail systems (Press 1 for...), self-check-out at supermarkets and any new newspaper revelations into the idiocy of techy systems.

35.2 Further reading and resources

Title and price	Author	Publisher and ISBN	Brief account
The Economist Guide to Management Ideas and Gurus £20	Hindle, T.	Profile Books 2008 978 1 84668 108 0	Three hundred pages of 1-2 page accounts that help to fill in holes, e.g. e-commerce, enterprise resource planning, mass customisation and disruptive technology.
50 Management Ideas you Really Need to Know £8.99	Russell-Walling, E.	Quercus Publishing plc 2008 978 1 84724 009 5	Two hundred pages, so again it's 2 pages per topic; relevant topics are customer relationship management (database mining, really) and the knowledge economy.
The Toyota Way £16.99	Liker, J.K.	McGraw-Hill 2004 0 07 139231 9	In essence the whole book is about how relatively unimportant new technology is, per se, compared with a motivated workforce and long-term goals.
Business Case Studies 3rd Edition £17.99	Marcouse, I. and Lines, D.	Longman 2002 0 582 40636-6	Case Study 60 'A Day in the Life of Teresa Travis' emphasises the limitations and disadvantages of electronic communications.

35.3 Answers to workbook questions

A Revision questions

(35 marks; 35 minutes)

1. A database could be used by an aircraft manufacturer such as Boeing to record the supplier and batch number of every part used on every aircraft. How might this information be used? **(3)**

    • For checking back in the case of an accident/air crash. (Were other parts in the same production batch defective? What planes are they in?)

    • To know when every part is nearing the end of its useful life and must be replaced.

2. State two benefits of good database management in achieving efficient stock control. **(2)**

    • Knowing what and when to reorder.

    • Helping record what's arrived and what's been sold, therefore pinpoints 'wastage'/stock losses; can carry out aged stock analysis.

3. Read the A-grade application on JCB Dieselmax. Identify two benefits of 'virtual safety testing'. **(2)**

    • avoids risks (of death) to test-drivers of early prototypes

    • enables all the safety implications to be recorded electronically

4. Look at Figure 35.3. Explain one possible implication for:

    (a) A UK factory owner feeling under pressure from competition from China. **(3)**

    • That the lower prices and greater efficiency of robots may provide a lifeline to keep producing in Britain.

    (b) A UK worker with few qualifications or skills, thinking of taking a job in a factory. **(3)**

    • That the future for such work is awful – one day, most of these jobs will be done by robots.

5. Explain one benefit and one drawback of computer aided manufacture (CAM). **(4)**

    • Benefit: when running smoothly, CAM can speed up production and ensure the right parts are ordered to be at the right place at the right time.

    • Drawback: CAM has often proved very difficult to establish at the start; the teething problems are often considerable, because of the complexity of the software.

6. From your reading of the whole unit, outline three ways in which technology can lead to improved quality. **(6)**

    • better quality of – and more interesting – design, e.g. the Guggenheim Museum

- greater consistency of production, by robots

- quicker response to changing customer tastes, through EDI

7. How significant might Internet retailing become for each of the following types of business?

   (a) a music shop specialising in 1960s classic pop and rock **(2)**

   (b) a builders' merchant (selling bricks, cement, etc.). **(2)**

   (c) a mail order clothing firm **(2)**

   - (a) Ideal: a specialised product with potential demand worldwide; could become the dominant part of the business.

   - (b) Useful: as builders on-site could order 4000 bricks to be delivered at 8.00 tomorrow, i.e. enable rapid deliveries to take place; but urgent needs are still likely to mean the builder must go to the outlet, i.e. that traditional retailing will not die.

   - (c) Important: there is no reason why people used to ordering from a catalogue wouldn't be willing to order electronically.

8. From your reading of the whole unit, explain two ways in which technology can reduce waste within a business. **(6)**

   - Automated stock control should reduce 'sell-by' wastage in grocers.

   - Sophisticated database management can stop firms having to send 'junk mail' to every household, as they get smarter about who is or is not a potential customer.

B1 Data response

Robots
(30 marks; 35 minutes)

(Refer to question on pages 225–6 of textbook.)

1a Explain in your own words the meaning of 'downtime'. **(3)**

   - Downtime is the length of time in which no production is taking place, perhaps due to machinery breakdown or time it takes to changeover and set up a new production process.

1b Why may firms be keen to minimise downtime? **(4)**

	Knowledge 2 marks	Application 2 marks
Level 2	**2 marks** Shows clear understanding of the subject content.	**2 marks** Answer is applied effectively to the specific case of 'firms'.

Level 1	1 mark Shows understanding of the subject content.	1 mark Some relationship to the scenario (perhaps indirectly).

Possible answers include:

- 'Time is money' is an important business cliché; firms have to keep costs down in order to generate a profit, so they have to minimise the time when staff are standing around idly, waiting for production to be restarted.

2. Examine the importance to this 'major UK manufacturer' of the accuracy and flexibility of these three robots. (6)

	Knowledge 1 mark	Application 2 marks	Analysis 3 marks
Level 2		2 marks Answer is applied effectively to the specific case.	3 marks Build-up of argument, making use of relevant business concepts.
Level 1	1 mark Shows some understanding of the subject content.	1 mark Some relationship to the scenario (perhaps indirectly).	2-1 marks Some build-up of argument, showing grasp of cause and effect.

Possible answers include:

- Accuracy is the key to reliability and therefore performance quality for a car manufacturer (and Toyota is famous for quality); 'major manufacturers' are usually competing with top firms from round the world, so accuracy is critical.

- Flexibility is important given that consumer preferences can change dramatically over quite short periods (e.g. the collapse in sales of 4×4s in 2008); 240 different product variants enable Toyota to cope with change.

3a Calculate the % increase in production speed now that the robots are producing rather than people. (3)

- Manual method took $7.8 + 4.2$ seconds $= 12$ seconds

Robot takes 4.2 seconds less time

% change $= 4.2/12 \times 100 = 35\%$ faster

3b Analyse two ways in which the manufacturer can benefit from the extra speed. **(6)**

	Knowledge 1 mark	Application 2 marks	Analysis 3 marks
Level 2		**2 marks** Answer is applied effectively to the specific case.	**3 marks** Build-up of argument, making use of relevant business concepts.
Level 1	**1 mark** Shows some understanding of the subject content.	**1 mark** Some relationship to the scenario (perhaps indirectly).	**2-1 marks** Some build-up of argument, showing grasp of cause and effect.

Possible answers include:

- Provides the ability to produce more per day, e.g. in the seasons when demand is especially high.

- Should lower the labour cost per unit, i.e. if a production supervisor earning £500 a week can supervise 20% more output, the labour cost per unit falls by 20%.

4. Using the information in the case and your own knowledge, discuss two ways in which human workers may be more valuable than robots. **(8)**

	Knowledge 1 mark	Application 2 marks	Analysis 2 marks	Evaluation 3 marks
Level 2		**2 marks** Answer is applied effectively to the specific case.	**2 marks** Build-up of argument, making use of relevant business concepts.	**3 marks** Shows judgement in drawing conclusions from own argument.
Level 1	**1 mark** Some understanding of the subject content; or one answer identified.	**1 mark** Some relationship to the scenario (perhaps indirectly).	**1 mark** Some build-up of argument, showing grasp of cause and effect.	**2-1 marks** Some judgement shown in argument or weighting of language.

Possible answers include:

- Workers can come up with ideas to improve the production process or the product itself, partly because they may be consumers as well as producers.

• The text says that 'a manual process can be advantageous' when there are regular production changeovers. For example, someone hand-finishing a custom-built Rolls Royce can finish one job and move on straight away to the next.

B2 Data response

An architect and her iPhone

(35 marks; 45 minutes)

(Refer to question on page 226 of textbook.)

1. Outline three benefits of the CAD system to this architectural business. **(6)**

	Knowledge 3 marks	Application 3 marks
Level 2	**3 marks** Answer is applied effectively to the specific case.	**3 marks** Answer is applied effectively to the specific case.
Level 1	**2-1 marks** Shows understanding of the subject content.	**2-1 marks** Some relationship to the scenario (perhaps indirectly).

Possible answers include:

• Easily access all their design and construction documents while on the move; so changes wanted on site can be recorded straight away onto the drawings – and saved safely.

• When customers come to the site a portable CAD system makes it much easier to communicate the design plans.

• CAD allows you to zoom in and see much greater detail than would be possible on paper.

2. Explain how the iPhone-linked CAD has reduced time wastage for the business. **(4)**

	Knowledge 2 marks	Application 2 marks
Level 2	**2 marks** Answer is applied effectively to the specific case.	**2 marks** Answer is applied effectively to the specific case.
Level 1	**1 mark** Shows understanding of the subject content.	**1 mark** Some relationship to the scenario (perhaps indirectly).

Possible answers include:

- Allows designer, customer and builder to work on-site, seeing the actual building and the drawings – therefore saving time shuttling to and fro from site to design office.

- Every aspect of information retrieval is quick and easy.

3. Examine Patti Stough's suggestion that having CAD on the iPhone leads to 'huge productivity gains'. **(6)**

	Knowledge 1 mark	Application 2 marks	Analysis 3 marks
Level 2		**2 marks** Answer is applied effectively to the specific case.	**3 marks** Build-up of argument, making use of relevant business concepts.
Level 1	**1 mark** Shows some understanding of the subject content.	**1 mark** Some relationship to the scenario (perhaps indirectly).	**2-1 marks** Some build-up of argument, showing grasp of cause and effect.

Possible answers include:

- Hers is a small architectural firm, which wants to find a way to sound cool, progressive and impressive. Here, she is publicizing herself through her own website, so her claims about the increased productivity could easily be exaggerated.

- ...Yet it is true that good communications is a key part of project management, so there may be a huge reduction in wasted time if the meetings are more effective because of the CAD-enabled iPhone.

4. To what extent is the portable CAD system likely to improve Patti's customer service? **(9)**

	Knowledge 1 mark	Application 2 marks	Analysis 2 marks	Evaluation 4 marks
Level 2		**2 marks** Answer is applied effectively to the specific case.	**2 marks** Build-up of argument, making use of relevant business concepts.	**4-3 marks** Shows judgement in drawing conclusions from own argument.
Level 1	**1 mark** Some understanding of the subject content; or one answer identified.	**1 mark** Some relationship to the scenario (perhaps indirectly).	**1 mark** Some build-up of argument, showing grasp of cause and effect.	**2-1 marks** Some judgement shown in argument or weighting of language.

Using Technology in Operations

Possible answers include:

- Customer service is best achieved by providing exactly what the customer wants; we cannot be sure what that is, but it is probably some combination of producing good designs, keeping the costs down and making the client's life as easy as possible – it is easy to see how portable CAD can help with the latter.

- There remain many other key aspects of customer service, though, that portable CAD cannot affect; most important of these is probably the willingness to listen to the client; high quality technology and low quality communications often exist side-by-side.

Integrated Operations Management Unit 36

36.1 Introduction

Operations management is a wide-ranging term, now broadened even further by the inclusion of customer service in the new A level specification. More than ever, students must appreciate that the way organisations deal with their customers plays a key role in their operations. Unless a business is able to match, and ideally exceed, customer expectations, it will struggle to survive in a competitive environment. However, efficiency and quality have vital roles to play in providing consistently high levels of customer service. Students should, therefore, be able to appreciate the link between all areas of operations management and business profitability. They should also be able to make the connection between a firm's operations and the other functional areas, in particular, marketing, finance and people management.

The ideal way to achieve an integrated understanding of operations management would be to take students to a local factory, small enough for the MD to show you round. A Google of 'Manufacturing Morden Surrey' provided contact details of ten local firms; ten emails later and there were two factory visits lined up.

36.2 Further reading and resources

Title and price	Author(s)	Publisher and ISBN	Brief account
Operations Management 5th Edition	Slack, N., Chambers, S. and Johnston, R.	Financial Times/ Prentice Hall 978 140 584 700X	A thorough and well-structured introduction to operations management, offering views from the service sector as well as manufacturing.
101 Ways to Improve Business Performance	Waters, D.	Kogan Page Ltd 1999 0 7494 2981 X	A student-friendly guide on how to improve operations.
The Customer Service Pocketbook	Newby, T. and McManus, S.	Management Pocketbooks Ltd 2002 1 903 776 007	A practical guide to customer service aimed at practitioners, containing a number of useful exercises, checklists and quizzes.
Business Case Studies 3rd Edition £17.99	Marcouse, I. and Lines, D.	Longman 2002 0 582 40636-6	Case Study 42 'Workforce Performance and the Skoda Supplier' gives good coverage of ops and people, though ask students to ignore Q3b.

36.3 Answers to workbook questions

A Revision questions

(60 marks; 60 minutes)

1. What is meant by the term capacity utilisation? **(2)**

   • Capacity utilisation measures the level of a firm's existing output as a percentage of the maximum output possible, given its existing level of resources.

2. A firm's fixed costs are £100,000, its variable costs per unit are £2.50 and its maximum output is 20,000 units a week. Calculate the cost per unit of production for the firm if it operates at:

   (a) 50% capacity **(3)**

   (b) 90% capacity **(3)**

   • At 50% capacity:

Fixed costs p.u.	= £100,000 /10,000 units
a.	= £10.00
Plus variable costs p.u.	= £2.50
Therefore, cost p.u.	= £12.50

   • At 90% capacity:

Fixed costs p.u.	=£100,000 /18,000 units
b.	= £5.56
Plus variable costs p.u.	= £2.50
Therefore, costs p.u.	= £8.06

3. Suggest two benefits for a firm from increased capacity utilisation. **(2)**

   • Reduced costs per unit allowing firms to reduce prices and become more competitive

   • …or increased profit margins.

4. Outline two ways in which a firm could increase its capacity utilisation. **(4)**

   1. Increase the level of sales by selling to new customers/markets.

   2. Use spare capacity to produce new products.

   3. Reduce spare capacity by selling off or renting out unused factories or machinery.

5. Explain why a firm may choose not to operate close to 100% capacity utilisation over long periods of time. **(3)**

   • In order to create down-time in order to service or repair machinery.

   • In order to be able to meet any unexpected orders that may arise.

6. Explain why average costs are likely to fall as production increases. (4)

   • Fixed costs are spread over a greater level of production.

   • Bulk buying can reduce variable costs per unit as production increases.

7. Briefly explain what is meant by total quality management (TQM). (3)

   • Total quality management (TQM) is a management philosophy to improve quality throughout the organisation (not just production) and at all levels within the workforce.

8. Identify three features of TQM. (3)

   • Emphasis on quality assurance rather than quality control.

   • The use of quality circles to generate ideas from all areas of the business.

   • A focus on customer service, both within the firm (internal customers) and outside the firm (external customers).

9. Explain, using examples, what is meant by quality. (3)

   • Quality means that a product is fit for purpose, i.e., it meets customer needs. Thus, a cheap, disposable razor is a quality product if it provides a good, comfortable shave.

10. Identify two costs for a business that fails to meet acceptable quality standards for its products. (2)

    • The costs of replacing products and/or offering compensation to customers who complain.

    • The loss of sales from customers who remain dissatisfied because of an inadequate response to customer complaints.

    • The loss of sales from existing and potential customers as a result of a poor customer service image.

11. Briefly explain the distinction between quality control and quality assurance. (3)

    • Quality control involves inspectors checking the accuracy of work that has already been completed by others.

    • Quality assurance means applying methods (and paperwork systems) to show how an external quality mark such as ISO 9000 is being met.

12. Identify two areas of business where technology could be introduced to improve performance. (2)

    • Using robotics or automating the production process to improve productivity and/or quality.

    • The use of accounting software to improve the speed and accuracy of storing and retrieving financial data, in order to improve decision-making.

    • The use of company websites as an effective marketing tool.

13. Identify two ways in which a restaurant could introduce technology to improve the service offered to its customers. (2)

    • Creating a database of customers, so that they can be contacted with customer satisfaction surveys or about special offers, seasonal events, etc.

    • To create a website to promote the business.

14. Give two reasons why it is important for a business to establish and maintain good relationships with its suppliers. (2)

    • In order to maintain regular supplies when they are needed.

    • In order to provide supplies for unexpected orders.

    • In order to secure trade discounts.

15. State three factors that might affect the choice of supplier for a business. (3)

    • Reduces warehousing and insurance costs

    • Frees up working capital for other uses, e.g. paying bills

    • Forces workers to get quality right first time, due to the lack of buffer stock.

16. Outline one benefit and one problem of operating a just-in-time (JIT) system of stock control. (4)

    • Benefit: Cuts the amount of (your) cash tied up in stock.

    • Problem: It leaves the firm vulnerable to problems with suppliers, e.g. industrial action or transportation problems.

17. Explain why customer service is so important to a modern business. (4)

    • Increased competition makes it relatively easy for customers to go elsewhere.

    • Customers are more aware of their consumer rights, making them more likely to complain.

18. What is the difference between a customer and a consumer? (3)

    • A customer is an individual/firm that buys the product…

    • … a consumer is the individual/firm who actually consumes or uses it. For example, a parent (the customer) may book a party at MacDonald's for a child (the consumer) to celebrate a birthday.

19. Identify three criteria that could be used to assess the quality of customer service at a hotel. (3)

    • the cleanliness of the room

    • the friendliness and efficiency of the staff

    • the ability to cater for special needs, e.g. vegetarian meals, disabled access, etc.

20. Suggest two ways in which a high-street retailer such as Debenhams could improve the service offered to its customers. (2)

• improved facilities, such as restaurants, toilets, etc.

• the ability to buy online from a website

• home delivery

B1 Data response

The perfect curry – in a box!
(25 marks; 30 minutes)

(Refer to question on pages 229–30 of textbook.)

1. Describe one advantage and one disadvantage to Spice-N-tice of blending its herbs and spices by hand. (4)

	Knowledge 2 marks	Application 2 marks
Level 2	2 marks Good understanding of the subject content.	2 marks Answer is applied effectively to the specific case.
Level 1	1 mark Shows some understanding of the subject content.	1 mark Some relationship to the scenario (perhaps indirectly).

• Advantages:

– High quality standards of quality – workers can be trained to blend a wide variety of ingredients to the same standards as the owners.

– Likely to be cheaper to produce relatively low volume levels by hand – the cost of purchasing machinery to do this may be prohibitive until the business has grown sufficiently.

• Disadvantages:

– The possibility of human error – resulting in a negative impact on quality.

– Labour intensive method of production likely to be more expensive than using machinery as the volume of output increases.

2. Examine two ways in which the introduction of technology could increase productive efficiency at the company. **(8)**

	Knowledge 2 marks	Application 2 marks	Analysis 4 marks
Level 2	**2 marks** Good understanding of the subject content; or two answers identified.	**2 marks** Answer is applied effectively to the specific case.	**4-3 marks** Build-up of argument, making use of relevant business concepts.
Level 1	**1 mark** Shows some understanding of the subject content.	**1 mark** Some relationship to the scenario (perhaps indirectly).	**2-1 marks** Some build-up of argument, showing grasp of cause and effect.

Possible answers include:

- The use of a website to promote Spice-N-tice's products and take orders from customers nationally and internationally.

- The use of machinery to control areas of the production process, such as measuring out ingredients and packaging.

- The use of accountancy packages to keep records and manage the company's accounts.

3. Discuss the main operational implications for Spice-N-tice from further expansion of the business. **(13)**

	Knowledge 3 marks	Application 3 marks	Analysis 3 marks	Evaluation 4 marks
Level 2	**3 marks** Good understanding of the subject content; or two answers identified.	**3 marks** Answer is applied effectively to the specific case.	**3 marks** Build-up of argument, making use of relevant business concepts.	**4-3 marks** Shows judgement in drawing conclusions from own argument.
Level 1	**2-1 marks** Some understanding of the subject content; or one answer identified.	**2-1 marks** Some relationship to the scenario (perhaps indirectly).	**2-1 marks** Some build-up of argument, showing grasp of cause and effect.	**2-1 marks** Some judgement shown in argument or weighting of language.

Possible answers include:

- Larger volumes of production would justify the cost of employing machinery that could help improve productivity and reduce waste.

- What would be the effect on the product's quality if the company switches from a relatively labour intensive to a more capital intensive method of production?

- Does Spice-N-tice have sufficient spare capacity to increase production? At what point will the business need to invest in new machinery, employ extra workers, move to new premises?

- Increasing the scale of production would be dependent on additional finance being secured – what sources of finance are available to the business and what are their implications?

B2 Data response

A unique service from the Pink Ladies
(30 marks; 35 minutes)

(Refer to question on page 230 of textbook.)

1. Explain, using examples from the case study, the difference between internal customers and external customers. **(6)**

	Knowledge 3 marks	Application 3 marks
Level 2	**3 marks** Good understanding of the subject content.	**3 marks** Answer is applied effectively to the specific case.
Level 1	**2-1 marks** Shows some understanding of the subject content.	**2-1 marks** Some relationship to the scenario (perhaps indirectly).

Possible answers include:

- 'Internal customers' are the employees within a business and the relationships that exist between them.

- External customers are the individuals or organisations that pay to use the good/services offered by a business.

- In the case of Pink Ladies the car drivers would act as internal customers to the staff who take bookings. External customers would be the members that use the company's car services.

2. Describe two ways of monitoring the levels of customer service provided by Pink Ladies Cars. (6)

	Knowledge 3 marks	Application 3 marks
Level 2	**3 marks** Good understanding of the subject content.	**3 marks** Answer is applied effectively to the specific case.
Level 1	**2-1 marks** Shows some understanding of the subject content.	**2-1 marks** Some relationship to the scenario (perhaps indirectly).

Possible answers include:

*   Carrying out regular customer satisfaction surveys with members – Pink Ladies keeps a database of members' details, so they could be contacted by post, telephone or email.

*   Recording and analysing any complaints made by members about the level of service received.

*   Using mystery shoppers, i.e. getting people to pose as members to use and assess the level of service offered.

3. Analyse the main methods used by Pink Ladies to meet customer expectations. (8)

	Knowledge 2 marks	Application 3 marks	Analysis 3 marks
Level 2	**2 marks** Good understanding of the subject content.	**3 marks** Answer is applied effectively to the specific case.	**3 marks** Build-up of argument, making use of relevant business concepts.
Level 1	**1 mark** Shows some understanding of the subject content.	**2-1 marks** Some relationship to the scenario (perhaps indirectly).	**2-1 marks** Some build-up of argument, showing grasp of cause and effect.

Possible answers include:

*   The use of trained women-only drivers for the target market – this should reassure female customers who are concerned about their safety when using normal taxi services, helping to attract new and repeat sales.

*   Additional details, such as the 'through the door' policy serve to further reassure customers concerned about safety.

Integrated Operations Management Unit 36

- Options for payment via telephone or online are facilities that are not generally available from taxi firms, offering greater convenience to customers.

4. To what extent do you believe that Pink Ladies' approach to customer service will guarantee its long-term success? **(10)**

	Knowledge 2 marks	Application 2 marks	Analysis 3 marks	Evaluation 3 marks
Level 2	**2 marks** Good understanding of the subject content; or two answers identified.	**2 marks** Answer is applied effectively to the specific case.	**3 marks** Build-up of argument, making use of relevant business concepts.	**3 marks** Shows judgement in drawing conclusions from own argument.
Level 1	**1 mark** Some understanding of the subject content; or one answer identified.	**1 mark** Some relationship to the scenario (perhaps indirectly).	**2-1 marks** Some build-up of argument, showing grasp of cause and effect.	**2-1 marks** Some judgement shown in argument or weighting of language.

Possible answers include:

- Pink Ladies offers a unique service to a specific target market – no other car hire firm offers this at the moment, giving it a unique selling point – but success may depend on how many women are concerned about safety.

- The company may maintain a competitive edge, even if other firms attempt to copy its services, if it can maintain customer loyalty. This may depend on factors such as price, reliability, other additional services, etc.

- The long-term success of Pink Ladies may depend on external factors, e.g. increase in violent crime, changes in legislation.

B3 Data response

SuperJam
(25 marks; 35 minutes)

(Refer to question on pages 230–1 of textbook.)

1. Identify two factors that a company like SuperJam might take into account when choosing its suppliers. **(6)**

	Knowledge 3 marks	Application 3 marks
Level 2	**3 marks** Good understanding of the subject content.	**3 marks** Answer is applied effectively to the specific case.
Level 1	**2-1 marks** Shows some understanding of the subject content.	**2-1 marks** Some relationship to the scenario (perhaps indirectly).

Possible answers include:

- the cost and or quality of supplies

- the credit terms offered and discounts for regular or bulk buying

- flexibility in terms of delivery

2. SuperJam operates a system of quality control. Examine one potential advantage and one potential disadvantage of doing this. **(9)**

	Knowledge 3 marks	Application 3 marks	Analysis 3 marks
Level 2	**3 marks** Good understanding of the subject content.	**3 marks** Answer is applied effectively to the specific case.	**3 marks** Build-up of argument, making use of relevant business concepts.
Level 1	**2-1 marks** Shows some understanding of the subject content.	**2-1 marks** Some relationship to the scenario (perhaps indirectly).	**2-1 marks** Some build-up of argument, showing grasp of cause and effect.

- Possible advantages include:

  - Any sub-standard products are more likely to be spotted and intercepted before reaching the market (especially if production staff are not interested in quality), avoiding any bad publicity and the need to compensate customers.

  - Specialist staff can be appointed to take the responsibility for quality control, avoiding the need to train and create additional responsibilities for production staff.

• Disadvantages include:

– The extra cost of employing staff responsible for quality control, adding to the overall costs of the business.

– The cost of wasted materials in faulty products that cannot be recycled – again, adding to costs and increasing the need to hold increased stocks of raw materials.

3. Discuss the importance of maintaining high standards of quality for a small and growing business such as SuperJam. (**10**)

	Knowledge 2 marks	Application 2 marks	Analysis 3 marks	Evaluation 3 marks
Level 2	2 marks Good understanding of the subject content; or two answers identified.	2 marks Answer is applied effectively to the specific case.	3 marks Build-up of argument, making use of relevant business concepts.	3 marks Shows judgement in drawing conclusions from own argument.
Level 1	1 mark Some understanding of the subject content; or one answer identified.	1 mark Some relationship to the scenario (perhaps indirectly).	2-1 marks Some build-up of argument, showing grasp of cause and effect.	2-1 marks Some judgement shown in argument or weighting of language.

Possible answers include:

• Consistently high standards of quality will support an integrated marketing mix for a product charging a premium price and distributed through an up-market retailer, such as Waitrose.

• Consistently high standards of quality should give the product a unique selling point and help a small business such as SuperJam break into a market dominated by much bigger companies.

However:

• How easy will it be for the company to maintain such high standards as it continues to increase production?

37.1 Introduction

You are likely to be tackling this material three or more months after going through market research. Therefore an early task will be a revision test on market research – not too searching, but getting at the basic terms and concepts from the earlier work. You will want to make it clear to them that there is no such thing as effective marketing without market research.

Almost all the material in the following units will be familiar to you. More difficult is when it is also familiar to the students. Topics such as Promotion or the Product Life Cycle need to be given quite a tough edge to empower the students in an exam situation. Common sense answers will be the bête noire of the examiners, so your job becomes harder. How much better to be able to quote Peter Drucker (see 37.2) in support of an argument.

When you get to the end of the section on marketing, make sure to return to the issue of defining the term. What *really* is meant by marketing? If the students think there's an obvious answer to the question, they're probably wrong. Many of the key issues are raised in Exercise B2 (which I'd especially recommend, Ed.)

37.2 Further reading and resources

Title and price	Author(s)	Publisher and ISBN	Brief account
Essentials of Marketing £32.99	Blythe, J.	Prentice Hall 2005 978 027 369 3581	The chapter on market research is practical and accessible. It doesn't explain different sampling methods, but apart from this is a very good match for the Spec
The Five Most Important Questions You Will Ever Ask About Your Organization £7.99	Drucker, P.	Jossey Bass 2008 978 0 470 225756 5	Short, sweet and powerful, especially 'Who is our customer' and 'What does our customer value?'.
The Economist Guide to Management Ideas and Gurus £20.00	Hindle, T.	Profile Books 2008 978 1 84668 108 0	Three hundred pages of 1-2 page accounts that help to fill in holes, e.g. branding, cannibalisation (no longer on the Spec, but an invaluable concept), differentiation (ditto!), niche markets, product life cycle and USP.

50 Management Ideas you Really Need to Know £8.99	Russell-Walling, E.	Quercus Publishing plc 2008 978 1 84724 009 5	Two hundred pages, so again it's 2 pages per topic; worth the money for 'the 4 Ps of marketing'; also Boston matrix and market segmentation.
Business Case Studies 3rd Edition £17.99	Marcouse, I. and Lines, D.	Longman 2002 0 582 40636-6	Case Studies 3, 6, 7, 12, 42 and 60 are still well worth using.
Fashion Marketing £22.95	Easey, M.	Blackwell 2008 978 0632 051 991	Marketing concepts applied to the fashion industry. Worth getting for Chapter 5 alone: Segmentation and the Marketing Mix. Pricey but worth it.

37.3 Answers to workbook questions

A Revision questions

(30 marks; 30 minutes)

1. In your own words, explain the meaning of the term 'marketing'. (**3**)

   • The all-embracing function that links the company with customer tastes to get the right product to the right place at the right time. (*A-Z Business Studies Handbook*)

2. Explain why some firms choose not to carry out market research. (**3**)

   • If a sole trader is coming into contact daily with customers, there may be little more that can be learned (as long as the sole trader is capable of listening effectively to negative comments).

3. Why do you think most firms decide to review their marketing strategy at fairly regular intervals? (**3**)

   • Marketing strategy hinges on three things: the objectives (which may change), the resources (which may be cut or increased) and the external environment, e.g. fashions may change or recessionary gloom may lift.

4. What is meant by the phrase 'target market'? (**2**)

   • The characteristics of the customers who represent the firm's main opportunity for sales, e.g. Stena Stairlifts at over-70s who live in houses.

5. Outline two reasons why it is important for firms to be able to identify their target market. (**4**)

   • To focus their marketing budget on the people most likely to buy.

   • To know where and how to distribute the products, e.g. Fat Face or Debenhams.

6a Distinguish between a production-orientated and a market-orientated approach to marketing. **(3)**

• A market-orientated approach will focus on what the customer wants and what the competitors offer, then design a product to meet that perceived need.

• A production-orientated approach will design the 'right' product, then try to sell it to customers. (And don't knock it; travellers should want a production-orientated, safety-conscious ferry business or airline, rather than one that is focused on the superficial aspects of customer service.)

6b Outline whether a production-orientated or market-orientated approach would be better for *one* of the following companies:

(a) Manchester United FC

(b) easyJet

(c) Topshop **(4)**

• e.g. Topshop: this is a tough question; a market-orientated Topshop might focus on fashion, speed-to-market and cost (and therefore price), because these are usually their customers' priorities. Yet ignoring the working conditions of its suppliers' Cambodian garment workers may result in extremely bad publicity. A paternalistic, production-orientated approach might be better in the long run.

7. Explain how market segmentation has helped companies such as BSkyB to improve their profitability. **(4)**

• By targeting niches such as kids, oldies or clubbers, BSkyB is able to increase its audience figures and make its advertising more attractive to advertisers (if you're advertising Thomas the Tank Engine games, you'd pay much more for an audience of 50,000 3-6 year-old boys than you would for 50,000 people in general).

8. What are the marketing advantages of not having a specialised marketing department? **(4)**

• Marketing is everyone's job – because every job in the organisation depends on customers, whether it's a school, a shop or a hospital.

• Without a specialised marketing department, everyone would need to go out regularly to meet and learn about the customers.

B1 Discussion point

The role of chance/luck
(Refer to question on page 236 of textbook.)

1. From your reading the text, is it really true that all Morgan's success is down to luck?

• Could be luck; in very few markets does nostalgia really translate into regular purchasing; Morgan Cars may have decided not to change due to lack of capital or lack of enterprise, and been lucky that it looks clever with hindsight.

- But it may just be that the managers understood the car buyer better than others, and were right to see the attractions of a very traditional British car.

2. What marketing problems might the business face if it attempts to expand?

- It will soon need to move away from its familiar market niche – perhaps targeting City traders with dough instead of people in posh families; this may prove very difficult (especially as City traders may regard the Morgan as a hot number one year, but a has-been the next).

- It will need a much bigger marketing budget, but the staff may lack the skills to use the budget effectively (as they usually rely on word-of-mouth).

B2 Case study

Wimbledon Quality Cars

(30 marks; 35 minutes)

(Refer to question on pages 236–7 of textbook.)

1. According to Roger, 'Marketing is just a set of tools to sell more products'. Explain the possible drawbacks of this approach (7)

	Knowledge 2 marks	Application 2 marks	Analysis 3 marks
Level 2	**2 marks** Good understanding of the subject content.	**2 marks** Answer is applied effectively to the specific case.	**3 marks** Build-up of argument, making use of relevant business concepts.
Level 1	**1 mark** Shows some understanding of the subject content.	**1 mark** Some relationship to the scenario (perhaps indirectly).	**2-1 marks** Some build-up of argument, showing grasp of cause and effect.

Possible answers include:

- Effective long-term marketing should be about building sufficient understanding of your customers that you build your business around them, e.g. effective marketing for Manchester United is not about advertisements and logos, it's about hanging on to Ronaldo for as long as he's the world's most exciting player.

- For Roger, the focus on selling appears to have led him to fail to ask exactly how and what was being sold.

An Introduction to Effective Marketing

2. How would you describe WQC's marketing philosophy? Is it production orientated or is it market orientated? **(7)**

	Knowledge 2 marks	Application 2 marks	Analysis 3 marks
Level 2	**2 marks** Good understanding of the subject content.	**2 marks** Answer is applied effectively to the specific case.	**3 marks** Build-up of argument, making use of relevant business concepts.
Level 1	**1 mark** Shows some understanding of the subject content.	**1 mark** Some relationship to the scenario (perhaps indirectly).	**2-1 marks** Some build-up of argument, showing grasp of cause and effect.

Possible answers include:

• Probably market orientated; they have identified a niche in 'cheap runaround' cars and are supplying that niche; Roger's concern is not for the cars (he perhaps doesn't even like cars), it's purely for the customer's money.

• However you could argue that the issue is not market v production orientation but a failure to (a) have reasonably high ethical standards or (b) to understand that, in the long run, business is very difficult if you have a poor reputation; even Dixons was rumbled eventually.

3. Using the example of WQC, explain why an unethical approach towards marketing can often yield profitable results in the short term. **(8)**

	Knowledge 2 marks	Application 3 marks	Analysis 3 marks
Level 2	**2 marks** Good understanding of the subject content.	**3 marks** Answer is applied effectively to the specific case.	**3 marks** Build-up of argument, making use of relevant business concepts.
Level 1	**1 mark** Shows some understanding of the subject content.	**2-1 marks** Some relationship to the scenario (perhaps indirectly).	**2-1 marks** Some build-up of argument, showing grasp of cause and effect.

Possible answers include:

• A cynical approach to selling can be very successful in the short term, especially in circumstances where the customers did not know how to judge the value of what they are being sold (in August 2008 six garage chains were fined £175,000 for mis-selling worthless Payment Protection Insurance to their customers).

- In the case of WQC, the profits can keep coming for quite a few years, especially if buyers are too embarrassed to tell friends of their awful purchase.

4. Outline two internal and two external factors that might affect the effectiveness of WQC's marketing. (8)

Knowledge 4 marks		Application 4 marks
Level 2	**4-3 marks** One mark for each relevant factor identified.	**4-3 marks** Answer is applied effectively to the specific case.
Level 1	**2-1 marks** Shows some understanding of the subject content.	**2-1 marks** Some relationship to the scenario (perhaps indirectly).

- Internal factors include:

  - Budget: the ability to afford £300 a week (especially if local papers put their prices up, i.e. less advertising for £300)

  - How well the advertisements are written and where they are placed in the papers; Roger knows how to do this, but an illness might force someone else to take on the job, yet be much less good at it.

- External factors include:

  - Whether WQC's rivals are in a good position to exploit the TV programme, e.g. run an advertising campaign locally: 'Come to Honest Jo's for genuine, quality cars'.

  - If a smarter car showroom was to open close to Roger's 'old, run-down' one, this might reduce significantly the ability of WQC to persuade customers to buy from them.

Niche versus Mass Marketing

38.1 Introduction

The contrast between niche and mass markets and marketing provides a huge opportunity for every student to lift her/his answers from common sense into technical language. Whereas the language of price elasticity is inaccessible to some students, none will struggle with niche marketing. The problem is that so few use the terminology we teach them.

When they start with us, students think that marketing is about selling more goods. They also assume that more sales = more profits (forgetting that it depends on the price being charged). Niche marketing is both a more sophisticated approach – linking in with value added and price elasticity – and a section of accessible theory that can be revised effectively.

With all the above in mind, it is wise to treat this topic with care, i.e. use either B1 or B2 in class and set the other material for homework. Also see the note below on Case 6 in *Business Case Studies*.

38.2 Further reading and resources

Title and price	Author(s)	Publisher and ISBN	Brief account
Even More Offensive Marketing	Davidson, H.	Penguin 1997 0 14 025691 1	This is an outstanding book, highly readable, full of cases, but fundamentally analytic and academic. There is a short section on niche marketing on pages 276-9 and a whole chapter on segmentation.
In Search of Excellence £9.99	Peters, J. and Waterman, R.	Profile Books 2004 1 861 97716 6	There are a half dozen pages explicitly on 'Nichemanship' in the chapter called 'Close to the Customer'.
Business Case Studies 3rd Edition £17.99	Marcouse, I. and Lines, D.	Longman 2002 0 582 40636-6	Case Study 6 is the Coca-Cola story – a bit long, but it's still interesting, and very pertinent re the company's switch from its original 'One pack, one price' philosophy to today's niche marketing.

In addition, the following websites may be helpful.

Site	Web address	Brief account
Marketing Magazine	www.marketing.haynet.com/others.htm	Very nicely set out gateway to other marketing-related sites, such as advertising agencies, Key Notes and the National Readership Survey. Also a good source of latest stories, some of which will fit into the mass v niche category.
Marketing Week Magazine	www.marketing-week.co.uk	Up-to-date stories, largely derived from the latest magazine. Useful to gain information on strategies such as mass v niche marketing.
Key Notes (market intelligence data)	www.keynote.co.uk	Provides free access to the Executive Summaries of many Key Note reports. Could provide data on market segments or niches.
Euromonitor (publishers of the respected Mintel source of secondary data)	www.euromonitor.com	Valuable top-line secondary research findings across a wide range of consumer markets. Can provide data for discussion on mass v niche strategies.

38.3 Answers to workbook questions

A Revision questions

(20 marks; 20 minutes)

1. Identify three advantages of niche marketing over mass marketing. **(3)**

    • niche markets can act as safe havens for small firms

    • niche brands can add value

    • identifying new niches provides growth opportunities

2. Give three reasons why a large firm may wish to enter a niche market. **(3)**

    • in order to diversify

• profit growth might be higher in a niche market

• as a defensive measure to combat a fast-growing niche market operator

3. Why may small firms be better at spotting and then reacting to new niche market opportunities? (3)

    • small firms might be closer to the market

    • out of necessity, they have to spot them in order to survive

4. Give two reasons why average prices in niche markets tend to be higher than those charged in most mass markets. (2)

    • Lower price elasticity of demand makes high prices possible.

    • Short production runs mean higher unit costs therefore, prices have to be higher.

5. Outline two reasons why information technology has made niche marketing a more viable option for large firms. (4)

    • Quick computer set-up can enable firms to produce small production runs more easily.

    • Selective mailing e.g. Tesco's use of its Clubcard database makes it more economic to target small niches.

6. Explain why it is important for a large firm to be flexible if it is to successfully operate in niche markets. (2)

    • Market conditions can change quickly therefore firms need to be flexible in order to adapt.

    • Production runs will need to be kept short therefore production will need to be flexible too.

    • Niche markets are often more fashion/change-sensitive.

7. In your own words, explain why the price elasticity of niche-market products may be lower than for products in the mass market. (3)

    • Products have low price elasticity when they face little direct competition; this is more likely in a small niche than in a mass market.

B1 Data response

The return of mass marketing
(40 marks; 45 minutes)

(Refer to question on pages 241–2 of textbook.)

1a What is a niche-market product? (2)

    • A product designed for a relatively small segment of a market, e.g. those with a particular passion for the environment.

Niche versus Mass Marketing

1b Explain why the Toyota Prius is a good example of a niche-market product. **(2)**

- Because it was designed to meet the wishes of a small segment of the worldwide car market; but in every country there are people willing to pay to have a more environmentally-friendly car.

2. Explain two reasons why the Indian car market has grown. **(4)**

- Income per head within India 'has grown rapidly'...

- ... from an extremely low base (7 cars per 1000 people), i.e. no question of market saturation.

3a What is a mass-market product? **(2)**

- One designed to appeal to as many people as possible, probably by making it attractive but not distinctive.

3b Explain why the 'People's car' is a good example of a mass-market product. **(4)**

- The People's car is designed to be sold for less than £1500, making it possible for ordinary (middle class) people to afford it.

- It is not designed to be special, simply cheap.

4. Analyse two advantages and two disadvantages for European car manufacturers, such as Renault, of mass marketing £2000 cars in India. **(8)**

	Knowledge 2 marks	Application 2 marks	Analysis 4 marks
Level 2	**2 marks** Good understanding of the subject content.	**2 marks** Answer is applied effectively to the specific case.	**4-3 marks** Build-up of argument, making use of relevant business concepts.
Level 1	**1 mark** Shows some understanding of the subject content.	**1 mark** Some relationship to the scenario (perhaps indirectly).	**2-1 marks** Some build-up of argument, showing grasp of cause and effect.

- Possible advantages include:

  – Get in early into a growth market of staggering potential (7 out of 1000 penetration means there's 993 to go amidst a population of nearly 1200 million.

  – Can provide the critical mass of high sales that makes it possible to get costs per unit down to the point where (a) a profit can be made and (b) it's hard for late-comers to compete.

- Possible disadvantages include:

  – Establishing a mass market image now may make it very difficult to appeal to the upper middle class.

– The image of Renault may always be 'downmarket' in India as a result of this – making it easy for German firms such as BMW and Mercedes to capture the Executive Car market of 2015.

5. £2000 pound cars can be profitably made in India. Explain why UK consumers are unlikely to benefit from similar low prices. **(4)**

   • Although it may be possible to deliver the cars to the UK for £2000, UK retailing and marketing costs will push the selling price up sharply; renting a UK car showroom would add hugely to the costs.

   • As the cheapest car in Britain at the moment costs more than £5000, Tata Motors would be likely to price their car at, say, £4500 rather than £2000 – to enjoy higher profit margins.

6. Discuss whether companies such as Tata Motors should take into account the concerns of environmentalists when making their business decisions. **(14)**

	Knowledge 3 marks	Application 3 marks	Analysis 4 marks	Evaluation 4 marks
Level 2	**3 marks** Good understanding of the subject content; or two answers identified.	**3 marks** Answer is applied effectively to the specific case.	**4-3 marks** Build-up of argument, making use of relevant business concepts.	**4-3 marks** Shows judgement in drawing conclusions from own argument.
Level 1	**2-1 marks** Some understanding of the subject content; or one answer identified.	**2-1 marks** Some relationship to the scenario (perhaps indirectly).	**2-1 marks** Some build-up of argument, showing grasp of cause and effect.	**2-1 marks** Some judgement shown in argument or weighting of language.

Possible answers include:

   • It depends where the environmentalists are from and what their perspective is; Western governments and individuals have no right to say 'OK, we became wealthy on the back of pollution and CO_2, but we don't think you should do the same (subtext: stay poor; not everyone can drive a BMW).

   • Local environmentalists might be able to persuade a car producer to cut environmental damage to a minimum, e.g. designing a higher level of fuel efficiency; this might be helpful to everyone.

   • Ultimately, though, wherever there's a trade-off between environment and jobs/profits/growth, the producer and the local population will always stand together against environmentalists; Tata has a greater duty to (all) its stakeholders than it does to environmental campaigners.

Niche versus Mass Marketing

B2 Data response

Winter melon tea
(30 marks; 35 minutes)

(Refer to question on page 242 of textbook.)

1a What is a niche market product? (**2**)

  • a product designed for one type of customer

1b Explain why Asian traditional drinks are examples of niche-market products. (**3**)

  • they are designed for the tastes of a small section of the community

2. Explain two ways in which the producers of traditional drinks, such as winter melon tea and grass jelly drink, created product differentiation. (**4**)

  • created an image as healthier than Coke and Pepsi

  • use nationalism ('Asian Heritage') to differentiate them from the American brands

3. Niche-market products are normally more expensive than most mass-market products. Using the example of traditional Asian drinks, explain why this is usually so? (**7**)

	Knowledge 2 marks	Application 2 marks	Analysis 3 marks
Level 2	2 marks Good understanding of the subject content.	2 marks Answer is applied effectively to the specific case.	3 marks Build-up of argument, making use of relevant business concepts.
Level 1	1 mark Shows some understanding of the subject content.	1 mark Some relationship to the scenario (perhaps indirectly).	1 mark Some build-up of argument, showing grasp of cause and effect.

Possible advantages include:

  • Unit costs may be higher, perhaps because they aren't being made in such high production runs.

  • Even if the unit costs were no higher, the producers may find that they are able to push prices up, no matter what the production cost, because the price elasticity is lower.

4. Discuss whether the local producers of Asian traditional drinks will be able to survive in the long term given that their products now have to compete against me-too brands produced by foreign multinationals such as Coca-Cola and Pepsi. (**14**)

Niche versus Mass Marketing

	Knowledge 3 marks	Application 3 marks	Analysis 4 marks	Evaluation 4 marks
Level 2	**3 marks** Good understanding of the subject content; or two answers identified.	**3 marks** Answer is applied effectively to the specific case.	**4-3 marks** Build-up of argument, making use of relevant business concepts.	**4-3 marks** Shows judgement in drawing conclusions from own argument.
Level 1	**2-1 marks** Some understanding of the subject content; or one answer identified.	**2-1 marks** Some relationship to the scenario (perhaps indirectly).	**2-1 marks** Some build-up of argument, showing grasp of cause and effect.	**2-1 marks** Some judgement shown in argument or weighting of language.

Possible answers include:

- It will depend on whether the local firms have built sufficient brand loyalty to mean that the US rivals are cut out.

- It will depend on the financial circumstances of the local producers – or whether they find new backers with deep enough pockets to finance the hole.

- The likely truth is that Coke and Pepsi will steadily carve out a bigger share of the market, but as long as the market grows in size it should be possible for the smaller local suppliers to keep enough market share to survive.

Designing an Effective Marketing Mix Unit **39**

39.1 Introduction

Perhaps surprisingly, the 2008 Specification has built up the role of the marketing mix still further. That forces us to find a way to move it forward from GCSE. The title of the unit, of course, is 'Designing an *Effective* Marketing Mix' and there's the rub. Students can say what a marketing mix is, but rarely apply it effectively to different business situations. To many, prices should always be cut 'to sell more', ignoring the possibility that the sales may be unprofitable; ditto, more advertising is always seen as a good thing – perhaps TV, maybe, which would certainly increase the turnover at the local chippie, though fatally.

There is simply no substitute for up-to-date cases. *The Grocer* magazine is always worth buying in the weeks you're teaching marketing, as its inside knowledge gives you some thought-provoking discussion lessons. The time to discuss the marketing of Coffee KitKat is at launch, not with the benefit of hindsight.

39.2 Further reading and resources

Title and price	Author(s)	Publisher and ISBN	Brief account
Essentials of Marketing £32.99	Blythe, J.	Prentice Hall 2005 978 027 369 3581	The chapter on marketing strategy is very effective. Definitely for staff not students.
The Five Most Important Questions You Will Ever Ask About Your Organization £7.99	Drucker, P.	Jossey Bass 2008 978 0 470 225756 5	Short, sweet and powerful, especially: 'Who is our customer' and 'What does our customer value?'
50 Management Ideas you Really Need to Know £8.99	Russell-Walling, E.	Quercus Publishing plc 2008 978 1 84724 009 5	Two hundred pages, so again it's 2 pages per topic; worth the money for 'the 4 Ps of Marketing'; also Boston Matrix and market segmentation.
Business Case Studies 3rd Edition £17.99	Marcouse, I. and Lines, D.	Longman 2002 0 582 40636-6	Case Study 3 (Marketing McDonalds) is another ageing classic. Worth using as it's a constant reminder of the power of marketing.

Designing an Effective Marketing Mix   Unit 39

Fashion Marketing £22.95	Easey, M.	Blackwell 2008 978-1405139533	Marketing concepts applied to the fashion industry. Worth getting for Chapter 5 alone: 'Segmentation and the Marketing Mix'. Pricey but worth it.

39.3 Answers to workbook questions

A Revision questions

(30 marks; 30 minutes)

1. Briefly outline each of the four ingredients of the marketing mix. (8)

    • Two marks for an outline of each of the four ingredients – product, promotion, price, place.

2. Pick the marketing mix factor (the 'P') you think is of most importance in marketing any two of the following brands. Give a brief explanation of why you chose that factor.

    (a) *The Sun* newspaper

    (b) The iPod

    (c) Cadbury's Creme Eggs

    (d) A top-of-the-range BMW (6)

    • Perhaps: Sun = Price; iPod = Product; Crème Eggs = Place (impulse purchase); BMW = Product

3. Outline how the marketing mix for Mars bars may affect their level of impulse sales in a small corner shop. (4)

    • Well-known product: brand may attract impulse purchaser.

    • Price compared to other similar products.

    • Place: product may be easy to see.

    • Promotion: advertising may help to recall the product.

    Credit should be given for understanding of the nature of an impulse buy.

4. What is meant by a market segment? (3)

    • A market segment is a distinct part of the main market, i.e. more mainstream than a niche.

5. Explain why new products are so important to businesses. (**3**)

   • Can generate new markets/customers.

   • Help to keep a brand alive.

   • Generate new income when existing products are in the mature stage.

6. List three different ways of promoting a product. (**3**)

   • point of sale

   • direct mailing

   • advertising

   • web promotion

7. Explain why it might be difficult for a new, small firm to get distribution in a supermarket chain such as Sainsbury's. (**3**)

   • Limited shelf space means that new/small firms may not be able to negotiate shelf space.

   • Small firms may be unable to meet quantity requirements.

   • Small firms with limited marketing budgets may find it difficult to get their products seen by the supermarkets.

B1 Case study

The battle for customers
(30 marks; 35 minutes)

(Refer to question on pages 248–9 of textbook.)

1. What is meant by 'the home market is saturated'? (**2**)

1 mark for a simple explanation such as 'too many suppliers'; 2 marks for a fuller explanation, such as 'too many suppliers fighting for a limited customer base'.

2. What are the marketing implications for a business in a saturated market? (**6**)

   • Constant competition for customers reduces margins as suppliers are forced to take marketing action such as additional promotion or pricing cuts.

   • This often results in price/competitive wars that are counter-productive.

   • Ways need to be found to differentiate the product(s), or new markets or customers need to be found.

3. Why might expansion allow economies of scale? (**4**)

   • Purchasing power will be greater so it can reduce purchasing costs.

- Distribution costs can be reduced by spreading over larger number of units.

- Fixed costs will be spread over larger sales volume, thereby reducing unit costs

4. What problems might a British retailer have in marketing its service in India? (6)

- Different cultures could mean that there is difficulty for the British firm in understanding the market.

- British firm may have difficulty in obtaining products and ensuring that usual levels of quality are maintained.

- Language difficulties.

- Possible staffing difficulties.

- As mentioned above, cost problems due to infrastructure and high cost of property.

- As in the case study, problems with competition from local stores.

5. Using the marketing mix, analyse the existing market and evaluate the UK firm's chances of success. (12)

	Knowledge 2 marks	Application 2 marks	Analysis 4 marks	Evaluation 4 marks
Level 2	2 marks Good understanding of the marketing mix.	2 marks Good points made about the existing market.	4-3 marks Good analysis of the existing market using the marketing mix.	4-3 marks Judgement shown with a conclusion on the likelihood of the firm's success.
Level 1	1 mark Some understanding of the mix.	1 mark Some understanding of the existing market.	2-1 marks Some analysis of the market.	2-1 marks Some judgement shown on the likelihood of success.

Possible answers include:

- A market is saturated when supply has reached a point where all of the demand within the market has been satisfied, there is little, if any, chance of attracting new customers to the market and the only way for firms to increase their individual sales is by poaching customers from rivals.

Product and Product Differentiation Unit 40

40.1 Introduction

This is the only unit of this book that can be regarded as optional. Oddly, the term product differentiation is not mentioned at AS. It is regarded as an A2 marketing strategy. Yet that leaves the odd notion that students can learn effectively about marketing in general – and price elasticity in particular – without the term differentiation. This seems problematic. If there is a ten-mark question on how a firm might seek to reduce the price elasticity of its products, how can it be answered effectively without product differentiation?

So the unit is here to encourage people to teach differentiation in AS. Nevertheless if you had serious staffing problems, this would be the first unit to drop.

For homework, the ideal combination is Section A plus B1.

40.2 Further reading and resources

Title and price	Author(s)	Publisher and ISBN	Brief account
Essentials of Marketing £32.99	Blythe, J.	Prentice Hall 2005 978 027 369 3581	Terrific reference book on all marketing topics, including ways to achieve effective differentiation.
The Five Most Important Questions You Will Ever Ask About Your Organization £7.99	Drucker, P.	Jossey Bass 2008 978 0 470 225756 5	Short, sweet and powerful, especially: 'Who is our customer' and 'What does our customer value?'
The Economist Guide to Management Ideas and Gurus £20.00	Hindle, T.	Profile Books 2008 978 1 84668 108 0	Three hundred pages of 1-2 page accounts that help to fill in holes, e.g. branding, differentiation, niche markets, product life cycle and USP.
50 Management Ideas you Really Need to Know £8.99	Russell-Walling, E.	Quercus Publishing plc 2008 978 1 84724 009 5	Two hundred pages, so again it's 2 pages per topic; worth the money for 'the 4 Ps of marketing'; also market segmentation.

Even More Offensive Marketing	Davidson, H.	Penguin 1997, 0 14 025691 1	This is an outstanding book, highly readable, full of cases, but fundamentally analytic and academic. In effect, the whole book is about differentiation (standing out from the crowd).
Pricing Strategies for Small Business £10.99	Gregson, A.	Self-Counsel Press 2008 978 1551 807 973	Cancel all other book orders until you've bought this book! Chapter 4 is terrific on 'Positioning for Price – the role of the USP'. This book's a gem.

40.3 Answers to workbook questions

A Revision questions

(40 marks; 40 minutes)

1. Outline two reasons that might explain the success of products such as Coca-Cola and Stella Artois. **(4)**

    • clearly differentiated brands

    • sustained marketing commitment to these brands over many decades

2. Analyse how training might be used to improve the quality of the product produced by a service sector business such as a supermarket. **(3)**

    • More polite, warmer dealings with customers.

    • Greater efficiency might speed up till service and therefore reduce queuing times.

3. Explain how technological advances can influence the direction of new product development. **(3)**

    • New technology can provide huge opportunities to a business smart enough and quick enough to develop a new product (e.g. Apple turned 'flash memory' into the iPod).

4. What is the first-mover advantage? State two benefits firms receive if they can achieve the first-mover advantage. **(4)**

- It is the benefit that comes from being the first product into a new market, e.g. the first company into hand-held consoles was Nintendo.

- Benefits: can charge higher prices before competitors arrive; the reputation as the first-mover (the 'real thing') can confer image benefits, e.g. Coke v Pepsi.

5. What is a me-too product and why do some firms choose to launch them? (4)

- A me-too is a copy of an original product, though often with a subtle tweak to try and make it seem different, e.g. longer battery life.

- May help to stop the progress of your rival, to avoid them becoming too profitable; may lead to success, e.g. Innocent Drinks, who stole the idea of Smoothies from 'PJ Smoothies'.

6. Explain the meaning of the term product differentiation, using your own example. (4)

- The extent to which customers perceive one product as being different from rivals, e.g. Skoda has a distinctly different image from other mass-market car brands.

7. Outline two ways in which a clothes shop might differentiate itself from its competitors. (6)

- It might use loud music and loud décor to mark it out from rivals.

- It might showcase local clothes designers to show that it's not just another branch of a chain such as Topshop.

8. Explain two benefits a firm can gain from selling a differentiated product. (4)

- Higher prices as distinctiveness adds value.

- Less vulnerable to the actions of competitors as your own products are seen as distinctly different, e.g. sales of Minis would be unaffected by price cuts or promotions on the Ford car range.

9. Why is it particularly helpful to have a product that is differentiated by a USP? (4)

- A USP is the ultimate in differentiation; it isn't just different, it's unique! That strengthens its ability to command a higher price.

10. Outline two examples of USPs in current products or services you buy. (4)

- Obviously will change over time, but:

  - Bounty – *A Taste of Paradise* (well, over-sweetened coconut, anyway)

  - Maltesers – *The Lighter Way to Enjoy Chocolate* (yum)

B1 Data response

(25 marks; 30 minutes)

(Refer to question on page 253 of textbook.)

1a Define the term 'unique selling point' (**2**)

  • Highlighting a feature of the product that is unique, i.e. no rival has the same consumer benefit.

1b Identify the original unique selling point that made San Paulo a successful business in South America (**2**)

  • the Italian coffee bar in Brazil

2. Using the data in the case as a starting point, discuss whether constant innovation is required to maintain product differentiation. (**12**)

	Knowledge 2 marks	Application 2 marks	Analysis 4 marks	Evaluation 4 marks
Level 2	2 marks Good understanding of the subject content.	2 marks Answer is applied effectively to the specific case.	4-3 marks Build-up of argument, making use of relevant business concepts.	4-3 marks Shows judgement in drawing conclusions from own argument.
Level 1	1 mark Some understanding of the subject content.	1 mark Some relationship to the scenario (perhaps indirectly).	2-1 marks Some build-up of argument, showing grasp of cause and effect.	2-1 marks Some judgement shown in argument or weighting of language.

Possible answers include:

  • The issue is that – ultimately – everything that differentiates a product or service can be copied; most of San Paulo's original USP (classic Italian interior design) has been copied by rivals, so the uniqueness has been eroded.

  • Accordingly, it may be that constant innovation is needed to keep ahead of the competition; a famous business quote from the boss of Intel (microchips) is that 'only the paranoid survive', i.e. unless you're always looking over your shoulder wondering who's out to get you, you won't see them coming.

3. You have been hired to manage the new bar in Croydon. Despite your concerns about the strength of the competition locally, your English boss wants you to charge high prices. Outline three ways that could be used to create the high product differentiation required for your coffee bar. (**9**)

- Emphasise the South American heritage instead of the Italian one; there are too many Italian coffee bars such as Caffe Nero and Costa's.

- Offer a range of eats that is completely different from rivals, perhaps including South American tortillas and South American hot chocolate.

- Create a culture of generosity among staff, from free coffee refills to free delivery locally, no matter how low the order size.

B2 Data response

Absolut Vodka

(30 marks; 35 minutes)

(Refer to question on page 254 of textbook.)

1. What is a premium priced product? **(2)**

    - One that sells well even when its price is above the level of its competitors. This would not be possible for Ryanair flights or Kingsmill bread.

2. Explain why product differentiation can create premium prices **(6)**

	Knowledge 2 marks	Application 2 marks	Analysis 2 marks
Level 2	**2 marks** Good understanding of the subject content.	**2 marks** Answer is applied effectively to the specific case.	**2 marks** Build-up of argument, making use of relevant business concepts.
Level 1	**1 mark** Shows some understanding of the subject content.	**1 mark** Some relationship to the scenario (perhaps indirectly).	**1 mark** Some build-up of argument, showing grasp of cause and effect.

Possible answers include:

- Differentiation makes premium prices possible, as no one would pay a price premium if they could buy the same from a rival at a lower price.

- Yet differentiation does not always create the opportunity for higher prices; a lime-green BMW would be different, but most people might dislike it and therefore pay no more then the standard price.

3. Outline two factors that might influence the direction of new product development in the alcoholic drinks industry (**6**)

	Knowledge 3 marks		Application 3 marks
Level 2	**3 marks** Good understanding of the subject content.		**3 marks** Answer is applied effectively to the specific case.
Level 1	**2-1 marks** Shows some understanding of the subject content.		**2-1 marks** Some relationship to the scenario (perhaps indirectly).

Possible answers include:

• Increasing concerns about young people's drinking habits: this might lead producers to be far more wary about designing fun, young drinks such as WKD.

• Britain has always had a good level of import and export trade in alcoholic drinks. If the £ continued to be low in value it would be worth developing more drinks for export.

4. Analyse two ways in product differentiation was created for the Absolut brand (**6**)

	Knowledge 2 marks	Application 2 marks	Analysis 2 marks
Level 2	**2 marks** Good understanding of the subject content.	**2 marks** Answer is applied effectively to the specific case.	**2 marks** Build-up of argument, making use of relevant business concepts.
Level 1	**1 mark** Shows some understanding of the subject content.	**1 mark** Some relationship to the scenario (perhaps indirectly).	**1 mark** Some build-up of argument, showing grasp of cause and effect.

Possible answers include:

• To create the award-winning bottle design and therefore make it distinctive.

• Creating the image as a 400-year-old 'heritage' brand.

Product and Product Differentiation Unit 40

5. Discuss the ethics of the marketing of Absolut vodka. **(10)**

	Knowledge 2 marks	Application 2 marks	Analysis 3 marks	Evaluation 3 marks
Level 2	**2 marks** Good understanding of the subject content.	**2 marks** Answer is applied effectively to the specific case.	**3 marks** Build-up of argument, making use of relevant business concepts.	**3 marks** Shows judgement in drawing conclusions from own argument.
Level 1	**1 mark** Some understanding of the subject content.	**1 mark** Some relationship to the scenario (perhaps indirectly).	**2-1 marks** Some build-up of argument, showing grasp of cause and effect.	**2-1 marks** Some judgement shown in argument or weighting of language.

Possible answers include:

- Among the more minor matters, the goal from the off was to create the impression that the flavour and purity of the brand was exceptional (whereas it wasn't really).

- More crucially is the moral question about the ethics of marketing (or producing) an alcoholic drink that will be abused by some people, leading to drink-drive deaths, fights or whatever; the fact that the brand is marketed so stylishly just makes the situation worse.

41.1 Introduction

For most of the period 1990-2005 sales of frozen food were melting away. It was clear that the sector was in terminal decline as sales of chilled food raced ahead. So Unilever decided to dispose of its Birds Eye frozen food empire. It announced this strategic move in early 2005 and by August 2006 had clinched the sale of the business. From about the time of signing the deal, the market swung back in the direction of frozen food. Now it's Iceland that's leading the way in food retail, with like-for-like sales of 12-15%. And Birds Eye reports a resurgence of interest as people have finally realised that frozen may be 'fresher' than chilled food. The moral of the story is, of course: don't treat the product life cycle (or the Boston Matrix) in a deterministic way. Both are interesting and helpful models of what usually happens, but neither is a substitute for applied thought.

Within the Workbook, Section A and B1 are probably the outstanding picks.

41.2 Further reading and resources

Title and price	Author(s)	Publisher and ISBN	Brief account
The Five Most Important Questions You Will Ever Ask About Your Organization £7.99	Drucker, P.	Jossey Bass 2008 978 0 470 225756 5	Short, sweet and powerful, especially: 'Who is our customer' and 'What does our customer value?'.
Fashion Marketing £22.95	Easey, M.	Blackwell 2008 978-1 40513 953 3	Marketing concepts applied to the fashion industry. Pages 129–133 are on product life cycle; super stuff, especially the diagram on p133.
The Economist Guide to Management Ideas and Gurus £20.00	Hindle, T.	Profile Books 2008 978 1 84668 108 0	Three hundred pages of 1-2 page accounts that help to fill in holes, e.g. cannibalisation (no longer on the Spec, but an invaluable concept), differentiation (ditto!) and the product life cycle and USP.

Product Life Cycle and Portfolio Analysis

50 Management Ideas you Really Need to Know £8.99	Russell-Walling, E.	Quercus Publishing plc 2008 978 1 84724 009 5	Two hundred pages, so again it's 2 pages per topic; worth the money for 'the 4 Ps of marketing'; also Boston Matrix and market segmentation.
Business Case Studies 3rd Edition £17.99	Marcouse, I. and Lines, D.	Longman 2002 0 582 40636-6	Case Study 2 (PLC) and 7 (Boston Matrix) are the ones to go for.

41.3 Answers to workbook questions

A Revision questions

(35 marks; 35 minutes)

1. Identify the different stages of the product life cycle. Give an example of one product or service you consider to be at each stage of the life cycle. (4)

   • Introduction (HD DVD)

   • Growth (iPhone)

   • Maturity (Indian restaurants)

   • Decline (smoking)

2. Explain what is meant by an 'extension strategy'. (4)

   • medium-long term strategies for prolonging a product's profitable life, e.g. modifying the product or changing its image

3. Outline the likely relationship between cash flow and the different stages of the life cycle. (4)

   • Introduction (severely strained cash flow)

   • Growth (still strained, especially if growth is rapid)

   • Maturity (cash flow positive at last, perhaps substantially)

   • Decline (cash flow can be very positive, especially if the business is investing nothing into its declining product)

4. How is it possible for products such as the Barbie doll to apparently defy the decline phase of the product cycle? (6)

   • due to extension strategies. Also, some products seem to go beyond fashion and become part of growing up for every generation of children.

Product Life Cycle and Portfolio Analysis

5. What is meant by 'product portfolio analysis'? **(3)**

   • Assessing the position of a firm's products in terms of their market share and market growth.

6. Distinguish between a cash cow and a rising star in the Boston Matrix. **(4)**

   • A rising star has a high share of a growth market.

   • A cash cow has a high share of a static (or declining) market.

7. Explain how the Boston Matrix could be used by a business such as Cadbury. **(4)**

   • to assess the performance of each of its brands

   • to decide how to prioritise its marketing spending in the coming year

8. Firms should never take decline (or growth) for granted. Therefore they should never take success (or failure) for granted. Explain why this advice is important if firms are to make the best use of product life cycle theory. **(6)**

   • There is a danger that the life-cycle is self-fulfilling; if managers believe sales will decline they may fail to promote the products effectively. If, however, they assume the life cycle could be prolonged they might adopt policies which do actually increase or maintain sales. They should not assume sales will fall. Similarly they should not assume sales will grow or they may fail to take actions necessary to make this happen.

B1 Data response

Fire Angel

(30 marks; 35 minutes)

(Refer to question on pages 262–3 of textbook.)

1. What is meant by 'market growth'? **(2)**

   • an increase in the size of the market this year compared with last, either in volume or value terms

2. Outline the unique selling point of the Fire Angel and explain how this can benefit the business. **(6)**

   • USP: a smoke detector based on plug-in instead of battery; this makes the product a permanent life-saver.

   • The USP enabled the business to look at a £20 price tag instead of the £5–£10 charged by competitors, i.e. it added value.

3. Analyse the possible benefits to Sam of undertaking market research before launching the Fire Angel. **(7)**

	Knowledge 2 marks	Application 2 marks	Analysis 3 marks
Level 2	**2 marks** Good understanding of the subject content; or two answers identified.	**2 marks** Answer is applied effectively to the specific case.	**3 marks** Build-up of argument, making use of relevant business concepts.
Level 1	**1 mark** Shows some understanding of the subject content.	**1 mark** Some relationship to the scenario (perhaps indirectly).	**2-1 marks** Some build-up of argument, showing grasp of cause and effect.

Possible answers include:

- He needed to know not just whether there was a 'need' for this product, but also a desire to buy it.

- It may have made it easier to persuade the retailers to stock the product if research had shown it to be attractive.

- Research might have shown him ways to improve the name or the packaging.

4. Explain why Sam might have had cash flow problems in the first few years of his business. **(6)**

	Knowledge 2 marks	Application 2 marks	Analysis 2 marks
Level 2	**2 marks** Good understanding of the subject content; or two answers identified.	**2 marks** Answer is applied effectively to the specific case.	**2 marks** Build-up of argument, making use of relevant business concepts.
Level 1	**1 mark** Shows some understanding of the subject content.	**1 mark** Some relationship to the scenario (perhaps indirectly).	**1 mark** Some build-up of argument, showing grasp of cause and effect.

Possible answers include:

- It took three years to get from the idea to a product ready to launch; then more months persuading retailers to stock it – in all that time, no money would have been coming in from sales.

- Even when retailers receive the Fire Angels, they'll take another stretch of time to pay.

5. At the moment the Fire Angel is still in its growth phase. Discuss the ways in which the marketing mix of the Fire Angel might change as it enters the maturity phase (9)

	Knowledge 2 marks	Application 2 marks	Analysis 2 marks	Evaluation 3 marks
Level 2	**2 marks** Good understanding of the subject content; or two answers identified.	**2 marks** Answer is applied effectively to the specific case.	**2 marks** Build-up of argument, making use of relevant business concepts.	**3 marks** Shows judgement in drawing conclusions from own argument.
Level 1	**1 mark** Some understanding of the subject content; or one answer identified.	**1 mark** Some relationship to the scenario (perhaps indirectly).	**1 mark** Some build-up of argument, showing grasp of cause and effect.	**2-1 marks** Some judgement shown in argument or weighting of language.

Possible answers include:

- In the early stages, the focus must be on gaining awareness of the product and what it does; later, the need may be to fight off competition, if others arrive on the market; in that case, branding will be important.

- There will also be a need to look for extension strategies for the Fire Angel or some completely new products.

- Pricing may change as well. Quite often, people start with quite low prices, wanting to maximise sales, but later choose to push the price up, especially if the brand 'Fire Angel' has achieved its own recognition. In effect, pushing the price up would be a way to milk the product, i.e. to treat it as a cash cow.

B2 Data response

Mackie's ice cream

(30 marks; 35 minutes)

(Refer to question on page 263 of textbook.)

(Refer to question on page 263 of textbook.)

1. What is meant by the term 'market share'? (2)

- the percentage of total sales in a market achieved by one brand or business

2. Explain the factors that Mackie might have considered before expanding its capacity. **(5)**

	Knowledge 2 marks	Application 3 marks
Level 2	**2 marks** Good understanding of the subject content; or two answers identified.	**3 marks** Answer is applied effectively to the specific case.
Level 1	**1 mark** Shows some understanding of the subject content.	**2-1 marks** Some relationship to the scenario (perhaps indirectly).

Possible answers:

- the cost of the extra capacity and the cost of financing it (e.g. interest rates if the money was borrowed)

- the opportunity cost of the capital

- the level of demand and therefore how well the extra capacity might be used

3. Explain how the promotion of a new Mackie's ice cream might vary at different stages in its life cycle. **(5)**

	Knowledge 2 marks	Application 3 marks
Level 2	**2 marks** Good understanding of the subject content; or two answers identified.	**3 marks** Answer is applied effectively to the specific case.
Level 1	**1 mark** Shows some understanding of the subject content.	**2-1 marks** Some relationship to the scenario (perhaps indirectly).

Possible answers:

- At the introductory stage the key would be awareness-raising advertising, first to the trade (e.g. *The Grocer* magazine) and then to potential customers.

- To help growth, it would be necessary to find more new customers who had not tried the product.

- During the maturity phase it would be more economic to encourage existing customers to buy more frequently than to keep trying to find new customers.

4. Examine the possible benefits to Mackie of having a portfolio of products (8)

	Knowledge 2 marks	Application 2 marks	Analysis 4 marks
Level 2	**2 marks** Good understanding of the subject content; or two answers identified.	**2 marks** Answer is applied effectively to the specific case.	**4-3 marks** Build-up of argument, making use of relevant business concepts.
Level 1	**1 mark** Shows some understanding of the subject content.	**1 mark** Some relationship to the scenario (perhaps indirectly).	**2-1 marks** Some build-up of argument, showing grasp of cause and effect.

Possible answers include:

• The idea of a portfolio is to help a business get round the two forces that determine success: the product life cycle and the way that different niches grow at different rates – totally outside your own control.

• If you have only one product you will inevitably suffer as and when its product life cycle starts to turn downwards.

• The Boston Matrix shows the need to have a range of brands, with at least some that are rising stars or have the potential to become so.

5. Consider whether new product development is likely to be essential for success in the ice cream market. (10)

	Knowledge 2 marks	Application 2 marks	Analysis 3 marks	Evaluation 3 marks
Level 2	**2 marks** Good understanding of the subject content.	**2 marks** Answer is applied effectively to the specific case.	**3 marks** Build-up of argument, making use of relevant business concepts.	**3 marks** Shows judgement in drawing conclusions from own argument.
Level 1	**1 mark** Some understanding of the subject content.	**1 mark** Some relationship to the scenario (perhaps indirectly).	**2-1 marks** Some build-up of argument, showing grasp of cause and effect.	**2-1 marks** Some judgement shown in argument or weighting of language.

Product Life Cycle and Portfolio Analysis

Possible answers include:

- Yes, because customers like to try new flavours and like to associate with a producer that has some innovative flair; furthermore, although some flavours last for ever, e.g. vanilla and chocolate, many are enjoyed for a time, but then lose their appeal, e.g. Bailey's ice cream.

- No, because although new flavours are fun, the vast majority of people like to buy the flavours they've always bought. So there will always be room in the market for a classic ice cream producer that concentrates on producing fantastic vanilla, chocolate and strawberry ice creams.

Promotion

42.1 Introduction

The major issue with promotion is to move students away from only thinking about advertising and to get them to think more widely about other ways of promoting the product or business. It is also important to stress that the methods of promotion suggested in a case study or data response section should be appropriate for the business. A small new business is unlikely to be able to afford a TV advertising campaign. A good way to start is to analyse the business and its promotional needs and then try to find a method of promotion that suits the business in its particular market.

Although the AS is not about objectives and strategy, it is difficult to understand promotion without realising that firms require more from marketing than simply selling more goods. Sometimes the key is to find a way to reposition a brand so that it appeals to a younger demographic. Promotion is successful, of course, when it helps to achieve the business objectives.

In this unit, the Section A questions plus B1 will provide a very worthwhile homework.

42.2 Further reading and resources

Magazines such as *Marketing Week, Sales Promotion,* and *The Grocer* provide up-to-date articles that are useful for classroom material. There are many books written for marketing professionals that have good case studies. The following might be useful as background material.

Title and price	Author(s)	Publisher and ISBN	Brief account
Essentials of Marketing £32.99	Blythe, J.	Prentice Hall 2005 978 027 369 3581	Chapter 9 on marketing communications gives good coverage of promotion; check out the table on p 222.
The Five Most Important Questions You Will Ever Ask About Your Organization £7.99	Drucker, P.	Jossey Bass 2008 978 0 470 225756 5	Short, sweet and powerful, especially: 'Who is our customer' and 'What does our customer value?'
The Economist Guide to Management Ideas and Gurus £20.00	Hindle, T.	Profile Books 2008 978 1 84668 108 0	Three hundred pages of 1-2 page accounts that help to fill in holes, e.g. branding, niche markets, product life cycle and USP.

Promotion

50 Management Ideas you really need to know £8.99	Russell-Walling, E.	Quercus Publishing plc 2008 978 1 84724 009 5	Two hundred pages, so again it's 2 pages per topic; worth the money for 'the 4 Ps of marketing'.

42.3 Answers to workbook questions

A Revision questions

(35 marks; 35 minutes)

1. Why is promotion an important element of the marketing mix? (**4**)

    • If customers do not know about the product they will not buy it. Customers need to be aware of the product's features to make informed choices. Customers need to know where the product is available in order to purchase.

2. Outline one advantage and one disadvantage of TV advertising. (**4**)

    • Pro:

    – can reach a large number of people

    – increases the prestige of the business

    – can be targeted to viewer watching specific programmes

    • Con:

    – expensive

    – may not reach the target audience

    – viewers can skip the advert

3. What is meant by the promotional mix? (**2**)

    • the mix of different forms of promotion used in a promotional campaign

4. Explain what form of promotion you think would work best for marketing:

    (**a**) a new football game for the PS3 (**3**)

    (**b**) a small, family-focused seaside hotel (**3**)

    (**c**) organic cosmetics for women (**3**)

        • One mark for suggested relevant method of promotion. Two marks for the reason why the method was chosen.

(a) TV, perhaps in centre breaks in televised football matches

(b) advertising in local publications, e.g. *What's On in Brighton* – not too expensive, and work on the assumption that those in need of a hotel will find you

(c) look for sponsorship of a relevant green-ish TV series

5. Why is it important for businesses to monitor the effect of their promotional activity? **(4)**

    • to ensure that the promotion is working

    • to compare the costs to the results

    • to enable better planning in the future

6. What is meant by the phrase: 'promotion needs to be effective'? **(3)**

    • Promotion needs to give value for money. Cost versus response (the contribution generated by the response must outweigh the cost of the promotion).

7. Explain why promotion is essential for new businesses. **(4)**

    • New business needs to let the market/customers know of its existence. Few firms can afford to wait for word of mouth to spread.

8. Discuss whether Pepsi-Cola would be wise to sponsor the *X-Factor* TV programme. **(8)**

Two marks for an understanding of how sponsorship works. Up to six marks for the explanation of why it is a good/not so good idea. This might include:

    • large coverage – the *X-Factor* is a popular show, but therefore expensive

    • Pepsi-Cola would gain prestige from being associated with such an event

    • it is targeting an audience that would want the product

    • hard to measure impact – may not actually have any effect on sales

Promotion

B1 Data response

Green & Black's second bite

(30 marks; 35 minutes)

(Refer to question on page 270 of textbook.)

1. Outline two possible explanations of why the 2005 biscuit launches failed. **(6)**

	Knowledge 3 marks	Application 3 marks
Level 2	3 marks Shows clear understanding of the subject content.	3 marks Answer is applied effectively to the specific circumstances.
Level 1	2-1 marks Shows some understanding of the subject content.	2-1 marks Some relationship to the circumstances (perhaps indirectly).

Possible answers include:

- Over-ambitious pricing may have stopped consumers from trying the biscuits.

- The biscuits may have been disappointing, making the level of repeat purchase rather low.

2. Explain how the sales of the new biscuit varieties could be helped by a programme of in-store merchandising. **(5)**

	Knowledge 2 marks	Application 3 marks
Level 2	2 marks Shows clear understanding of the subject content.	3 marks Answer is applied effectively to the specific circumstances.
Level 1	1 mark Shows some understanding of the subject content.	2-1 marks Some relationship to the circumstances (perhaps indirectly).

Possible answers include:

- Merchandising means ensuring that a brand's in-store presence receives regular upgrades, e.g. smartening up the product display, or arranging for a special 'dump-bin' to be placed near to the cash tills.

- This can help boost sales, especially for products that rely a lot on impulse purchases.

3. Discuss whether 'sampling in-store' is likely to be a sufficiently powerful form of promotion for the new biscuit range. (12)

	Knowledge 2 marks	Application 2 marks	Analysis 4 marks	Evaluation 4 marks
Level 2	2 marks Good understanding of the subject content.	3 marks Answer is applied effectively to the specific case.	4-3 marks Build-up of argument, making use of relevant business concepts.	4-3 marks Shows judgement in drawing conclusions from own argument.
Level 1	1 mark Some understanding of the subject content; or one answer identified.	1 mark Some relationship to the scenario (perhaps indirectly).	2-1 marks Some build-up of argument, showing grasp of cause and effect.	2-1 marks Some judgement shown in argument or weighting of language.

Possible answers include:

- A long-standing marketing idea is that new products need to move through a process known as AIDA: Awareness, Interest, Desire, Action. In other words it's not likely that someone would buy a product just because they've tried it in-store; they need to have been made aware of the product beforehand and come to want to try it; something like TV advertising would have been necessary to achieve that.

- Of course, if the new biscuit range was so perfectly tuned into latest customer desires ('Oh wow! An organic Almond, Cherry and Apricot cereal bar!') perhaps the in-store sampling would work.

4. Outline the other aspects of the marketing mix being used by Green & Black's. (7)

	Knowledge 3 marks	Application 4 marks
Level 2	3 marks Shows clear understanding of the subject content.	4-3 marks Answer is applied effectively to the specific circumstances.
Level 1	2-1 marks Shows some understanding of the subject content.	2-1 marks Some relationship to the circumstances.

Possible answers include:

- Place: launching seasonal products into 'selected supermarkets'; this is very wise, as the creation of a credible image depends on where your products are distributed; at this early stage it is very wise to appear in Waitrose, not Lidl.

• Price: Green & Black's seem to want to price the product very boldly; £2.49 for three products suggests 83p per bar, which is probably twice the price of most rivals. This is bold, price-leading behaviour; of course, if they cannot get this to stick, they may have to cut the prices to achieve acceptable sales levels.

B2 Data response

Getting your furniture noticed
(46 marks; 60 minutes)

(Refer to question on pages 270–1 of textbook.)

1a What is a corporate logo? **(2)**

  • a name or symbol that is associated solely with a particular company

1b Why do companies have logos? **(4)**

  • as a form of branding

  • to make the company easy to recognise

  One mark could be given for a good example.

2. What is meant by 'target market'? **(4)**

  • Groups or individuals that the product is designed for and therefore the marketing is aimed at. Group that you wish to sell to.

3. The initial promotional efforts did not reach the target market. Explain why this might have happened. **(8)**

	Knowledge 2 marks	Application 2 marks	Analysis 4 marks
Level 2	2 marks Shows clear understanding of the subject content.	2 marks Answer is applied effectively to the specific case.	4-3 marks Build-up of argument, making use of relevant business concepts.
Level 1	1 mark Shows some understanding of the subject content.	1 mark Some relationship to the scenario (perhaps indirectly).	2-1 marks Some build-up of argument, showing grasp of cause and effect.

Possible answers include:

  • Methods were too general so did not reach target (business) market.

  • Methods were not specific to business customers so attracted individual customers.

- Wording did not attract the right customers.

- The wrong media was used for the target market.

- Not enough research had been done to identify the correct method of promotion.

4a Explain how promoting a unique product might differ from promoting a mass-market product. **(4)**

	Knowledge 2 marks	Application 2 marks
Level 2	**2 marks** Shows clear understanding of the subject content.	**2 marks** Answer is applied effectively to the specific circumstances.
Level 1	**1 mark** Shows some understanding of the subject content.	**1 mark** Some relationship to the circumstances.

Possible answers include:

- You'd just focus promotion on the target market for the unique product, which would often be a different type of customer than those within the mass market.

- Promotion for the mass market might include TV or mass direct (junk) mail; for the unique product it might be possible to identify a medium that is better focused on the relevant type of buyer.

4b Discuss the advantages and disadvantages of two forms of promotion for a unique product such as Heaton & Jeremiah's. **(12)**

	Knowledge 2 marks	Application 2 marks	Analysis 4 marks	Evaluation 4 marks
Level 2	**2 marks** Shows clear understanding of the subject content.	**2 marks** Answer is applied effectively to the specific case.	**4-3 marks** Build-up of argument, making use of relevant business concepts.	**4-3 marks** Shows judgement in drawing conclusions from own argument.
Level 1	**1 mark** Some understanding of the subject content; or one answer identified.	**1 mark** Some relationship to the scenario (perhaps indirectly).	**2-1 marks** Some build-up of argument, showing grasp of cause and effect.	**2-1 marks** Some judgement shown in argument or weighting of language.

Promotion

Unit **42**

- Credit should be given for any promotional method selected. The application marks are awarded for the suggestions being relevant to the business. Analysis marks can be given even if the suggested methods are not relevant to the business. If the suggestions are not relevant it is unlikely that the evaluation marks would be given.

5. Discuss why word of mouth might be the best form of advertising for a new business. (**12**)

	Knowledge 2 marks	Application 2 marks	Analysis 4 marks	Evaluation 4 marks
Level 2	**2 marks** Shows clear understanding of the subject content.	**2 marks** Answer is applied effectively to the specific case.	**4-3 marks** Build-up of argument, making use of relevant business concepts.	**4-3 marks** Shows judgement in drawing conclusions from own argument.
Level 1	**1 mark** Some understanding of the subject content; or one answer identified.	**1 mark** Some relationship to the scenario (perhaps indirectly).	**2-1 marks** Some build-up of argument, showing grasp of cause and effect.	**2-1 marks** Some judgement shown in argument or weighting of language.

Possible answers include:

- Word of mouth is cheaper than other forms of advertising. It means that a happy customer will do the promotion for the business. For a new business with limited resources, it is a good way to spread the word to its target market.

- If the product is also new it is a way of gradually building knowledge about the product.

- Other methods of promotion may be too expensive. Other methods may not reach the target market. A new business may find it difficult to find the best way of reaching its customers.

43.1 Introduction

The 2008 Specification has reduced the number of terms to be used in relation to pricing. In particular, it has dropped the term 'pricing methods'. This has allowed other terms to be dropped such as cost-plus (and mark-up). Regrettably, the delisting also includes price discrimination.

However one feels about this, it is important to follow the new Spec, and therefore drop completely the terms that have been excluded. From the student perspective, there's still a lot to learn in order to distinguish effectively between: pricing strategies, pricing tactics, price-taker, price-leader, price skimming, price penetration, loss-leaders and psychological pricing – not to mention price elasticity.

Unit 43 is a particularly important unit for students to read, as it is accessible and well applied to the real world, yet provides the level of detail students need on all these terms. The Evaluation is especially worthwhile. All the exercises at the end of the unit are worthwhile, and the Section A ones should be mandatory.

43.2 Further reading and resources

Title and price	Author(s)	Publisher and ISBN	Brief account
Pricing Strategies for Small Business £10.99	Gregson, A.	Self-Counsel Press 2008 978 1551 807 973	Cancel all other book orders until you've bought this book! Good on skimming and penetration and on 'Positioning for Price – the role of the USP'. This book's a gem.
The Five Most Important Questions You Will Ever Ask About Your Organization £7.99	Drucker, P.	Jossey Bass 2008 978 0 470 225756 5	Short, sweet and powerful, especially: 'Who is our customer' and 'What does our customer value?'
The Economist Guide to Management Ideas and Gurus £20.00	Hindle, T.	Profile Books 2008 978 1 84668 108 0	Three hundred pages of 1-2 page accounts that help to fill in holes surrounding the issue of pricing, e.g. branding, differentiation, niche markets, product life cycle and USP.
50 Management Ideas you Really Need to Know £8.99	Russell-Walling, E.	Quercus Publishing plc 2008 978 1 84724 009 5	Two hundred pages, so it's 2 pages per topic; worth the money for 'the 4 Ps of marketing'.

Pricing

Fashion Marketing £22.95	Easey, M.	Blackwell 2008 978-1405139533	Marketing concepts applied to the fashion industry. Chapter 7 on pricing garments will provide you with some useful background.

43.3 Answers to workbook questions

A Revision questions

(35 marks; 35 minutes)

1. Explain why price 'is fundamental to a firm's revenues'. **(3)**

   • It is both a part of the calculation of revenue (quantity × price) and a fundamental influence on the quantity part of the equation, i.e. if you price too high, the quantity sold may be very low.

2. Look at Figure 43.1. Outline two factors that would affect the 'psychologically right price range' for a new Nokia phone. **(4)**

   • If a high-spec phone was too cheap, potential customers might be put off, suspecting that features such as the camera were of poor quality.

   • If a phone was too expensive, people would switch to a cheaper alternative.

3. Explain how the actions of Nike might affect the footwear prices set by Adidas. **(3)**

   • If Nike chose to increase all its prices by 15%, Adidas might do the same, both to increase its profit margins and to avoid any appearance of being 'a cheap trainer'.

4. Look at Table 43.1 on the price sensitivity of products, brands and services. Think of two more examples of highly price sensitive and two examples of not-very-price-sensitive products, services or brands. **(4)**

   Answers will change over time. Here are a few:

   • Price sensitive: Fosters beer at Asda; sales of The Sun; long-life orange juice.

   • Low price sensitivity: Fosters beer at a hot night club; sales of the Financial Times; Innocent smoothies.

5. Explain the difference between pricing strategy and pricing tactics. **(3)**

   • A pricing strategy positions a product's price over the medium-long term.

   • A pricing tactic is a short-term response to an opportunity or threat.

6. For each of the following, decide whether the pricing strategy should be skimming or penetration. Briefly explain your reasoning.

   (a) Richard Branson's Virgin group launches the world's first space tourism service (you are launched in a rocket, spend time weightless in space, watch the world go round, then come back to earth). (4)

   • Skimming: there's no competition, and a few wealthy people will pay a huge price premium to obtain a cool image as early flyers.

   (b) Kellogg's launches a new range of sliced breads for families in a hurry. (4)

   • Penetration: there's no clear customer benefit, so Kellogg's will struggle to break into a market with highly established bread brands such as Hovis and Warburtons.

   (c) The first Google Phone is launched (called G-Fone) with free, instant WiFi access to Google. (4)

   • Hard to say, but probably penetration, as this will probably seem an unoriginal idea by the time your students tackle this question!

7. Is a cash cow likely to be a price maker or a price taker? Explain your reasoning. (3)

   • A cash cow is usually a price maker, because it has a high market share and therefore has a great deal of influence over the market, e.g. Cadbury's Dairy Milk.

8. Identify three circumstances in which a business might decide to use special offer pricing. (3)

   • launching a new product

   • when trying to break into a new distribution outlet (e.g. all BP petrol stations)

   • when a rival is about to launch a directly competitive product

B1 Data response

(25 marks; 30 minutes)

(Refer to question on page 277 of textbook.)

1. Briefly explain why it might be fair to describe Elvive Anti-Dandruff shampoo as a price-taker. (3)

   • Because its managers seem to feel the need to price it at a discount to the presumed price-leader (among anti-dandruff shampoos), which is Head & Shoulders.

2. Neutrogena shampoo is priced at nearly 100 times the level of supermarket budget shampoos (per ml). Explain why customers might be willing to pay such a high price. **(6)**

	Knowledge 2 marks	Application 2 marks	Analysis 2 marks
Level 2	**2 marks** Good understanding of the subject content.	**2 marks** Answer is applied effectively to the specific case.	**2 marks** Build-up of argument, making use of relevant business concepts.
Level 1	**1 mark** Shows some understanding of the subject content.	**1 mark** Some relationship to the scenario (perhaps indirectly).	**1 mark** Some build-up of argument, showing grasp of cause and effect.

Possible answers include:

- They must believe that the shampoo has a significant consumer benefit, e.g. makes one's hair shinier or sexier; this might be because of clever marketing, or because there really is something special about the product.

- An alternative explanation might be that the brand has its own value for money, e.g. that it's produced in specially concentrated form, making the price worth paying.

3. Examine the position of the long-established brand Pantene Pro-V within the UK market for shampoo. What pricing strategy does it seem to be using and why might it be able to use this approach? **(7)**

	Knowledge 2 marks	Application 2 marks	Analysis 3 marks
Level 2	**2 marks** Good understanding of the subject content.	**2 marks** Answer is applied effectively to the specific case.	**3 marks** Build-up of argument, making use of relevant business concepts.
Level 1	**1 mark** Shows some understanding of the subject content.	**1 mark** Some relationship to the scenario (perhaps indirectly).	**2-1 marks** Some build-up of argument, showing grasp of cause and effect.

Possible answers include:

- It seems to be a price leader, setting a price that other brands such as Herbal Essences cannot approach. The implication is that Herbal Essences cannot achieve satisfactory sales volumes at £2.99, and has to be priced at £1.99. That is testimony to the strength of the Pantene brand name.

• A brand can only price itself higher than rivals because customers are willing to pay; it seems that Pantene has achieved the ideal market position: to be respected by its customers so much that they are willing to pay a strong price premium (and perhaps feel good about paying the extra for a 'quality brand').

4. Discuss whether dogs should have 'better' shampoo than kids. **(9)**

	Knowledge 2 marks	Application 2 marks	Analysis 2 marks	Evaluation 3 marks
Level 2	**2 marks** Good understanding of the subject content; or two answers identified.	**2 marks** Answer is applied effectively to the specific case.	**2 marks** Build-up of argument, making use of relevant business concepts.	**3 marks** Shows judgement in drawing conclusions from own argument.
Level 1	**1 mark** Some understanding of the subject content; or one answer identified.	**1 mark** Some relationship to the scenario (perhaps indirectly).	**1 mark** Some build-up of argument, showing grasp of cause and effect.	**2-1 marks** Some judgement shown in argument or weighting of language.

Possible answers include:

• The question refers to the extraordinary implication from the table that people who pay 38p for shampoo for their kids are willing to pay £3.35 for shampoo for their dogs.

• The question then raises the issue as to whether an item priced nearly ten times higher is necessarily better than the alternative; if it is better, then why would anyone spend more on their dog than their child (do dogs have more sensitive skin?!?); if the dog product is no better, then why not use the kids' shampoo on the dog?

• Ideally students will find this question taxing, but learn that pricing is affected by – and affects – consumer psychology; the clever consumer always questions the price of everything.

B2 Data response

The $100 dollar laptop
(30 marks; 35 minutes)

(Refer to question on pages 278–9 of textbook.)

1. Describe the objectives behind the pricing of the XO laptop. **(4)**

• The idea is 'Buy One, Give One Free', i.e. as a way to give educational aid to developing countries.

Pricing

- It is not clear whether the underlying purpose is charitable or whether it is a smart business idea, i.e. tuning into the desire by many customers to show greater social concern for others.

2a Compare the 'breakdown of costs' pie chart in Figure 43.5 to the text to work out the recent profit per unit made on selling the XO laptop. **(3)**

- The pie total comes to $220. If these have been sold for $188, then a loss of $32 is made per sale; if, however, the figure of $220 relates to the US selling price of $399 for 2, then a significant profit is being made ($179 per sale). The data lacks clarity.

2b Given that level of profit, how could the company hope 'to sell the machines for $100'? **(4)**

- The price of $100 is only possible if there prove to be huge cost advantages in producing large volumes; this is possible and would help the producers to cut the unit costs, e.g. through bulk buying.

3a Explain what is meant by an 'early adopter'? **(3)**

- Someone who is willing to take the risk on a new product by buying it before having the reassurance of knowing that other people feel comfortable with it. In this case the early adopters were governments.

3b Why may early adopters be important to a business? **(4)**

- They provide an income, possibly at high prices (if a skimming strategy has been used).

- They can be the ones that spread the positive word of mouth that leads to further purchases.

4. Some people see the XO laptop as a brave charitable idea; others see it purely as a clever form of penetration pricing strategy. To what extent can you agree with either view? **(12)**

	Knowledge 2 marks	Application 2 marks	Analysis 4 marks	Evaluation 4 marks
Level 2	**2 marks** Good understanding of the subject content; or two answers identified.	**2 marks** Answer is applied effectively to the specific case.	**4-3 marks** Build-up of argument, making use of relevant business concepts.	**4-3 marks** Shows judgement in drawing conclusions from own argument.
Level 1	**1 mark** Some understanding of the subject content; or one answer identified.	**1 mark** Some relationship to the scenario (perhaps indirectly).	**2-1 marks** Some build-up of argument, showing grasp of cause and effect.	**2-1 marks** Some judgement shown in argument or weighting of language.

Possible answers include:

- There is no doubt about the potential benefits of the idea; providing millions of free laptops to schools in developing countries could have a significant influence upon the life chances of the kids; India has built a hugely successful IT sector – perhaps this initiative will help a country like Rwanda become Africa's IT hub in years to come.

- The idea of it being a form of penetration pricing seems harder to follow; clearly the pricing point of $399 is very low for a laptop, so perhaps there's an element of penetration; certainly there is a huge prize to be gained by any business that manages to break into the vast world market for computer hardware; but it is easier to see it as a form of product differentiation (or a USP) than to see it specifically as penetration pricing.

Price Elasticity of Demand

44.1 Introduction

Most A-level students find price elasticity of demand difficult to understand. A surprising number of A-level students struggle with simple percentage calculations. Consequently before starting to teach this topic it might be necessary to do some basic work on how to calculate percentages. In examinations price elasticity questions can come in various shapes and sizes. Some questions will involve a fair amount of number crunching. Other questions will involve analysing price elasticity figures that have already been calculated in order to draw conclusions. Both types of question will need to be practised in detail.

Price elasticity is a key discriminator in examinations. It can be used as a powerful tool of analysis within marketing, and in answers to many other questions, such as strategy. Price elasticity may be difficult to grasp initially and many reinforcing exercises might be required. Investment of time made by the teacher in this area is likely to pay real dividends in terms of examination success.

Students should be encouraged to do all the Workbook exercises for homework.

44.2 Further reading and resources

Title and price	Author(s)	Publisher and ISBN	Brief account
Even More Offensive Marketing	Davidson, H.	Penguin 1997, 0 14 025691 1	This is an outstanding book, highly readable, full of cases, but fundamentally analytic and academic. Pages 523 and 524 contain super material, including a correlation graph showing the price elasticity of Fairy Liquid. Regrettably it's not been updated, but it's still a marketing masterpiece.
The Five Most Important Questions You Will Ever Ask About Your Organization £7.99	Drucker, P.	Jossey Bass 2008 978 0 470 225756 5	Short, sweet and powerful, especially: 'Who is our customer' and 'What does our customer value?'
The Economist Guide to Management Ideas and Gurus £20.00	Hindle, T.	Profile Books 2008 978 1 84668 108 0	Three hundred pages of 1–2 page accounts that help to fill in holes, e.g. branding, differentiation, niche markets and USP.

Price Elasticity of Demand

Business Case Studies 3rd Edition £17.99	Marcouse, I. and Lines, D.	Longman 2002 0 582 40636-6	Case Study 15 is tough, but not too long and it hasn't dated. Well-worth using, though you'll have to tell students to ignore Q1c on semi-variable costs.

44.3 Answers to workbook questions

A Revision questions

(35 marks; 35 minutes)

1a If a product's sales have fallen by 21% following a price rise from £2 to £2.07, what is its price elasticity? **(4)**

$-21\% /+(\pounds0.07/\pounds2.00 \times 100) = -6$

1b Is the product price elastic or price inelastic? **(1)**

• Inelastic

2. Outline two ways in which Nestlé might try to reduce the price elasticity of its Aero chocolate bars. **(4)**

• Differentiate them even more clearly from standard chocolate, e.g. foil-wrap each stick within the bar.

• Improve the quality of the chocolate – make it yummier than Cadbury or Galaxy.

3. A firm selling 20,000 units at £8 is considering a 4% price increase. It believes its price elasticity is −0.5.

(a) What will be the effect upon revenue? **(5)**

• Old revenue $= 20,000 \times \pounds8 = \pounds160,000$
New revenue $=$ new price $\times$ new quantity
New price $= \pounds8.32$
Change in quantity $= 14 \times -0.5 = -2\%$
New quantity $= 19,600$
New revenue $= \pounds163,072$ $(\pounds8.32 \times 19,600)$
Change in revenue $= +\pounds3072$

(b) Give two reasons why the revenue may prove to be different from the firm's expectations. **(2)**

• competitors may have changed their prices at the same time

• unexpected changes in consumer tastes

4. Explain three ways a firm could make use of information about the price elasticity of its brands. (**6**)

   • Pricing decisions – decide whether a price increase or decrease would boost profit.

   • Sales forecasting – anticipate the effect upon sales of a given price change.

   • Identifying brands with low product differentiation – and devise new strategies.

5. Identify three external factors that could increase the price elasticity of a brand of chocolate. (**3**)

   • The competition launches a new product.

   • End of the product's life cycle.

   • Competitors increase above the line support for their brands.

6. A firm has a sales target of 60,000 units per month. Current sales are 50,000 per month at a price of £1.50. If its products have a price elasticity of –2, what price should the firm charge to meet the target sales volume? (**4**)

   • Percentage change in sales required = 20%
     20% / –2 = 10% price cut
     £1.50 – 10% = £1.35

7. Why is price elasticity always negative? (**2**)

   • There is a negative correlation between price and quantity demanded.

8. Explain why the manager of a product with a price elasticity of −2 may be reluctant to cut the price. (**4**)

   • Demand might increase but does the necessary spare capacity exist?

   • How will other firms respond? Will a price cut cause a price war?

B1 Data response

(20 marks; 25 minutes)

(Refer to question on page 285 of textbook.)

1. Given that the price elasticity of the product is believed to be –0.4, calculate:

   (**a**) the old and the new sales volume (**3**)

      • Old volume = £500,000 / £10
                    = 50,000 units (**1**)

      • New volume = +10% × –0.4
                    = 4% fall in sales (**1**)

      • New sales   = 50,000 × 0.96
                    = 48,000 units (**1**)

(b) the new revenue **(3)**

- New revenue = new price × new quantity **(1)**
  New price   = £11
  New revenue = £11 × 48,000 units **(1)**
             = £528,000 **(1)**

(c) the expected change in profit following the price increase **(6)**

- Old profit   = (£10 − £4) × 50,000 **(1)**
             = £300,000 − £100,000 (fixed costs)
             = £200,000 **(1)**

- New profit   = (£11 − £4) × 48,000 **(1)**
             = £336,000 − £100,000
             = £236,000 **(1)**

- Change in profit = +£36 000 **(1)** + **(1)** for the £ sign

2. If the firm started producing mass-market white pillow cases, would their price elasticity be higher or lower than the Manchester United ones? Why is that? **(8)**

	Knowledge 2 marks	Application 2 marks	Analysis 4 marks
Level 2	2 marks One or more benefit explained, showing good understanding.	2 marks Relevant points consistently applied to the case.	4–3 marks Good analysis of identified advantage and disadvantage.
Level 1	1 mark One or more benefit identified, but not explained, showing limited understanding.	1 mark Some attempt to apply point(s) to the case.	2 – 1 marks Limited analysis of identified advantage and/ or disadvantage.

Relevant answers might include:

- price elasticity will be higher

- main USP lost

- reduced product differentiation

- increased product substitutability

- however, if the new pillow cases had a different USP, e.g. superior quality, ped might actually fall

Price Elasticity of Demand Unit **44**

B2 Data response

The iPhone

(20 marks; 25 minutes)

(Refer to question on pages 285–6 of textbook.)

1. Explain the likely logic behind Apple's decision to sign an exclusive deal with the O$_2$ network. **(6)**

	Content 2 marks	Application 2 marks	Analysis 2 marks
Level 2	**2 marks** One or more benefit explained, showing good understanding.	**2 marks** Relevant points consistently applied to the case.	**2 marks** Good analysis of identified advantage and disadvantage.
Level 1	**1 mark** One or more benefit identified, but not explained, showing limited understanding.	**1 mark** Some attempt to apply point(s) to the case.	**1 mark** Limited analysis of identified advantage and/ or disadvantage.

Relevant answers might include:

- To 'keep competition down'; this would enable Apple to tell O$_2$ about pricing and display, and keep everything within Apple's control (they wouldn't want the image of the iPhone being damaged by a retailer using the product as a loss-leader.

- It would be a way to contain demand at this early stage, and make it easier to charge a higher price; later on, when production levels were higher, Apple could to sell through all the networks.

2. Use your understanding of price elasticity to discuss whether or not Apple was right to price the iPhone in this way. **(14)**

	Content 3 marks	Application 3 marks	Analysis 4 marks	Evaluation 4 marks
Level 2	**3 marks** Relevant issue(s) explained, showing good understanding.	**3 marks** Arguments are consistently applied to the case material.	**4-3 marks** Good analysis of question, arguments are fully developed.	**4-3 marks** Judgement offered with limited justification.
Level 1	**2-1 marks** Relevant issue(s) identified but not explained, showing limited understanding.	**2-1 marks** Limited attempt to apply arguments to the case material.	**2-1 marks** Limited analysis of question.	**2-1 marks** Some judgement offered but unjustified.

Price Elasticity of Demand

Possible answers include:

- With such an innovative product with its highly attractive branding, price elasticity was bound to be low during the launch period, therefore high pricing was the right business approach.

- The only downside would be that the high prices would attract other rivals into this market – making Nokia desperate to find a comparable phone.

- Price elasticity isn't a constant and isn't laid down in tablets of stone: it can be influenced. In this case, setting a relatively high price might signal to customers that the iPhone really is a classy phone; this, in turn, would help establish the product as desirable whatever the price – which is the definition of a product with low price elasticity.

45.1 Introduction

Students 'get' most aspects of marketing, but not 'place'. The name doesn't help, because it implies that it's something you do ('I think I'll place *Business Review* in WHSmith'), i.e. it's within your control. In fact, of course, nothing is harder for an entrepreneur than getting distribution. That's why the Dragons are so smug about the power or influence they wield. Duncan Goose (One Water) speaks eloquently but chillingly about how difficult it was to get distribution and how hard it is to retain it.

So please make an effort to stress to students that shelf space is precious and decidedly finite. Only the best new products have any serious chance of getting distribution and in order to keep it the producers often have to run promotions such as 'Buy One Get One Free', just to keep the retailer happy. Yet those same promotions can damage the brand image.

All the questions in the Workbook are worthwhile. Particularly strong is Question B2.

45.2 Further reading and resources

Title and price	Author(s)	Publisher and ISBN	Brief account
Essentials of Marketing £32.99	Blythe, J.	Prentice Hall 2005 978 027 369 3581	Good coverage here of 'place' and its importance within marketing strategy.
The Five Most Important Questions You Will Ever Ask About Your Organization £7.99	Drucker, P.	Jossey Bass 2008 978 0 470 225756 5	Short, sweet and powerful, especially: 'Who is our customer' and 'What does our customer value?'
50 Management Ideas you Really Need to Know £8.99	Russell-Walling, E.	Quercus Publishing plc 2008 978 1 84724 009 5	Two hundred pages, so again it's 2 pages per topic; worth the money for 'the 4 Ps of marketing'; also a good piece on 'place', called 'Channel Management'.
Business Case Studies 3rd Edition £17.99	Marcouse, I. and Lines, D.	Longman 2002 0 582 40636-6	Case Study 10 (Even Levi Can Make Mistakes) is terrific on market research and market segmentation, but it also has a lot to teach about distribution.

Place

Even More Offensive Marketing	Davidson, H.	Penguin 1997 0 14 025691 1	This is an outstanding book, highly readable, full of cases, but fundamentally analytic and academic. Chapter 15 is entirely on 'place' (Channel Marketing).

45.3 Answers to workbook questions

A Revision questions

(30 marks; 30 minutes)

1. Outline the meaning of the term 'place'. (**2**)

    • 'Place' is the means by which you get the product in front of the customer, whether in a shop, a restaurant or a website. It is the means of achieving distribution.

2. Explain in your own words why it may be that 'place is the toughest of the 4 Ps'. (**4**)

    • With the other 'Ps' the firm can make its own decisions on the price to charge, the design of the product, etc. With place, success depends on others, e.g. you can only get distribution in Tesco if the Tesco buyer decides you're worth it.

3. Outline what you think are appropriate distribution channels for:

    (**a**) a new magazine aimed at 12–15-year-old boys. (**3**)

    • sweetshop/newsagents

    • the internet

    (**b**) a new adventure holiday company focusing on wealthy 19-32 year olds. (**3**)

    • the internet

    • high class travel agents and consultants

4. Retailers such as WHSmith charge manufacturers a rent on prime store space such as the shelving near to the cash tills.

    (**a**) How might a firm work out whether it is worthwhile to pay the extra? (**4**)

    • Estimate the extra sales due to the better location.

    • Subtract the variable costs generated by the extra sales (to find the contribution).

    • Take the WHSmith fee from the contribution to work out the profitability of the deal.

    (**b**) Why might new small firms find it hard to pay rents such as these? (**4**)

• They may already be quite short of cash, so this could be an extra cost too far.

• Their profit margins may be too low to afford this extra charge.

5. Explain in your own words what is meant by the phrase 'a better mousetrap'. (**4**)

• 'A better mousetrap' means a product that has a function of real value to buyers, so customers make the effort to find it and buy it.

6. Outline three reasons for the success of direct distribution over the Internet in recent years. (**6**)

• Awful traffic turns 'going shopping' from fun to an effort.

• The greater speed and power of the Internet makes it quicker and easier to make your purchases.

• People may have become more price conscious.

B1 Data response

Getting distribution right
(20 marks; 25 minutes)

(Refer to question on page 290 of textbook.)

1. State the meaning of the term 'market size'. (**2**)

• Market size means all the sales made by all the companies in the course of year – by volume or by value.

2a The Year 1 sales target for Kitten Milk is £5 million. What share of the total market for cat food would that represent? (**3**)

• 0.61%, i.e. less than a hundredth of the market

2b Explain why it might be hard to persuade retailers to stock a product with that level of market share. (**6**)

	Knowledge 3 marks	Application 3 marks
Level 2	3 marks One mark for each relevant factor identified.	3 marks Answer is applied effectively to the specific case.
Level 1	2-1 marks Shows some understanding of the subject content.	2-1 marks Some relationship to the scenario (perhaps indirectly).

Possible factors include:

• Shelf space is precious, especially in a city centre; products with such a tiny market share struggle to justify their place on the shelves.

- It is likely that there would be a higher selling product that would therefore generate more profit for the supplier.

3. The marketing manager for Kitten Milk is planning to focus distribution efforts on getting the brand placed in pet shops. Discuss whether this seems wise. **(9)**

	Knowledge 2 marks	Application 2 marks	Analysis 2 marks	Evaluation 3 marks
Level 2	**2 marks** One mark for each relevant factor identified.	**2 marks** Answer is applied effectively to the specific case.	**2 marks** Build-up of argument, making use of relevant business concepts.	**3 marks** Shows judgement in drawing conclusions from own argument.
Level 1	**1 mark** Some understanding of the subject content; or one answer identified.	**1 mark** Some relationship to the scenario (perhaps indirectly).	**1 mark** Some build-up of argument, showing grasp of cause and effect.	**2-1 marks** Some judgement shown in argument or weighting of language.

Possible answers include:

- Yes, because it may emphasise the special nature of the product, and make it possible to charge a higher price than for ordinary milk (and if there's no value added by the Kitten Milk branding, there's no hope for the product).

- No, because the text says that 81% of cat owners buy pet foods at supermarkets, so it seems odd to ignore such a major outlet; especially as it says that pet food shoppers are willing not to buy rather than buy what they don't want (they spend only 80% of the sum they want to spend).

B2 Data response

An arm's length from desire
(25 marks; 30 minutes)

(Refer to question on pages 290–1 of textbook.)

1. Explain how a vending machine can be a 'barrier to entry' to new competitors. **(5)**

	Knowledge 2 marks	Application 3 marks
Level 2	**2 marks** One mark for each relevant factor identified.	**3 marks** Answer is applied effectively to the specific case.

Level 1	1 mark Shows some understanding of the subject content.	2-1 marks Some relationship to the scenario (perhaps indirectly).

Possible factors include:

- A barrier to entry is a factor that makes it hard for new firms to enter a market.

- In many places there is not enough room for more than one vending machine, so if you've got your own cola (or chocolate bar) vending machine distribution network, it will be hard for others to follow.

2. Explain what the text means by the difference between 'maximum availability' and 'maximum visibility'. (5)

- Maximum availability means stocked by the largest possible number of retail outlets (100% of the possible outlets).

- Maximum visibility means having your brand situated in the most visible position in every outlet, e.g. a small Coke fridge by every cash till in every shop in the country.

- Maximum availability is effectively achieved by a few superstar brands such as Cadburys Dairy Milk; maximum visibility is a terrific – but probably unobtainable – goal.

3. Explain why 'an arm's reach from desire' might be less important for a business that does not rely upon impulse purchase. (7)

	Knowledge 2 marks	Application 2 marks	Analysis 3 marks
Level 2	2 marks One mark for each relevant factor identified.	2 marks Answer is applied effectively to the specific case.	3 marks Build-up of argument, making use of relevant business concepts.
Level 1	1 mark Shows some understanding of the subject content.	1 mark Some relationship to the scenario (perhaps indirectly).	2-1 marks Some build-up of argument, showing grasp of cause and effect.

Possible answers include:

- If someone has a headache and sets out to buy aspirin, this planned purchase will not be affected by in-store location or visibility; that person will go to the nearest chemist and look/ask for the product; similarly, any planned purchase makes the in-store location irrelevant; this is important to firms, because WHSmith effectively charges suppliers a higher rent for highly visible shelf space than for a shelf at the back of the store.

Place

- If your product is an impulse purchase, your marketing budget must be spent largely on 'place'; if your product is a planned purchase, the budget is better spent on influencing the plan, e.g. by spending on branding and advertising.

4. From all that you know about today's Coke, Diet Coke and Coke Zero, discuss whether Coca-Cola's distribution strategy was at the core of the firm's marketing success. (8)

	Knowledge 1 mark	Application 2 marks	Analysis 2 marks	Evaluation 3 marks
Level 2		2 marks Answer is applied effectively to the specific case.	2 marks Build-up of argument, making use of relevant business concepts.	3 marks Shows judgement in drawing conclusions from own argument.
Level 1	1 mark Some understanding of the subject content; or one answer identified.	1 mark Some relationship to the scenario (perhaps indirectly).	1 mark Some build-up of argument, showing grasp of cause and effect.	2-1 marks Some judgement shown in argument or weighting of language.

Possible answers include:

- Yes, at the core, but not necessarily the single most important factor.

- The single most important factor has been the brand image, affected over the years by the iconic bottle and logo, plus the sustained excellence (and expense) of the advertising; this was at the heart of the brand's dominance of the cola market.

- Nevertheless the distribution strategy was very important, because Coke has often had little competition, and in order to grow it has had to build up the size of the market; this has effectively been done by encouraging existing customers to buy Coke more often because it's so easy to do so.

Marketing and Competitiveness

46.1 Introduction

The curious thing about the AQA AS Specification is the absence of an external context. Until now. So this unit is very important to give students the opportunity to see a further dimension to marketing. Examiners will give high rewards for analysis to any student able to discuss the difference between marketing for an oligopolist compared with marketing for a firm in a highly competitive market.

Furthermore, the factors referred to in the Spec as 'Determinants of competitiveness' give the opportunity to take a broader look at business. Operational factors such as quality and efficiency clearly impinge on the issue of competitiveness from a marketing point of view. Therefore this section acts as a bit of synopticity, giving the Unit 2 examiner the opportunity to write a question that encourages students to write about business as a whole, instead of treating the functional areas as discrete.

The obvious homework exercises here are Section A plus B2. Exercise B1 is very valuable, though, and could be tackled as a group exercise in class.

46.2 Further reading and resources

Title and price	Author(s)	Publisher and ISBN	Brief account
The Five Most Important Questions You Will Ever Ask About Your Organization £7.99	Drucker. P.	Jossey Bass 2008 978 0 470 225756 5	Short, sweet and powerful, especially: 'Who is our customer' and 'What does our customer value?'
The Economist Guide to Management Ideas and Gurus £20.00	Hindle, T.	Profile Books 2008 978 1 84668 108 0	Three hundred pages of 1-2 page accounts that help to fill in holes, e.g. branding, cannibalisation (no longer on the Spec, but an invaluable concept), differentiation (ditto!), niche markets, product life cycle and USP.
50 Management Ideas you Really Need to Know £8.99	Russell-Walling, E.	Quercus Publishing plc 2008 978 1 84724 009 5	Two hundred pages, so again it's 2 pages per topic; see the Boston Matrix and market segmentation.

Business Case Studies 3rd Edition £17.99	Marcouse, I. and Lines, D.	Longman 2002 0 582 40636-6	Case Study 13 on 'Marketing Myopia' is useful as an overview of marketing, in this case in relation to a monopolist competitor.
Pricing Strategies for Small Business £10.99	Gregson, A.	Self-Counsel Press 2008 978 1551 807 973	The short section called 'How do you know your pricing's not right?' is excellent on competitiveness, pages 11-14. This book's a gem.

46.3 Answers to workbook questions

A Revision questions

(35 marks; 35 minutes)

1. What is a competitive market? **(2)**

    • One in which no business can be complacent, as none has a dominant market position.

2. Explain how the marketing mix of Virgin Trains might be affected by a decision by government to allow other train operating companies to compete on Virgin's routes. **(4)**

    • It would probably have to focus more on price and value for money, e.g. free breakfast.

    • It would have to consider extending its distribution channels, making it easy to buy your weekly season ticket while completing your shopping at Asda.

3. Describe the main features of an oligopolistic market. **(3)**

    • competition between a few large firms

    • reluctance to compete on price; emphasis on new, 'improved' products (not necessarily improved from the consumer's point of view)

4a What is a price war and … **(3)**

    • a wave of price-cutting within a market in which neither side seems willing to give up; often the ones caught in the crossfire are smaller firms with weaker financial positions

Marketing and Competitiveness

Unit **46**

4b why are they rare? (**3**)

- They can be fatal, i.e. companies can be driven to the wall, so they are rarely started unless a business sees no way out of its own troubles. In 2008 Ryanair responded to rising oil prices and falling passenger numbers by slashing its prices; it probably hoped to see the death of one or two competitors.

5. Explain why product differentiation becomes more important as competition within a market increases. (**3**)

- Product differentiation is the extent to which customers perceive one product as being distinct from rivals.

- If the level of competition rises, it becomes increasingly important to be differentiated, to avoid being drawn into profit-sapping competitive actions such as price-cutting.

6. Identify four factors that could be used to identify whether or not a business is competitive. (**4**)

- Is its market share rising or falling?

- Are its sales rising or falling?

- Are its profits rising or falling?

- Is its productivity rising or falling?

7. How might the size of an organisation affect its efficiency? (**3**)

- Larger firms should be more efficient, because they can benefit from bulk buying...

- ...but in many cases smaller firms are superior because decision making is quicker so the business can respond better to changes in customer taste.

8. Why might a firm that is struggling to be competitive increase its training budget? (**3**)

- improved product quality

- better customer service

- higher productivity

9. Explain how the quality of management can impact upon an organisation's efficiency. (**4**)

- Good managers will find the funds for training and for effective communication with the workforce.

- Good managers will also make sure that modernisation of the business happens regularly, to always keep a step ahead of rivals.

10. Apart from market research, how might a firm achieve its goal of attempting to get closer to the consumer? (**3**)

- Get senior managers to spend a week a year serving customers, or working in the customer service call centre.

• Make sure that the profile of the staff reflects the customer profile, e.g. make sure that it's not just men running a business such as Boots, where most customers are women.

B1 Data response

(35 marks; 40 minutes)

(Refer to question on pages 296–7 of textbook.)

1. Using the table explain what has happened to the degree of competition within the UK Indian restaurant market over the last 50 years. **(6)**

	Knowledge 2 marks	Application 2 marks	Analysis 2 marks
Level 2	2 marks Good understanding of the subject content.	2 marks Answer is applied effectively to the specific case.	2 marks Build-up of argument, making use of relevant business concepts.
Level 1	1 mark Shows some understanding of the subject content.	1 mark Some relationship to the scenario (perhaps indirectly).	1 mark Some build-up of argument, showing grasp of cause and effect.

Possible answers include:

• Whereas an Indian restaurant in 1960 might have been the only one in town, by 2000 there might have been ten or more direct competitors.

• Only in recent years are there clear signs of market saturation and therefore fewer new entrants to the market.

2. Giving your reasons, discuss whether the Indian restaurant market in the UK is an example of a fiercely competitive market. **(6)**

	Knowledge 2 marks	Application 2 marks	Analysis 2 marks
Level 2	2 marks Good understanding of the subject content.	2 marks Answer is applied effectively to the specific case.	2 marks Build-up of argument, making use of relevant business concepts.
Level 1	1 mark Shows some understanding of the subject content.	1 mark Some relationship to the scenario (perhaps indirectly).	1 mark Some build-up of argument, showing grasp of cause and effect.

Possible answers include:

- The text says that 'in most British high streets … several Indian restaurants compete aggressively'; that is clear evidence that it's a fiercely competitive market.

- Later the text gives other examples of competition based on innovation (of which 'big-as-your-table Naan breads' sound the tops).

- Nevertheless, there must be small towns where there's only one Indian restaurant; these can prove to be poor quality and relatively expensive.

3a Explain how efficiency might affect the competitiveness of an Indian restaurant. **(4)**

	Knowledge 2 marks	Application 2 marks
Level 2	**2 marks** Good understanding of the subject content.	**2 marks** Answer is applied effectively to the specific case.
Level 1	**1 mark** Shows some understanding of the subject content.	**1 mark** Some relationship to the scenario (perhaps indirectly).

Possible answers include:

- The greater the efficiency, the easier it is for the proprietor to compete on price, especially if a new restaurant is opening nearby and s/he wants to stop it from gaining market share.

- Efficiency can also provide the profits to make it easier to finance improvements, e.g. upgrading the interior/toilets, etc.

3b How might an Indian restaurant set about improving its efficiency? **(4)**

	Knowledge 2 marks	Application 2 marks
Level 2	**2 marks** Good understanding of the subject content.	**2 marks** Answer is applied effectively to the specific case.
Level 1	**1 mark** Shows some understanding of the subject content.	**1 mark** Some relationship to the scenario (perhaps indirectly).

Possible answers include:

- It should make sure that the kitchen is close as possible to the customers – to minimise the time taken to get the food and serve it (many Indian restaurants have the cooking done in the basement).

- It should ensure that all staff work hard at preparing the restaurant/kitchen before customers arrive, to make it easy to cope when things get busy.

4. Identify and explain three internal factors that might affect the competitiveness of an Indian restaurant. (**6**)

   - the amount of training given to staff

   - the motivation of staff

   - the investment by managers in high quality cooking facilities

5. Product differentiation is essential if an Indian restaurant is to survive in the long-run. Discuss. (**9**)

	Knowledge 2 marks	Application 2 marks	Analysis 2 marks	Evaluation 3 marks
Level 2	**2 marks** Good understanding of the subject content; or two answers identified.	**2 marks** Answer is applied effectively to the specific case.	**2 marks** Build-up of argument, making use of relevant business concepts.	**3 marks** Shows judgement in drawing conclusions from own argument.
Level 1	**1 mark** Some understanding of the subject content; or one answer identified.	**1 mark** Some relationship to the scenario (perhaps indirectly).	**1 mark** Some build-up of argument, showing grasp of cause and effect.	**2-1 marks** Some judgement shown in argument or weighting of language.

Possible answers include:

- Not necessarily, if the Indian is the only one in a small town.

- But generally the statement is true; a few will survive on the basis of high efficiency and therefore low costs and low prices, but most will need to provide a differentiated offer.

- As people get more sophisticated, they want more than to just 'go for a curry'; they want something more distinctive; nevertheless, there will be scope for some to differentiate themselves not through the food but by the service; some people love to be schmoozed ('Good evening Mr Jenkins, so pleased that you have come again').

- In business, nothing is certain, therefore the statement in the question is overdone. Not every Indian restaurant will die if it fails to differentiate itself effectively; nevertheless the statement has a lot of truth in it.

Marketing and Competitiveness

B2 Case study

Tesco's £9 toaster
(35 marks; 40 minutes)

(Refer to question on page 298 of textbook.)

1. Describe three characteristics of a highly competitive market. (**6**)

   • many suppliers of a comparable size

   • little differentiation between products or services

   • all suppliers have to focus on keeping costs as low as possible

2. Why has the market for consumer electronics become more competitive? (**4**)

   • no longer sold just by specialist electrical goods retailers

   • supermarkets may be using some electrical items as loss leaders

3. Explain three factors that would affect the competitiveness of a manufacturer of consumer electronics. (**6**)

   • labour costs, hence Philips' decision to switch production from Holland to China

   • labour productivity, which can be affected by training and by the level of investment in equipment and machinery

   • the ability of the business to come up with new, more innovative products, e.g. the Wii console

4. What is a loss leader and why do supermarkets sell them? (**4**)

   • A loss leader is a product sold at below cost, i.e. the more you sell the more you lose.

   • It may be a worthwhile approach if customers come for the bargain, yet leave with shopping bags full of other, full-priced items.

Marketing and Competitiveness $\overset{\text{Unit}}{}$46

5. How might the degree of competition impact upon the marketing mix used by a Chinese manufacturer of own-label toasters? **(5)**

	Knowledge 2 marks	Application 3 marks
Level 2	**2 marks** Good understanding of the subject content.	**3 marks** Answer is applied effectively to the specific case.
Level 1	**1 mark** Shows some understanding of the subject content.	**2-1 marks** Some relationship to the scenario (perhaps indirectly).

Possible answers include:

- The most probable answer is that the Chinese manufacturer will spend nothing at all on marketing, as he is just meeting the retailer's requirement for the product, pack design and so on.

- There may be a possibility, though, that the manufacturer might spend some money on market research as part of a programme of innovation, i.e. in the attempt to design an innovative new type of toaster that will be highly desirable to buy.

6. In today's increasingly competitive market for consumer electronics, firms must constantly cut costs and prices if they are to survive. Discuss. **(10)**

	Knowledge 2 marks	Application 2 marks	Analysis 2 marks	Evaluation 4 marks
Level 2	**2 marks** Good understanding of the subject content; or two answers identified.	**2 marks** Answer is applied effectively to the specific case.	**2 marks** Build-up of argument, making use of relevant business concepts.	**4-3 marks** Shows judgement in drawing conclusions from own argument.
Level 1	**1 mark** Some understanding of the subject content; or one answer identified.	**1 mark** Some relationship to the scenario (perhaps indirectly).	**1 mark** Some build-up of argument, showing grasp of cause and effect.	**2-1 marks** Some judgement shown in argument or weighting of language.

Possible answers include:

- This is a strategy but not the only one. The alternative is to try to maximise the distance between the firm's products and those of the competition, i.e. maximise the product differentiation. If one producer can consistently produce a better TV picture than its rivals, customers will come (and pay a price premium).

• In the absence of innovation, a cost-cutting strategy will work best. It will allow the firm to choose between charging rock-bottom prices to customers and enjoying slightly better profit margins than its.